what
grows
here?
Indoors

what grows here?

Indoors

**favourite houseplants
for every situation**

Jim Hole

Photography by Akemi Matsubuchi

HOLE'S

Library and Archives Canada Cataloguing in Publication

Hole, Jim, 1956-
    What grows here? : indoors / Jim Hole.

Includes index.
ISBN 978-1-894728-06-5

    1. House plants. 2. Indoor gardening. I. Title.
SB419.H75 2007   635.9'65   C2006-905363-4

Hole's   Lone Pine Publishing
101 Bellerose Drive   10145-81 Avenue
St. Albert, Alberta, Canada   Edmonton, Alberta
T8N 8N8   T6E 1W9
www.enjoygardening.com

Contents

Acknowledgements

We are grateful to all the interior gardeners who so generously shared their experiences, ideas and passions for many indoor growing challenges and allowed us into their homes to photograph their prized plants.

Hilary Allen, the Citadel Theatre, Jill Cunningham and Terry Olsen, Heather Dolman, Judith Fraser, Susan Groves-Folkerts, Amanda Hentschel, Werner and Leni Hiob, Lori Johnson, Bruce Keith, Bob and June Kerrison, Stella Kozak, Benjamin McDonald, Sheri McEachern, Stephen Raven, Robert Rawlick, Nina Reshauge, Betty Sampson, Peter Scheffer, Lisa and Ted Smith, Darrell Soetaert, St. Albert Place, Lindsey Steffen, Gail Steiestol, John Leon and the Uplands Condominium Association, Harry Vriend, Marcie Wheele and Karen Wilson.

FOREWORD

Over the many years I spent caring for the houseplants area of the greenhouse, a lot of questions came my way. The two most common were "Which plant can go where?" and "What type of bug is destroying my plant?" This book has been written to answer those questions and many more.

Of all the advice I've offered throughout the years, the bits that ring truest are that there is no such thing as a 'stupid' question and that no one intends to kill their plants—but it happens. Buy your plants from a reputable garden centre, one that cares for its plants and can answer your questions, and your investment is more likely to survive and give you pleasure.

Plants come in and out of fashion, and it's been interesting to note the changes. Today, orchids are the plants to have, and growers are producing beautiful varieties that bloom for months and provide pleasure for the average houseplant lover and specialty grower alike.

So enjoy your plants. Bring them into your homes and don't be afraid of them. Most importantly, be adventurous and let your enthusiasm guide you. There's a whole world of indoor plants to discover, and the next big thing is right around the corner.

— Judith Fraser
*Judith Fraser was the indoor
plants manager at Hole's for
12 years and saw a lot of plants
come and go—she misses all
of them.*

Introduction

There's nothing new about people telling me their gardening stories; however, I've noticed a strange thing happens when I mention the word "houseplant" to people who, moments earlier, were raving about their green thumbs. Like magic, that one word seems to induce a chain reaction of grisly confessions. The interesting thing is that, although there is never any joy attached to these accounts, I don't think I come across bigger smiles than the ones I see on the faces of people who tell me their favourite I-killed-a-houseplant stories. More times than not, these conversations turn into bizarre competitions of who has the best (that is, most horrific) account.

At first glance, it might seem like people are proud of their failures, but I've realized (partly through my own houseplant nightmares) that this enthusiasm has more to do with relief than with masochism. By telling our happily-never-after stories, we get to tend to our enormous guilt and take ownership of our mistakes. It's a sense of responsibility that runs deep and one that I believe stems from the fact that nature didn't create houseplants—we did.

A book dedicated to indoor plants seemed like the natural next step in our *What Grows Here?* series. It's designed to strike a balance between the desire to bring nature indoors and the knowledge to do it properly. As with previous books in this series, this one offers helpful tips and information about how to select plants to suit a number of diverse locations and environments. Because people's experiences with houseplants seem to vary from terrific to tragic, I've included information for indoor gardeners of

We can use indoor plants for many of the same reasons we use plants outdoors: as stand-alone features grown for their beauty or form, as privacy screens that divide up spaces, as colourful accents or as decorative and seasonal elements that highlight architecture. Indoor plant gardening can be challenging or easy, depending on what we grow.

all levels, from the basics about light, water and soil to specific details about caring for orchids and grooming topiaries. So whether you're looking for a plant for that dark corner in your first apartment, wanting to make a terrarium with your kids or planning to create a plant border for your office, you'll be able to find the knowledge you need here.

Like all relationships, the one we have with houseplants is at its best when it's cultivated with understanding, respect and good advice. In fact, a relationship is exactly what you'll find at the core of *What Grows Here? Indoors*. It's our goal to turn information into knowledge, hesitation into confidence and problems into solutions.

Philodendron 'Brazil'

Collect all the tips you can at a garden centre. Ask about fertilizing and watering, and don't be shy about jotting down notes.

Choosing Indoor Plants

Plants are often impulse buys. You see a gorgeous display of seasonal plants at the grocery store, and before you know it, there's a violet or poinsettia sitting in your grocery cart next to the magazine you weren't going to buy and the bag of potato chips you swore off the week before. The best way to ensure the plant outlasts that bag of chips is to think before you buy. Simply taking a little extra time to think about what you want from the plant—and what it needs from you—will greatly increase your chance of bringing home a plant that you can enjoy for years.

Here are a few tips to make that happen:

• Come prepared. Know which directions your rooms face and how much sunlight they get. Light is key to growing all plants, so knowing the intensity of the light that shines through your windows is key to selecting appropriate plants.
• Note both the daytime and nighttime temperature of your room.
• Consider how much space you have for a plant. Be careful not to select one that will outgrow your space too quickly.
• Be honest about how much time and care you have to give a houseplant. If you know you are likely to water irregularly, be sure to select a plant that will be forgiving.
• Talk to knowledgeable staff.
• Don't be afraid to ask 'stupid' questions. Chances are you can't come up with anything that hasn't already been asked. Besides, when you take that little bit of time to strike up a conversation, knowledgeable staff will often offer answers to questions you may not have known to ask.

You can learn a lot about the health of a plant simply by inspecting its leaves.

- Describe that plant you have in mind. Even if you can't remember its name, you can still describe its form and growing habit.
- Select plants according to their light requirements. Different plants need different amounts of light, so read tags and note the suggestions.
- Inspect leaves for general health.
- Keep an eye out for pests and blotches that could indicate fungal or bacterial problems. In general, leaves should look shiny—not dusty or covered in residue.
- Look for new leaves. Sometimes it's hard to tell a new leaf from an old one, but colour is a clue. New leaves are often a lighter and brighter shade of green.
- Look for buds on flowering plants. Plants need to be healthy to support bud production, so an abundance of buds indicates that the plant isn't under stress.
- Buy seasonal plants early. They are usually very popular, so get yours before they get picked over.
- Ask about delivery. Large plants can be hard to get home, so take advantage of services that are available.

The Basics

Plants have several basic needs: light, comfortable temperature, humidity, soil, water, fertilizer and physical space. Placed together on one list, the basics look a little daunting, but understanding their significance requires a very small (but thoughtful) investment of your time. And when it comes to plants, a little knowledge really does go a long way.

Light

Plants, like people, need energy to grow. But whereas people seem to obsess over avoiding carbohydrates, plants obsess over making them. I am, of course, referring to photosynthesis—the process by which plants take energy from the sun and convert it into sugars that can be used to grow. This process has been called the most important chemical reaction in the world.

Measuring Light

Light is the single most important factor in determining whether your houseplants will thrive or die. Unfortunately, it is also the most poorly understood factor. It comes down to understanding that the amount of light your plants receive will determine whether they are rapidly dying plants, slow-dying plants, status quo plants (neither gaining nor losing growth), slow-growing plants or rapidly growing plants.

Don't be afraid to move plants around. Keep them in their ideal growing locations during the day, when people are usually away, and then move them to your preferred display sites when company arrives.

Because light can't be held in one's hands or poured into a glass and measured, you have to think of it in terms of intensity, quality and duration.

- **Intensity of light:** the strength of light available
- **Quality of light:** the wavelengths or colours of light
- **Duration of light:** the amount of time plants are exposed to light in a 24-hour period

The relationship between these three factors is important. For example, if the quality of light is high, but there isn't much of it (intensity), or it doesn't last very long (duration), will your plant do well? Not on your life! Ideally, you want to give your plants the perfect intensity of the highest quality spectrum light for the optimum amount of time. But that will never happen. So the situation comes down to compromise and manipulation. The fact is, as wonderful as a short burst of perfect light is, 12 hours of lower quality light is better.

Light Factors

By far, the greatest challenge you'll have is providing your houseplants with enough light. Providing the ideal quantity of light seems like a fairly easy task initially, but consider the complicating factors that reduce the amount of natural light that gets to a plant's leaves.

- Not as much sunlight enters your home in the winter as it does in the summer. In fact, winter light may be 20% of summer light. This, of course, is because the days are shorter and the sun is lower in the sky.

A light meter is one of my favourite gadgets to use around the greenhouse. It helps me determine if plants are receiving the best light.

Because a window is roughly two dimensional, the sunlight that passes through it doesn't envelope a plant the way outdoor sunlight does. The result is a plant with lots of new growth on one side and none on the other. To combat this problem, give plants a quarter turn each time you water.

- Moving plants even a few extra feet away from a window will cause a dramatic reduction in sunlight. A few feet doesn't sound like much, but it is not uncommon to see a 100-fold drop in light when a plant is moved from a windowsill to a table a few feet away.
- Windows are not a source of sunlight—they merely allow light to pass through with, at best, 93% sunlight transmission. The sunlight transmission may drop to less than 50% if the glass is tinted.
- South-facing windows usually provide the greatest amount of sun exposure due to the sun's apogee (or track across the sky). For us in the northern hemisphere, the sun tracks across the southern sky with a high angle in the summer and a low angle in the winter. Because of this angle, south-facing windows tend to get the greatest amount of year-round light exposure, with west-facing and east-facing windows coming in second and third respectively. North-facing windows receive little if any direct light but can capture enough indirect sunlight to grow a few low-light plants.

Zebra Plant

Other factors that contribute to inconsistent natural light

Many other factors may contribute to inconsistent natural light throughout the year, including fog, cloud cover, elevation, drapes and window treatments, the presence of ultraviolet-blocking coatings, dirt or dust on the window, reflections from light-coloured interior paint and the presence of awnings, overhangs or shade trees near windows.

Artificial Lights

Fortunately for plant lovers, artificial lights can be used to supplement the natural light that windows provide. What's unfortunate, however, is that there tends to be a lot of confusion about what artificial lights can and cannot do.

The majority of the lights available in garden centres are referred to as grow lights, implying that they have some magical ability to grow plants above and beyond that of standard lights. The reality is that virtually every common household light *is* a grow light. In other words, they all emit at least some light in the visible light spectrum—otherwise, why would we use them? Some of these lights are better than others when it comes to light spectrum, but all of them (with the exception of those used by professional growers) are quite wimpy. What I mean by that is typical grow lights from hardware stores kick out very little total light energy and, therefore, may starve your plants. Many so-called grow lights do have plant-friendly light spectrums, but they are equivalent to one wonderfully flavoured, but Lilliputian-sized appetizer at a dinner party—something that will satisfy your tastebuds but starve you if it's the whole meal.

To give you an idea of what grow lights can and can't do, let's compare some of the common 'grow lights' you might find in a store.

Simply moving plants off the floor and onto a table by a window will increase the amount of sunlight they receive.

Snake Plant 'Moonglow'

Plants prefer certain wavelengths of light over others—red and blue being the favourites. There are also green wavelengths, but they aren't used for photosynthesis. Instead, the green light that strikes a plant's leaves is reflected towards your eyes, which is why the plants appear green.

Stephanotis

Fluorescent Lights

Cool white-light fluorescent tubes
Cool white-light fluorescents emit a high percentage of blue light and green light (which is why people's complexions look a little dull under them). These lights are convenient, economical, energy efficient and—best of all—don't produce excessive heat. Although these lights stimulate some of the processes needed for growth, they don't provide enough of the entire spectrum of light that plants need to grow to their full potential.

Warm white-light fluorescent tubes
Warm white-light fluorescents are slightly better than cool white-light flourescents in that they provide a greater portion of the light spectrum (specifically the red band), but these lights don't entirely meet a plant's needs either.

Chloroplasts are structures that contain chlorophyll and give plants their green colour. The primary duty of chlorophyll is to take electromagnetic energy (sunlight) and change it into chemical energy. Without this conversion, electromagnetic energy can't be turned into the usable energy we call food.

As a general rule, plants receiving no outdoor light should receive 16–18 hours of artificial light each day. For plants that are supplemented with natural light, 12–14 hours of artificial light should be adequate. In such cases, artificial lights should be used at the same time that the plant is receiving natural light from a window.

Eucalyptus

Incandescent Lights

An incandescent light is any light that has a filament. Although incandescent light is the light people tend to prefer, plants don't really value it. Most of the electrical energy from an incandescent light is converted to heat, and only 6–12% is converted to usable light. Because incandescent lights produce a lot of red light, they need to be used in combination with fluorescent tubes in a ratio of about 1:3 to prevent plants from becoming stretched and lanky. So for 100 watts of fluorescent light, provide about 30 watts of incandescent light. This ratio ensures a better red-to-blue light balance.

Note: the intensity of light drops dramatically as distance increases between light bulb and plant, so height-adjustable fluorescent tubes are ideal for tweaking that optimum distance.

Managing Light Levels

It's important to realize that a plant that requires low light *can* be placed in a room with bright southern exposure. The key, however, to keeping that plant from becoming stressed is moving it an appropriate distance away from the window. The closer a plant is to a window or skylight, the more light it receives. Just remember that light intensity and duration change with the seasons.

I will admit to being a bit of a light-meter geek, but in my defence, the concept of measuring something you can't hold or touch is pretty cool.

Outdoors, the intensity of sunlight cast in the middle of a summer day may average between 10,000 and 12,000 foot-candles. Indoors, light intensity depends on a combination of artificial and natural light. The best way to measure light is with a light meter.

A light meter can show how light levels change as you move away from a window. At one time, light intensity for plants was measured in foot-candles, but that is a term more suited to measuring the human eye's sensitivity to light than it is to measuring the light energy that plants use. The correct term for plant light intensity is a bit of a tongue twister—*photosynthetic photon flux*. The actual units are measured as micromolecs per square metre per second. If this sounds complicated, try thinking of measuring light as we do raindrops. The volume of water that hits each square metre every second can be measured and quantified.

LIGHT IN THIS BOOK

The amount of light required by plants listed in this book is measured according to the following labels:

- **Direct:** sunlight strikes the plant's leaves for at least three hours a day.

- **Bright Indirect:** plants are very close to a sunny window but not in direct sunlight.

- **Indirect:** plants are in a bright sunlit room but not near a window.

Temperature

In an ideal world, you would make your houseplants feel at home by adjusting the temperature of their indoor environment to mimic their natural environment. The reality, however, is that, your comfort is likely to come before that of your plants. And even if you were to choose your plant's comfort over your own, homes have warmer and cooler spots just waiting to present problems.

Because there are so many species of indoor plants, it follows that there is a wide range of ideal growing temperatures. Fortunately, plants are reasonably tolerant of variations from the ideal. As a general rule, keep nighttime temperatures a few degrees cooler than daytime temperatures: 18–27°C during the day and no less than 15°C at night.

The cooler nighttime temperature is important because it allows plants to store energy. When nighttime temperatures are hot, plants have no choice but to burn a portion of the energy that they worked hard to accumulate during the day. Flowering plants are especially appreciative of a cool rest in the evenings because it prolongs flower life and colour intensity.

Swedish Ivy

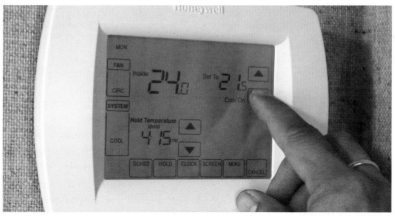

Most houseplants enjoy temperatures between 16°C and 27°C. Conventional wisdom says any lower and you run the risk of chilling injury; any higher, and houseplants burn up their energy reserves. Fortunately, indoor heat is fairly easy to control—just keep an eye on your thermostat. A good compromise between humans and plants is somewhere between 18°C and 27°C.

Here is a list of conditions houseplants generally dislike:
• Extreme changes in temperature
• Cold drafts from windows or exterior doors
• Hot air blasts from fireplaces, heat registers or radiators
• Close proximity to hot or cold window panes
• Night temperatures that dip below 14°C
• Daytime temperatures in the upper 20°C to lower 30°C range

Humidity

Relative humidity is simply a measure of the amount of water the air will hold at a given temperature. The reason it becomes an important factor in plant health is that it affects plant moisture loss.

Ideal relative humidity for most houseplants is about 60%, but during the winter months when our homes tend to be far less humid, a much more realistic percentage to aim for is about 25%. I have yet to see a plant that has died due to low relative humidity, and I don't even want to think about the condensation my windows would collect during the winter if I tried to keep my home at 60% relative humidity. So although your plants might appreciate your efforts, don't fall into the trap of believing you can't grow beautiful plants in a dry home or office. Remember, there are both deserts and rainforests in nature, and plants thrive in both environments.

Here is a list of ways to maintain ideal humidity:
• Use a humidifier.
• Group plants closely so they can benefit from one another's transpiration.

- Keep plants away from heat sources like registers and fireplaces.
- Grow especially humidity-sensitive plants in terrariums—if they're small enough.

Symptoms indicating that a plant may be suffering from a lack of water (including relative humidity) are brown leaf edges, abnormally small leaves, misshapen plant growth and drooping or wilting.

Note: in most cases, the real culprit at work is a lack of soil moisture—not low relative humidity.

Watering

There are many tools and gadgets on the market designed to measure soil moisture, yet very few are as reliable or as 'handy' as the 10 you already have. There's no secret method to checking whether a plant needs water. Just walk over and stick your finger in the potting soil, scratching down 2–3 cm into the soil. Moist soil should feel about as wet as a damp sponge. In fact, the soil should feel a little spongy, too. Even when the top layer of soil looks dry, there may still be plenty of moisture just beneath the surface.

How much water your plant needs and how often your plant needs it depend on the following factors:

- Type of plant
- Size of plant
- Size and type of container
- Soil composition
- Humidity of the growing environment
- Season

Window panes can allow plants to become too hot in the day and too cold at night, so use window coverings to help regulate the two extremes.

Home humidifiers can help reduce moisture loss a little bit, but simply paying close attention to the plant and keeping it well watered can alleviate the effects of low humidity. Many people advocate placing pots on top of pebbles sitting in water-filled trays as a means of raising humidity around plants, but it's just not so—can a couple of centimetres of water really raise the humidity enough to counteract the effects of a dry house? Not at all.

- Location of the plant in the room
- Average room temperature

Know your plant's preferences and water accordingly. Don't forget that although most plants will forgive you if you miss a watering here or there, some plants aren't as tolerant. Boston ferns, for example, hate dry soil. On the flip side, cacti hate being too wet.

Watering Methods

Most plants get watered from the top, but that says more about people's preferences than it does about plants. Most plants don't care whether they are watered from the top or from the bottom as long as they are watered regularly and sufficiently. A general way to gauge whether you've given your plant enough to drink is to check for water running through the drainage holes at the bottom of the container. This runoff is particularly important because it flushes excess salts from the soil. Just be sure to drain any water that remains sitting in the base of the saucer.

HOLD the FLUORIDE... and the CHLORINE, PLEASE

Plants are not as enamoured of fluoride as we are. In fact, the fluoride in our tap water can be quite a problem for dracaenas, palms and ti-plants. Spider plants (especially variegated ones) are extremely sensitive to fluoride, so watch for signs of damage such as browning of foliage tips. If you want to avoid complications related to fluoride, water with distilled water or rainwater when possible.

If soils have adequate lime and a proper pH level, fluoride in the water will be tightly bound in the soil and not be drawn up by the plant roots.

Chlorine is another nutrient that can be hard on plants. If you grow chlorine-sensitive plants, like African violets, fill your watering can in the evening and let it stand overnight. This will allow the chlorine to evaporate and will also bring the water to room temperature.

WATERING GADGETS

Many homes have great vertical spaces that are ideal for plants. The trouble is that while high ledges and tops of bookshelves are perfect spots for growing plants, they can also create inconvenient watering situations. Fortunately, there are many gadgets designed to make watering a little easier.

My best advice is to keep it simple. A lightweight stepladder and a long-necked watering can is all you really need. Just be sure to choose a watering can you can comfortably handle. A plastic watering can might not weigh much when it's empty, but fill it with water, hold it away from your body and watch just how quickly your arm starts shaking.

Allow plants to dry out partially between waterings to ensure that the root zone doesn't stay continuously wet. Soggy roots can introduce a host of health problems to your plants.

Watering from the top

- Consider grouping plants together in the bathtub and giving them a gentle watering and shower. After you've watered, let your plants stay in the tub for a few hours. This will allow them to drain properly and keep you from tracking water across your house.
- Don't water from high above your plant. Place the spout of your watering can close to the lip of the container and water from a different side each time. Watering from the same spot each time will wash away sections of topsoil and leave behind craters.

I don't care much for water meters. My fingers do a better job of telling me whether or not soil is dry—and for a lot less money.

Watering from the Bottom

Some plants, like African violets, prefer to wick water through the drainage holes in the bottoms of their pots, essentially drawing up water until the surface soil is moist. This method is particularly beneficial to fuzzy-leaved plants that tend to blemish when they come in contact with water.

Don't feel you have to hide your watering can in a closet. They've come a long way, and many of the sleek contemporary designs make attractive accessories.

Soil

The quality of potting mix can mean the difference between life and death for a houseplant, so invest in a high-quality mix—one that offers the correct balance of water and oxygen. This balance is important because the soil must be able to retain moisture long enough to sustain a plant between waterings yet also allow for proper drainage.

Don't reuse soil from the pots of 'plants past.' If the plant died because of pests or disease, the soil could be contaminated. Even if the plant died because you dried it out, chances are the soil has too few pore spaces (pockets of open spaces that can be filled with water) to sustain a new plant. As soil decomposes, it starts to lose pore space and becomes too dense for air to infiltrate and for roots to grow properly. Pots can, however, be reused—just be sure to scrub them clean and then soak them in a solution of 10% bleach and water.

If I wear one snobbish indulgence proudly, it has to be my penchant for correcting people when they refer to soil as dirt. Soil is not dirt. Soil is defined as a dynamic natural body composed of inert and organic solids, gases, liquids and living organisms, which can serve as a medium for plant growth. Dirt is just the stuff under your fingernails, thank you very much.

Hydroponics is a method of growing plants in the absence of soil. Instead, a plant's roots grow in nutrient-rich water. Hydroponics might seem like something new and high-tech, but the practice goes all the way back to the Hanging Gardens of Babylon.

Potting Mix vs. Soil Mix

Soil is the term most people use to describe the black medium in which we pot plants. But the truth is that most of the 'soil' to which we refer is actually soil-less—completely free of what we traditionally think of as garden soil. It looks like rich field or garden soil and even smells like it but is completely different.

Most potting mixes contain at least one of the following materials: peat moss, vermiculite, perlite, sand and lime (to neutralize the peat moss), bark, pumice or compost. Soil mixes, on the other hand, contain a blend of soil. So when you're looking for 'soil,' be sure to read the bags carefully and choose a high-quality soilless potting mix.

It's hard to tell what's in a potting mix just by looking at it, so always read the label carefully to make sure you're bringing home the right mix for your plant. Orchid mix, pictured here, is a mixture specifically formulated to meet the needs of orchids.

Specialty Potting Mixes

African violets, cacti and orchids require special potting mixes. Because of the popularity of these plants, distributors have come up with special commercial blends of each.

Orchid mixes: To the uninitiated, this planting medium might look unable to sustain anything other than a beaver. Many contain two or three types of bark, coarse sphagnum peat, fine-grade pumice and sponge rock. It's an odd combination, but one that serves an important purpose.

Some species of orchids grow on trees in their natural habitat. These orchids are referred to as *epiphytic* plants—those having roots exposed to the air. One of the reasons orchid mixes contain bark and moss is to allow air to move freely through the medium. This air movement allows an orchid's roots to absorb moisture and nutrients from the humid air.

Cacti mixes: Even someone who doesn't know much about cacti knows that these plants prefer dry soil. It should come as no surprise to find that the standard potting medium for cacti is composed of coarse sand, potting mix, peat and perlite. Although the formula varies from one commercial mix to another, all cacti mixes are designed to provide rapid drainage.

African violet mixes: African violets like a light, loose, porous soil, so most commercial African violet mixes consist of three parts peat moss, two parts coarse vermiculite and one part perlite. Lime is also often added to bring the pH level to the 5.8–6.0 range. Because African violets hate their roots sitting in water, the loose, porous soil is important for the health of these plants.

Fertilizer

Plants need fertilizer to supplement their diets. Although they feed on light and the nutrients in the soil, a boost of fertilizer can help promote and support strong, healthy growth.

Fertilizers contain three major nutrients to support stem and leaf production, flowering and healthy roots. These elements are nitrogen (N), phosphorous (P) and potassium (K). When you look at a container of fertilizer, pay special attention to the fertilizer analysis represented by three hyphenated numbers (for example, 20-20-20 or 10-6-16). The first number represents available nitrogen. The second number represents available phosphate, and the third number represents available potash. The higher the number, the greater the percentage by weight of that nutrient. Plants require nitrogen for leafy growth, so as a general rule, plants grown primarily for their foliage are given a fertilizer with a high first number, a lower second number and a third number that is comparable to the first. Plants grown primarily for their blooms are given a fertilizer with a high

Brassia Orchid

Different fertilizer should be applied for different purposes, but as a general rule, a plant will use five times as much nitrogen as it will phosphate.

third number (K or potash) that promotes flower development. For specific recommendations regarding fertilizer for individual plants see "Indoor Plant Favourites" begining on page 173.

Fertilizers are most beneficial to a plant during its growing season (February to October). During winter months there is less light, so hold back on fertilizing unless your plant is showing signs of new growth. A plant's fertilizer consumption follows its growth curve, which in turn follows a light and temperature curve.

General Rules for Fertilizing

• Granular and liquid fertilizers work similarly. Be sure to read the instructions and to mix and feed accordingly.
• Hold off fertilizing for at least a few weeks after plants are repotted. It's not that the plants don't need food; it's that they need only so much. Most soils contain unknown amounts of fertilizer and it's easy to overfeed your transplant.
• Water until water flows out the bottom of the container. This step will help flush any buildup of soluble salt deposits. As salts become more concentrated, it becomes harder for a plant to take up a proper supply of water.

Silver Shield

Containers

Your plant needs a suitable home to live successfully indoors. That's why container choice is so important—and there's a wide range of containers from which to choose.

The two most important factors to consider when choosing a container are size—in both depth and diameter—and drainage. Aesthetics are also a consideration.

Size

Make sure your plant has the proper root-to-soil volume. This means choosing a container that will accommodate a plant's root system and a sufficient amount of soil to sustain it. An oversized pot

The theory that layers of pebbles at the bottom of a pot is good for a plant is older than it is wise. Pebbles actually hinder drainage by reducing the soil depth. Most people who add rocks to a pot without drainage holes assume that the rocks will create a reservoir for the water to accumulate. While this is true, excessive salts will accumulate in the reservoir over time. Further, when you displace soil space with pebbles, you reduce the amount of living space for roots. To give your plants the best home possible, leave the rocks out of the bottom of their pots.

Containers come in a variety of shapes and colours. Choose one to meet your plant's specific needs and to suit your decorating style.

You can add interest to a potted plant by top-dressing the soil surface with colourful decorative pebbles.

holds more soil than is needed, and that soil can easily become saturated with water, disrupting the air/water balance and increasing the plant's chance of dying of root rot. Never increase soil volume by more than one pot size when repotting.

Drainage

Unless you're growing an indoor water garden, be sure to choose containers that have drainage holes. Water must be able to drain through the soil and out of the pot. Without proper drainage, a plant is likely to die. If you're thinking about putting rocks at the bottom of your pot to help with drainage, don't! It's a point that you'll hear repeated in this book—basically because it's worth repeating. Pebbles shorten the column of soil, allowing the soil to become more easily waterlogged.

This Rex Begonia takes on a whole new look each time its conatiner is changed.

Umbrella Tree

Beauty

Just because a container has to be functional doesn't mean it can't be attractive, too. Garden centres are full of beautiful containers that fit any style and budget. The right container can make just as big an impression as the plant itself, so take your time and pay attention to those finishing touches—they have a way of making all the difference.

Tips
- Remember to buy a saucer or tray to go under a container (many containers are sold with a matching saucer).
- Add caster wheels to the bottom of a large container for easy mobility.
- Use decorative moss, pebbles and driftwood on the soil surface to create visual interest and to discourage pets from digging.
- Conceal less attractive pots and saucers in decorative baskets, crocks or plant stands.

 How to Build a Terrarium
Building a terrarium is fun and easy!

Materials

Because a terrarium is a self-contained ecosystem, you must set it up properly the first time, using proper materials. Be sure to buy a high-quality potting mix and select the appropriate plants.

Supplies needed:
- One terrarium with air holes or a glass jar without a lid (such as a fishbowl or a pickle jar)
- Small gravel (pea rock or aquarium gravel will do)
- High-quality potting mix
- Sphagnum moss
- Plants (two or three for every 3 L of space; avoid fuzzy-leaved plants—they hold water and are susceptible to rotting)
- Decorative accessories (stones, drift wood, etc.)

Preparing the soil

Start by creating a 1 cm base of gravel at the bottom of the terrarium. The gravel provides proper drainage, which is important because the container has no holes.

Next, cover the gravel with a layer of potting mix. At least 5 cm of mix is required, but the mix can come up as high as half the height of the terrarium.

Note: charcoal is not necessary. The common belief is that charcoal will 'filter' the soil and keep it clean, but activated charcoal becomes inactive as soon as it's exposed to carbon in the air.

Transplanting

Space plants according to the mature height and spread listed on their tags.

Prepare holes in the soil where the plants will go by gently scooping away enough potting mix to bury the roots to the same depth as they were growing in their pots.

Remove plants from containers and examine the roots. Packed and tangled (rootbound) rootballs can be gently teased loose. Don't worry if the soil falls off plants while transplanting. Losing some is fine.

Place plants in prepared holes and gently firm the soil, being careful not to pack it. Remove any damaged leaves.

Watching it grow

Cover the terrarium with the lid and place it in a spot that receives bright indirect light (light that is filtered). Placing a terrarium in a bright window might seem like a nice treat for your plants, but it's the equivalent of steaming vegetables in a pot!

If you didn't use a container with air holes, don't cover your terrarium with a lid. Although it's possible to grow plants in a self-contained environment, it's incredibly difficult and requires perfect light, temperature and humidity conditions.

Trimming the terrarium

Decorate the soil with bits of moss or add other finishing touches such as driftwood or decorative stones. You're creating your own little world, so let your imagination guide you.

Watering

Give plants a thorough watering but don't overwater. A terrarium sustains itself, so the first watering is essential to establishing a correct moisture level.

Caring
for Your Plant

Neglect seems to be inevitable when it comes to caring for house-plants. Let's face it, there are days—occasionally weeks—when just getting one's self ready and out the door on time is a feat of heroic proportions. Because plants don't whine, bark or leave messages on our answering machines, they occasionally fall victim to neglect. To ensure that your plants are around to enjoy years of life in your home or office, set up a maintenance schedule and do your best to stick to it.

Cleaning

Plants clean the air for us, so it's only fair that we take a turn cleaning them. When a plant's leaves are dirty, they can't absorb as much sunlight, which makes photosynthesis more difficult.

Cleaning a plant not only removes sun-blocking dust and helps it to look its best, but it also gives you an opportunity to inspect leaves for general health. Although the job may sound like a lot of work, it's a great way for plant enthusiasts to get closer to their plants and for gardeners to keep their green thumbs in shape for the next growing season.

Use a soft cloth or a natural sponge to clean smooth leaves. Old T-shirts also work well; just cut them into quarters for easier handling. Paper towels may seem like a good idea, but besides being expensive and wasteful, they also leave lint on leaves.

How often should I clean my plants?

Aim to clean your plants every month. You probably won't get around to doing it that often, but the more often you attempt it, the more likely you are to get it done. Depending on what kind of heating system you have, you may find that your house gets dustier at certain times of the year than it does at others.

Always clean or mist plants with tepid water. Cold water can cause leaves to spot, and hot water is damaging.

Tips for cleaning

- Dry dust delicate, fuzzy-leaved or crinkly leaved plants with a soft paintbrush.
- Use tweezers to remove debris from cacti. Tweezers are ideal for reaching between hairs and spines, and your hands are sure to thank you.
- Plants with small, smooth leaves that can't be practically wiped down can be cleaned by placing a plastic bag over the pot and gently cinching it around the plant's base with your hand to protect the soil. Hold the plant under a gently running spray of tepid water.
- In warm weather, take plants outside and give them a good shower—just be sure to use tepid water and to let it drain before you bring plants back into the house.

Flamingo Flower

Pruning and Deadheading

It's surprising how easily even tough houseplants can be damaged. When leaves or stems are damaged or broken, it's important to reach for the scissors. You might be tempted to let the plant repair itself, but that will only leave it vulnerable to diseases and pests.

Here are some other reasons to prune your houseplants:

• **For shape:** Prune back plants that become overgrown or straggly. Dieffenbachia, for instance, have a tendency to run out of ceiling space. To remedy this problem, simply prune the top at the spot where you would like to encourage branching. Throw the top away, or reroot it in a new pot. In the case of tree-form plants, prune branches that cross through the centre of a plant. It will help maintain a pleasing form and allow sunlight into the centre of these plants.

Tip pruning is a great way to encourage new growth on the lower branches of indoor trees. Prune tips regularly and you'll be rewarded with a bushy plant and a quieter space—the more leaves a tree has the more sound it buffers.

Deadheading spent blooms keeps your indoor plants looking tidy.

- **To encourage growth:** Keep in mind that the biological purpose of all plants is to reproduce. When you deadhead (remove spent flowers), you are also removing the seeds. By doing so, you trick the plant into thinking it hasn't fulfilled its reproductive goal. The plant responds by producing more flowerbuds and, eventually, more flowers.
- **To remove disease:** Yes, it's that simple—prune out disease. It's a good habit to clean your shears after every use, but it's especially important to wipe them with a solution of water with 10% bleach after pruning out disease. Dry your shears to prevent rust.

TRUTH and FICTION

It never ceases to amaze me how much bad information gets passed on from generation to generation. I'm not sure what makes us so eager to cling to bad advice, but we all seem to do it.

In an attempt to dispel some of the myths floating around the indoor plant world, here is a list of advice to set the record straight.

- No, you shouldn't use milk to shine leaves (a soft cloth will do).
- No, pebbles won't help with drainage in a pot (buy pots with drainage holes).
- No, poinsettias aren't poisonous (but that doesn't mean you should eat them).
- Talking to houseplants will not make them grow (but it might make *you* feel good!).
- Plants won't take the oxygen out of the room (in fact, during photosynthesis they release oxygen).
- Soil doesn't have to be moist before you fertilize plants (parched plants won't absorb more water than they need, so their fertilizer uptake is still controlled).
- Fertilizer doesn't cause plants to grow (but light does).

Most plants have a natural growth season, and that time tends to be in the spring and summer when the days are longer. Giving a plant a larger pot and a fresh supply of soil at this time of the year will promote root growth and benefit the general health of the plant.

Repotting

In nature, roots go where the living is good. They search for water and nutrients in the soil and don't stop until they find them. Because houseplants are restricted to pots, their roots can spread only so far. In order to support plant's root systems, it's necessary to repot to a larger container from time to time.

An easy way to tell whether a plant needs repotting is simply to tip it upside down (while cradling the plant in your hand) and tap it gently out of its pot—if a plant is large, this may take a team of people to accomplish. If the bottom half of the container contains mostly roots and very little soil, it's time to repot. The reason is simple: at this stage, the roots have penetrated nearly every pore space in the soil, leaving little room for air or water. By repotting the plant, you're giving it much-needed physical space and a fresh supply of soil and essential nutrients.

Other signs that indicate it's time to repot include exposed roots, yellowing leaves, slow growth or little new growth and top-heavy plants that tip over easily.

How to Repot a Plant

Repotting a plant isn't as difficult as it may seem. All you need
to do is plan ahead and follow a few easy steps.

1. Do the prep work.

A little preparation can save you a lot of cleanup. Moments after you've
started removing the plant from its container is a bad time to realize
you've forgotten to pick up potting mix, so make a list of everything you
need to get the job done properly: potting mix, water, a bigger container,
gloves and scissors. I tend to get soil everywhere, so for me a huge drop
cloth is also essential. I also recommend using a beneficial fungus, available
as a product called MYKE. It contains mycorise fungi that colonize on a
plant's roots, increasing phosphate uptake, which in turn stimulates root
development (the fungi colonize on most plants, with the exception of
members of the *Crassula*, *Orchidaceae* and *Ericaceae* families).

2. Water your plant the day before you plan to repot.

Watering will soften the roots, leaving them pliable and easy
to manipulate.

3. Select a pot.

Choose a practical container that is only one size larger than the one
you are currently using. There are lots of decorative containers, but sometimes beauty and creativity must bow to functionality. One of our staff
members found this out when he planted a collection of cacti in a strawberry pot. It was an impressive display and seemed like a great idea until it
was time to repot. There was no way to get the plants out without break-
ing the container—and no way to break the container without damaging
the cacti.

*A cactus may look as though it has outgrown its
shallow containers, but the only way to know for
sure is to turn it over and to check the roots. More
often than not, you'll find that the root system is
healthy and has enough room and soil to sustain
new growth.*

*Don't give a small plant an oversized pot to grow
into. The container will hold too much soil and,
therefore, too much water.*

Tease roots free with the same gentleness you'd use to untangle a knot from your hair.

4. Take it outside.

Repotting can become quite an ordeal, so whenever possible, make the mess outside. If going outdoors isn't possible, line a table or countertop with newspaper that can be rolled up and discarded when you're done. Dishwashing basins also make great portable potting sinks.

5. Be brave.

Getting started is sometimes the hardest part, so be confident and go for it! Put on gloves if you require them, and then tip the plant out of its container and into your hand.

6. 'Tease' the roots.

Gently tease tightly bound roots free to encourage them to explore the new potting soil. If the plant is very rootbound, use a gardening claw to loosen the rootball.

When the roots have been gently loosened, use scissors to cut away any damage.

7. Prepare the soil.

Shake 3–4 cm of soil mix into the bottom of the new container. Gently insert the plant into the pot, ensuring that it sits at the same height as it was in the original pot. If necessary, remove the plant and add more soil.

Use a repotting service if your plant is very big. Some jobs are too difficult to tackle alone, so if you have a plant that requires more time, muscles, expertise or patience than you have, get a garden centre professional to take care of it for you (there may be a charge for this service).

8. Gently fill the pot around the plant with soil mix.

Use hand movements that mimic those you would use to tuck a shirt into your pants. Be sure not to pack down the soil. If you do, you'll end up with drainage problems.

9. Water the plant thoroughly.

Don't stop until water flows out from the holes in the bottom of the container.

Caring for Seasonal Plants

Holiday plants are hard to resist. Not only are they readily available, but their beauty and great value make them perfect guests in our homes. Yet the holidays are hard on plants, too. One of the reasons that holiday plants take such a beating is that most people think of them as disposable—and, for the most part, they are. Of course, we all know people who manage to keep a poinsettia from one year to the next, but the bragging rights that come with that coup are usually more impressive than the plant itself.

The secret to keeping a holiday plant looking healthy isn't really much of a secret. Simply make time to water and deadhead. It comes down to recognizing that you don't need to grow the plant—you simply need to maintain the status quo. What I mean is that a holiday plant is on holiday. It has spent months working and growing to its peak of perfection, and now all that it has to do is retain its beauty. This fact makes your job relatively easy— putting the plant in the right environment and watering properly is often all that is required. It does take a bit of effort and patience on your part, but no more than it does to be nice to well-meaning relatives and friends who overstay their holiday welcome.

Amaryllis

Troubleshooting
& Common Problems

aphids

Pests and Diseases

Dealing with pests and diseases is difficult because the process involves considerable diagnosis. It's natural for people to focus on the remedy that promises to 'cure' a sick plant, but the cure is only one piece of the puzzle. To put the whole puzzle together, you have to know what kind of a plant you have, the kind of insect that's attacking it, the treatments available and the frequency of those treatments. If you miss even one of these pieces, you lessen your chances of solving your problem. With that said, don't lose hope! Knowledge is the key to identifying and dealing with pests and diseases, and you're about to acquire it.

Pests

The joy of purchasing a beautiful houseplant quickly fades when the first 'pet' is discovered on a leaf. The pet I am referring to, of course, is not the four-legged, furry kind, but rather the six (or more!) legged variety that loves plants as much as we do.

When most people try to take on the insects and pests that attack houseplants, their goal is usually to annihilate them—to destroy every last

One weapon in dealing with insect pests, like the mealy bug pictured here, is remembering that they are cold blooded and completely vulnerable to temperature. Therefore, the speed of insect reproduction, growth and feeding is influenced by the temperature of your home. The higher the temperatures, the greater the potential for insect problems.

one! While I agree that eradication is the ultimate goal, I have yet to see an instance where anyone has successfully implemented a program without first having a thorough understanding of the enemy.

The good news about insect and insect-like enemies is that of the millions of insect species in the world, only a handful are pests of houseplants. The bad news is that handful is a bit like the Dirty Dozen—a tough bunch to kill. Many of the pests we battle have adapted extremely well to our attempts at controlling them, pesticide resistance being a prime example. But, by far, the number one reason I see pest control fail is due to a failure to understand the pest.

Part of understanding pests is understanding their place in nature. It's hard to look past the fact that pests cause a lot of frustration, but they are part of the ecosystem—not extraneous to it. In nature, pests are kept in balance by a well-functioning system of predators and prey. Of course, household environments can't support the diversity required to keep plant pests in check, so the inevitable result is an exploding pest population and a trail of dead and dying plants.

So beyond seeking to help you identify your pest problems properly, I hope to inspire in you an unlikely appreciation for the pests themselves. Now, I didn't say love; I said appreciation…as in new-found respect. After all, as much as their destructive tendencies drive us crazy, they are fascinating enemies and amazingly successful creatures—despite our best efforts to obliterate them.

Given 30 days at 30°C, one female spider mite is capable of giving rise to 30 million offspring. Of course, these numbers are theoretical, requiring the perfect environment and no enemies feeding on them, but you get the idea.

 Spider mites have truly amazing fecundity (reproductive rates) that is second to none in the arena of houseplant pests. The typically male-to-female ratio of offspring is roughly three females for each male. But don't let the shortage of males fool you—spider mites don't need to mate to produce offspring. Fertilized females produce both males and females, while unfertilized females produce only males.

Spider Mites

Physical description: Spider mites—just one of the many types of mite that attack plants and probably the worst of the lot—are generally 5 mm long and oval shaped, varying in colour from yellowish to greenish and even reddish to brownish. Spider mites are difficult to see, so they usually go unnoticed until they become a full-blown problem.

The damage and the signs: Spider mites are polyphagous (meaning they eat many different plants) and spend most of their time piercing plant tissue and feeding on sap. The first indication of a problem is usually mottled leaves. Heavy infestations produce frail, silky webbing that can cause plants to die.

Where to look for them: Spider mites live on the underside of leaves.

Seriousness of the problem: Severe if not controlled early. One of the reasons mites spread quickly is that they produce threads that act as crude parachutes, enabling mites to glide on drafts from one plant to another. They can also hitch a ride on our clothing.

Preferred environment: Spider mites like hot, dry conditions, so they are well suited to living indoors. They prefer plants with soft easily pierced tissues and tend to avoid those with foliage that is waxy.

Treatment and prevention: Spider mites can be challenging to get rid of. Because the eggs are resilient to most sprays, treatments must be applied at five- to seven-day intervals. For best results, use a good insecticidal soap and cover these pests thoroughly.

Scale Insects

Physical description: Scale insects earn their name because their protective shells look like scales. They are difficult to see without a magnifying glass, but even when you can see them, you're not seeing their bodies per se but rather their shell-like, waxy protective coverings. Most scale insects are 1.5–3 mm in diameter and round or oval shaped. To the naked eye, scale looks like brown scabs.

The damage and the signs: Scales cause discoloration, stunting and even leaf drop if the infestation is bad enough. The greatest problem is usually the honeydew (the clear, sticky secretion the scale leaves behind) and the sooty mould that grows on it. Unfortunately, the scales tend to stick to the plant long after the insect is dead.

Where to look for them: Scale insects can be found on stems, leaf veins, undersides of leaves and leaf joints.

Seriousness of the problem: Scale problems are often overlooked for two reasons. First, they look like part of the bark, and second, they are immobile for a good part of their lives and conceal themselves in the plant.

Preferred environment: Scale insects don't like extreme weather and prefer warm, humid, shady conditions.

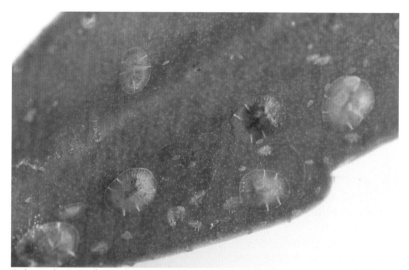

Scale reproduction is often parthenogenetic (without mating) with females giving rise to entirely female offspring. In some species of scale, the males live for only one or two days and are rarely seen. In a greenhouse, six or seven generations are possible in a year.

Treatment and prevention:
Females can lay a huge number of
eggs—up to 3000 over several
weeks. The crawlers that emerge
from the eggs are most sensitive to
sprays because they haven't devel-
oped their protective shell-like
armour. Scale can be removed with
your fingers when the insects are
adult size, but you'll have the best
chance of controlling the problem
if you apply a thorough coating of
insecticidal spray or horticultural
oil on the young crawlers every
7–10 days until all signs of these
pests are gone. As hard as scale is
to battle, you can get rid of it.

Mealy Bugs

Physical description: Mealy
bugs have soft, slender, waxy bodies
that are 12 mm long and dusty
looking. Many mealy bugs are covered with waxy threads. Females
are wingless and tend to move very
little.

*Female mealy bugs are sometimes viviparous,
meaning they produce live young, bypassing the
egg stage.*

The damage and the signs:
Mealy bugs suck the sap from
leaves and leave behind a trail of
sticky honeydew. Other signs of
damage are yellowing or dropping
leaves.

Where to look for them:
Mealy bugs can live on the undersides of leaves, on leaf joints, below
the surface of the soil or on newly
pruned stems.

Seriousness of the problem: A
mealy bug's waxy coat keeps it well
protected from predators and pesticides, so controlling the problem is
a serious issue. Because pesticides
are often absorbed through the
exoskeleton, the waxy coat on a
mealy bug acts like a safety suit,
shucking off the spray and render-
ing many pesticides useless.

Preferred environment: Mealy
bugs tend to inhabit leaf axils (the
spots where leaves meet stems) and
leaf veins. They reproduce quickest
in warm, humid environments but
manage to survive in less than ideal
environments.

Although mealy bugs are
notorious pests, one
species produces bright-red pigments
that have been used as a dye. In fact,
I'm willing to bet that if you have ever
had strawberry ice cream, chances are
good that you have eaten mealy bugs—
the pink colour of the ice cream was
often intensified with the dye extracted
from the cactus-loving cochineal mealy
bug.

Treatment and prevention:
Mealy bugs are easy to deal with
on a bug-by-bug basis, but if neglected they can become a big
problem. Simply picking off of-
fenders when you notice them
and following up by dabbing rub-
bing alcohol directly on the insects
will often do the trick. For bigger
infestations, aim for a thorough
application of horticultural oil or
insecticidal soap, every 7–10 days
for as many applications as needed.

Thrips

Physical description: Thrips
are insects from the order *Thy-
sanoptera*, which means *fringed wings*,
and are generally just a few milli-
metres long and a fraction of a
millimetre wide. They are also very
mobile and able to run, fly and
jump. Most thrips are tan or dark
coloured.

The damage and the signs:
Thrips feed on foliage, buds and
flowers by scraping and piercing
the cells of plant tissue and drawing
out the nutrient-rich contents.
Infested leaves have a silvery, stippled appearance that resembles the
damage caused by mites. An easy
way to distinguish a thrip infestation from a mite infestation is to
look for the brownish specks of
excrement that thrips leave behind
where they feed. Besides causing
leaves to shrivel, thrips transmit
viruses that can cause more damage
than the pests do.

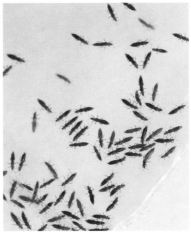

Thrips have eyelash-like hairs along their wing margins, and although they aren't strong flyers, they can open their wings and drift along on air currents.

Where to look for them:
Thrips can be found on leaves,
buds, flowers and under plant
debris. Females make slits in plant
tissue and lay the eggs within.
When larvae mature, they often
fall into the soil to pupate before
emerging as adults.

Seriousness of the problem:
Thrips aren't a problem for tropicals with tough, waxy leaves, but
they love to live and feed on flowers. Although they feed on both
pollen and petals, petals are at
greatest risk of becoming stippled
from the thrips' rasping mouths.
Yellow flowers are particularly
prone to attack.

Preferred environment: Thrips
prefer direct sunlight and very
warm temperatures. These pests are
thigmotactic, meaning they love to
be in tight spaces, literally 'hugged'
by plant tissue.

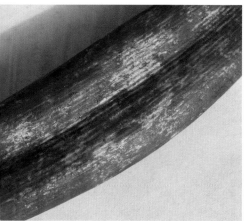

Thrips themselves are hard to see, but the damage they cause often looks silvery and stippled.

Treatment and prevention:
Prevention is the key to controlling this pest. Once thrips get into the flowers, there are few options for control other than snipping off the damaged flowers and disposing of them. Thrips are far worse when the weather is hot, so growing plants in cooler temperatures can slow thrip damage substantially.

Fungus Gnats

Physical description: Fungus gnats are generally 3–4 mm long; the adults resemble small fruit flies.

The damage and the signs:
The lifespan of an adult fungus gnat is only about three weeks. Adult fungus gnats are unable to feast on plants, but the larvae eat the young tender roots, allowing the entry of root rot. Pull plants out of their pots and check the soil for chewed roots and small, white larvae with black heads. Damage is usually restricted to the plant's roots, but tender stems can also be attacked.

Where to look for them:
Fungus gnats live in the soil.

Seriousness of the problem:
Although fungus gnats do minimal damage to plants, they are notorious for flying around and annoying people.

Preferred environment:
Damp soil is a fungus gnat's favourite place to live.

Treatment and prevention:
Fungus gnats love moist soil surfaces, so avoid infestations by not overwatering. Pesticides are also available and are very effective if applied to the soil surface.

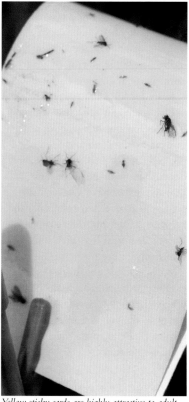

Yellow sticky cards are highly attractive to adult fungus gnats and can be used to monitor their presence and to provide some control.

Aphids

Physical description: Aphids are pear shaped and usually green, but watch for them in shades of black, brown, grey, yellow, red and purple. It's interesting to note that aphids come with and without wings. Wingless aphids are called *apterous*, and winged adults are called *alate*.

The damage and the signs: Aphids seek protein and, therefore, feed on plant sap, but because sap is sugar rich and protein poor, aphids must extract large quantities to get enough protein. Aphids rid themselves of the excess sugar by excreting it in the form of visible sticky honeydew. Aphids may also transmit viruses to plants through their saliva, sometimes causing malformation of leaves. Another sign to watch for is the white skins that aphids shed as they grow.

Where to look for them: Aphids prefer to cluster on stems and under leaves.

Seriousness of the problem: Aphids have a huge capacity for rapid reproduction, and young aphids reach maturity in only six to seven days.

Preferred environment: Aphids react to plant leaf colour and prefer those that are yellowish-green. They also prefer to live on new growth. Some species are very specific feeders, while others are polyphagous (eat many different species of plants), like the green peach aphid.

Treatment and prevention: An insecticidal soap works best. Apply the soap thoroughly and often until the problem is under control. If the soap doesn't cover the aphids' bodies, it won't kill the pests.

Aphids develop wings as a result of crowding, reduction of food quality, drop in temperature or significant changes in day length.

Whiteflies

Physical description: Whiteflies have wedge-like wings and are commonly described as looking like tiny bits of ash. When infested plants are disturbed, clouds of winged adults swarm into the air.

The damage and the signs: Whiteflies feed by sucking juices from leaves. The leaves often become covered in a sticky honeydew, turn yellow and fall off. Leaves may also appear covered in sooty mould. Because whiteflies need a lot of protein for development, they consume large amounts of plant sap. Thus, like aphids, whiteflies secrete a large amount of honeydew on which sooty mould often grows.

Where to look for them: Look for wingless nymphs on the underside of leaves and for adults on stem ends and the tops of plants.

Seriousness of the problem: Whiteflies can transmit plant viruses. They are similar to aphids and mites in that their populations can explode. Although they are slow moving, whiteflies spread to nearby plants quite effectively.

Preferred environment: The optimum relative humidity for whitefly is 75–80%. Eggs can survive for only a few days at slightly freezing temperatures, but even moderately sub-freezing winters will kill whitefly in any of its developmental stages.

Treatment and prevention: Thorough applications of insecticidal soap, neem oil and botanical insecticides can be used repeatedly to spot-treat heavily infested areas until the infestation is under control. Yellow sticky traps are also useful for trapping and monitoring the presence of adult whitefly populations.

Whiteflies aren't really flies at all. In fact, they are more closely related to aphids. As their name suggests, whiteflies have a waxy coating on their bodies that give them a white appearance.

Diseases

When it comes to plant diseases, *prevention*, not *cure*, is the operative word. This is the reason most treatments for plant disease usually involve protecting plants before they get a disease rather than trying to eliminate a disease once it has established itself.

There aren't many products available to control diseases, so the principles of disease control are rather simple: always start with healthy, disease-free plants, don't introduce disease to those plants and always grow your plants in a healthy, stress-free environment.

Once again, knowledge is key to identifying and dealing with disease problems, so take the time to learn about what you're battling. It's important to know what you're up against and whether you can beat it.

Biotic Diseases

Powdery Mildew

What is it? Powdery mildew is a fungus that forms a white powder-like growth on leaf and stem surfaces. It also commonly appears as dry, brown, papery leaf spots. There are numerous powdery mildew species that infect a wide range of plants, but as unattractive as they are, they are rarely fatal. Large amounts of powdery mildew can, however, impair photosynthesis. The one good thing about powdery mildew fungi is that they are fairly host specific, meaning the powdery mildew on your umbrella plant isn't going to spread to your African violet.

Some chemicals are very effective for combating plant diseases, but chemicals are only one tool in a solid disease-prevention program.

Powdery mildew is unattractive and can cover enough of a plant to actually hinder photosynthesis.

What causes it? Powdery mildew is caused by fungi that survive in dead and decaying plant materials. Spores are often carried to plants by both wind and insects. Contrary to popular belief, powdery mildews aren't caused by a wet environment; however, they do require high humidity for spores to germinate and invade plant tissue. Grouping plants too closely together and depriving them of adequate air circulation will also encourage a powdery mildew problem.

Control and prevention: Powdery mildew loves thin, weak, leaf tissue, so providing the best growing environment possible goes a long way to preventing an invasion. Unfortunately, fungicides are effective only prior to the mildew becoming established, so stay on top of the problem and remove infected growth as soon as you notice it.

A cactus with stem rot.

Root and Crown Rot

What is it? Root and crown rot is a catch-all term for a series of plant diseases that attack plant roots and the transition zone between roots and stem, known as the crown. Fungi are usually the culprits, but bacteria can also cause the damage. As the name suggests, root and crown rot causes stems, crowns and roots to turn brownish-black and become soft and mushy. Lesions will normally form on stems near the surface of the soil. When it comes to African violets, the symptoms are slightly different. Watch for older outer leaves that show signs of drooping and for younger inner leaves that are stunted or are turning brownish-black.

What causes it? Root and stem rot diseases are caused by micro-organisms that live in the soil. The disease organisms are, by and large, various species of fungi, but they need the right environment to do their dirty work, such as soil that doesn't drain easily or has been over-compacted. In fact, I would say 90% of root rot problems can be eliminated by choosing high-quality potting soils and watering properly.

Control and prevention: Your best means of control and prevention is to use high-quality pasteurized soilless mixes, to avoid over-watering and not to repot plants too deeply.

Unnecessary stress and injury can render a plant particularly susceptible to Botrytis *fungi.*

Gray Mould

What is it? Gray mould (or *Botrytis* sp.) is a fungal disease that forms a fuzzy, grey mould on young foliage and flowerbuds—old, tough, waxy leaves are rarely attacked. For gray mould to get established, it must find foliage that's had free water sitting on it for a few hours. If there is no free water, it is impossible for gray mould to attack plant tissue. African violets and begonias are susceptible to gray mould. Stem and crown rot may also occur as a result of this disease.

What causes it? The gray mould fungus requires water sitting on susceptible plant matter for an extended period of time. Overwatering, extended periods of cool, damp conditions and improper maintenance (such as lack of deadheading) can all lead to a problem with gray mould.

Control and prevention: Water your plants close to the soil level. Letting water shower over the leaves creates the moist environment in which the *Botrytis* fungi loves to live—dry leaves are a poor environment for the mould. Let the soil dry out slightly between waterings and space susceptible plants to allow for adequate air circulation. Removing infected leaves and tissue won't get rid of the disease, but will slow its spread. Use a proper fungicide. Remember that the fungi tend to thrive on weakened or injured tissue, so keep plants healthy by deadheading and maintaining an appropriate fertilizing and watering schedule.

Prevent the spread of gall by sterilizing all gardening tools that come into contact with infected plants in a solution of 10% bleach and water (one part bleach to nine parts water) for 30 minutes. Dry tools completely to prevent rust.

Trunk Gall

What is it? Gall looks something like a brown knot and is usually found growing on the tree's crown or trunk. Most galls won't kill a tree, but they will disfigure it.

What causes it? Gall is caused by the soil-borne bacteria *Agrobacterium tumafaciens,* which enters the tree through wounds in the crown or stem. In most cases, gall is not lethal. If the gall cannot be cut out without extensively damaging the tree, I suggest leaving it alone.

Control and prevention: The best way to prevent gall is to use high-quality, pasteurized soilless mixes and to take care not to nick or wound the crown or trunk of trees.

Environmental Diseases (Abiotic)

Edema

What is it? When plant cells absorb more water than they can transpire, the cells literally burst, leaving cork-like swellings on the leaves and stems.

What causes it? Edema is caused by high humidity, over-watering and cool air temperatures.

Control and prevention: Improving light levels so that plants photosynthesize at an increased rate can help prevent edema. Increasing air circulation and allowing plants to dry out slightly between waterings will also help.

Edema appears as blisters or cork-like swellings on stems and leaves.

Chlorosis

What is it? Chlorosis is a nutrient deficiency that causes leaves and stems to look pale. When nutrients are lacking, chlorophyll, DNA, RNA, proteins and lipids cannot be manufactured. As a result, enzymes are less able to carry out important chemical transformations. Growth is slowed and susceptibility to disease may increase. Infected flowering plants may become dwarfed and produce fewer flowers.

What causes it? Chlorosis may be caused by a lack of nutrients in the soil, poor functioning roots, cold temperatures and waterlogged soils.

Control and prevention: Maintain plants in the healthiest condition possible, and be sure to fertilize when needed. Chlorosis is often caused by iron deficiency and soil pH that is too high, so have a soil test done if problems persist.

Chlorosis is a nutrient deficiency that causes leaves and stems to look pale.

Leaf Drop

What is it? Leaves dropping off plants.

What causes it? All plants shed leaves, but if a plant suddenly drops healthy green leaves, it is usually an indication of low light. If the dropped leaves are brown or yellow, you might be dealing with soil that is too dry or too wet, natural shed or even disease or insect problems.

Control and prevention: Give the soil a scratch before you water it. Soil that appears dry on the surface may have plenty of moisture below. Green leaf drop is common with plants that are brought indoors after having spent the summer outside. Plants may take a while to adjust to the lower light levels indoors (usually two to three weeks). Remember also to repot plants when necessary—a pot that is too small won't hold enough soil to support proper leaf development.

Leaf Scorch

What is it? Leaf scorch results when intense sunlight hits leaves that aren't adapted to high light conditions—such as when low light plants are suddenly moved to high light areas. The result is patches of dead tissue on the areas of leaves that are most exposed to the sun.

What causes it? During hot, dry weather, a plant's stomata or pores close up and heat builds up. Strong sunlight can destroy chlorophyll in leaves. Prolonged exposure to these environmental factors, combined with an insufficient amount of water, will cause leaves to become scorched and dried out.

Be vigilant about watering plants during hot, dry spells. If you take plants outdoors for the summer, be especially mindful of leaf scorch.

Control and prevention: Be vigilant about watering plants during hot, dry spells. If you take plants outdoors for the summer, be especially mindful of leaf scorch. Mulch the soil surface to improve its water-holding capability, and use a high-quality potting mix. Provide diffused light for your plants during months when sun is most intense. There is no 'cure' for leaf scorch. When tissue turns brown, it is dead.

A combination of consistent training and covering plant's soil with decorative pebbles or moss will help discourage pets from nosing about where they are not welcome.

Pets

Keeping houseplants and pets in the same space can create its own special brand of frustration. Houseplants are magnets for curious pets. As sweet and obedient as our cats and dogs may be the majority of the time, there are some cases when no amount of scolding can deter our four-legged friends from doing what they want. In a battle of keep-the-plant or keep-the-pet, there is only one winner—and nine times out of ten, that winner has four feet.

In dealing with stubborn pets, it comes down to a balance between compromise and conceit. Are we higher on the food chain? Yes. Do our pets care? Not in the least. The good news is that all is not lost. There are things you can do to keep pets from eating, digging in and toppling houseplants.

• Keep tempting or tasty plants up and out of the way. Cats love to nibble on or bat at long, cascading foliage. Whether your cat is seeking roughage or entertainment, it can easily be deterred from nibbling if you simply move your plants to locations that are up and out of the way. Depending on the age, agility and determination of your cat, a trek to a high shelf or counter-top might prove too much of a bother.

Although dogs have less of a penchant for batting around plants than cats do, they are more likely to knock them over. If your dog plays hard in the house, keep your plants away from high-traffic areas—and remember, those areas aren't always the spots that see a lot of traffic from us. Most dogs have favourite paths that lead to windows or doors. They often navigate these paths at full speed, cutting corners a little too tightly and occasionally miscalculating when it's time to lay on the brakes. By keeping plants out of these areas, you greatly reduce the likelihood of having a rambunctious dog topple a plant.

- Supervise your pets. There are many commercial sprays and home-spun deterrents (like placing double-sided tape on planters) designed to keep pets away from plants, but the best prevention is supervision. Puppies in particular need lots of watching. Besides being incredibly curious, they are also teething, which makes them more likely to search for a plant to chew. Of course, supervision is not always possible, but knowing where your pet is at is often the best way to know where it shouldn't be.

- As a last resort, grow cat grass. A pot of cat grass might be all that's needed to keep your favourite feline away from your houseplants. It is available at most garden centres and pet stores, and it is easy to grow. All you need is seed, a shallow container and a sunny window. Your cat will take care of keeping it trimmed. While it doesn't discourage your plant from eating indoor plants, cat grass does focus your pet's attention on a single plant.

Plants and pets often compete for the same sunny spot in front of windows, but there is room for both.

Heart Leaf Philodendron

Poisonous Plants

Safety is always an issue when it comes to house-plants. Whenever people ask me about toxic plants, I always end up saying, "It's the dose that makes the poison." What this means is *anything* taken in suffi-cient quantity will eventually poison you. Even the consumption of too much pure water (a condition known as hyponatremia) has resulted in deaths. That said, I would by no means suggest that we shouldn't be concerned about accidental poisoning. In fact, I think it's everyone's responsibility to know what kind of plants he or she has and whether or not those plants are toxic. After all, we wouldn't let our families and pets venture about in an unsafe outdoor environment, so why wouldn't we make them as safe as possible in their own homes?

Toxic is not an absolute term. We tend to think of it in an ingest-and-die way, but it can also refer to less dire symptoms, such as skin irritations, photosensitivity, soreness of the mouth and cramps. If you have concerns regarding plant toxicity, consult your local poison control centre.

Some plants may have only parts (sap, foliage, fruit, etc.) that are toxic. Others, like Jerusalem cherry (Solanum capsicastrum) *pictured here, are entirely poisonous.*

Asparagus Fern

Going on Vacation

Whenever my family and I go away on vacation, there's always that initial dread of "Who will water the plants?" Let's face it, sometimes having to ask someone to water your plants is as bad as being the person who is asked. To make the experience a little less traumatic for all involved, plan ahead, put the right person in charge and leave detailed watering instructions. After that, the rest is up to chance.

What to Write

Regrettably, the watering instructions we should leave are rarely the ones we do leave. The problem is that most people are afraid to sound obsessive or bossy. And as tempted as you might be to draft a note that begins with, "Please water the plants once a week—not when you feel like it, or when you re-member to," and that ends with, "When you 'check' my bathroom for a plant I may have neglected to tell you about, please keep your nose out of my medicine cabinet,"

Button Fern

fight the urge! There are better ways to increase your likelihood of coming home to happy, healthy plants.

Plan Ahead

- Make time to give your plants a proper once-over before you leave. Cleaning even a few of the leaves will allow you to check for pests or diseases that could cause problems in your absence. While you're cleaning, don't forget to deadhead any spent flowers and to remove any unsightly foliage. Follow that up with a proper watering and you're halfway there.

- Move small plants to a temporary holding area in one room. This is a great option if you're not keen on having someone walk through your entire house. If you're lucky enough to have a bright bathroom, you can gather your small low-light plants and give them a temporary home in the bathtub. It's an option that removes any worries about water spills and messy cleanups.

- Plan for disaster. It never hurts to leave a few bath towels out and ready for accidents that might require cleaning up. Leaving out a broom and a dustpan is also a good idea.

- Pre-measure fertilizer. If you're going to be gone for an extended period, pre-measure your fertilizer and leave it in disposable baggies, marked with clear application instructions and then put them back in the fertilizer container to prevent mishaps.

Dragon Tree

Leave Detailed Instructions

- Be clear about how much water each plant needs and how often each needs it. Writing the schedule on a calendar is a great way to deal with this, but I think anyone asking someone else to water their houseplants must specify both the quantity and the frequency of water each plant needs. If nothing else, it takes the pressure off friends and family who worry about wiping out your plants and goes a long way toward sustaining good relationships.

- Make note of any plants or issues that require special attention. If you have a saucer that tends to overflow, for example, mention it.

- Note whether any window coverings need to be opened or closed.

Home Again, Home Again

So you gave it your best. You planned ahead. You wrote the perfect note. You still came home to sickly-looking plants. Now what? Unfortunately, not all plants can be resuscitated, but you can increase your plants' survival rate by following the emergency revival techniques in the following section.

Croton

Over-watered plants can literally drown in their pots—throw them a lifeline by taking them out of the pot, allowing extra moisture to drain away and roots to be exposed to air. Return them to the pot a few hours later.

Plant 911

How to Save a Waterlogged Plant

The key to saving a waterlogged plant is getting it out of its container, allowing excess water to drain away and letting air get to its roots. The easiest way to do this is simply by slipping a plant out of its container and placing it on a pile of paper towels. Gently blot the rootball with the towels, being careful not to compact the soil. After you've removed some of the surface water from the soil, place a few more paper towels on a cookie rack or in a basin or colander, and rest the plant on the toweling. Next, move the plant to an out-of-the-way spot that's not in direct sunlight. In a day or two, your plant should be dry enough to be returned to its container.

How to Save an Over-fertilized Plant

If your plant has browning leaf tips, misshapen leaves and a white crust on the rim of its pot, it's likely suffering from over-fertilization. Excess soil nutrients put tender plant roots at risk of being burnt. Some plants suffering from over-fertilization will also show signs of wilting. This is because high concentrations of nutrient salts prevent the plant from taking up a

To rehydrate a severely dried-out plant, let the plant soak in the sink in water for 30 minutes.

sufficient amount of water. To repair damage caused by over-fertilization, flush out your plant with water. When done properly, water should flow out the holes in the bottom of the container. A fancy name for this nutrient-laden water is *leachate*, and it's important to discard it from your saucer after watering.

How to Rehydrate a Dried-out Plant

If your plant is so parched that it has begun to droop, fill your sink or a basin with lukewarm water and immerse the plant, container and all. The water level should be a few centimetres higher than the container. If the plant is extremely dry, you might have to hold it down for a few seconds to prevent it from floating. Let the plant soak for 30 minutes. Once it's had a good drink, drain the water and let the plant sit in the empty sink or basin for about an hour (use a large drip tray if your plant requires more space).

Learn a Little
Grow a Lot...

When I sat down to write this book, I didn't expect that I would learn as much about people as I would about houseplants. But that's exactly what happened. As you have discovered from reading this introduction, people's relationships with houseplants are personal. At first glance, it's a relationship that might appear somewhat dysfunctional—and truthfully, why wouldn't it? We go out of our way to find time we don't have to care for plants that will never thank us and never compromise their demands. As unrewarding as that sounds—and in spite of the moments when I've questioned whether plants are worth the effort—I know that the rewards are there. And the reason I choose to put in the effort is the same reason everyone else does—because we know that what we give to a houseplant in care will be returned to us in comfort.

As with all the books in our *What Grows Here?* series, this one is loaded with practical, expert advice that will give you the knowledge you need to grow the plants you've always admired. If you're feeling a little over-whelmed by the sheer volume of information in this introduction, take comfort in knowing that we were too. Fortunately for all of us, it's not necessary to memorize everything in order to grow beautiful indoor plants. As you will find in the 50 questions and answers that make up the next section of the book, an example is just as valuable as a fact. We've made a special effort to include as many of the places that people grow plants as possible and to offer solutions to novice and experienced house-plant growers alike. So, as you read and become inspired to tackle your own indoor plant challenges, be reassured by the fact that plants already know how to grow. The roots know how to draw up water, the leaves know how to react with sunlight and the flowers know when it's time to emerge. Think of yourself as a companion to a plant rather than as its boss. With that mindset in place, all you need to do is give your plant a healthy environment and marvel that it knows how to do the rest. Enjoy!

Kimberly Queen Fern

Private Spaces

"That's private!" It's quite amazing how much attention that tiny sentence demands. It seems instinctual, really. With little to no encouragement, we learn to strain our ears to hear the private conversations of others, to interpret those fragments as information and to draw conclusions based on little more than first impressions. Our understanding, it seems, is that all things private reveal (or at least suggest) who we are and how we want to be perceived. It comes as no surprise, then, that the plants we fill our private spaces with also provide clues to our personalities, sensibilities and indulgences. It sort of follows the old adage "You are what you eat." Only in this case, it's more of a "You are what you grow."

When people welcome plants into their private home or work spaces, they do so for their own reasons. But whatever the reason for keeping them, indoor plants are part of most of our daily lives. And as you will find from reading the questions and answers that follow in the next section, choosing the right plant for personal spaces comes down to understanding a lot about your space and a bit about yourself, too.

From major issues concerning light and humidity, to the smallest details regarding aesthetics and practicality, there are things about every individual and every space that make growing plants indoors challenging. The good news, however, is that the solutions for even those hardest challenges are limited only by imagination.

Plants at Home

Plants make personal statements about who we are. They can be reminders of places we visited, things we saw, people we loved. For me, indoor plants represent a combination of all three. Having grown up in the family business, I don't remember a time when my parents didn't have plants growing in the house. Plants were simply parts of our lives and livelihoods.

Today, I feel much the same about indoor plants as I did when I was growing up, which is why, like my parents, I choose to fill my home with plants. When it came time to choose those plants, I found that my love of science influenced my purchasing decisions. Unfortunately, whereas I was more curious about mutant varieties and what made them tick, my wife, who has a vested interest in keeping our home from turning into a scene from *Little Shop of Horrors*, wanted to choose plants for their (gasp!) beauty. Inevitably, we ended up making compromises and practising the difficult task of softening our judgements. When it was all done, we ended up with a home full of plants that represented, well, us.

So the plants we grow in our homes represent who we are—no shock there—but it must be noted that there are also individuals who become known *for* their plants. These are those indoor plant enthusiasts who grow spectacular collections of plants and inspire—occasionally frighten—the rest of us with their knowledge and passion. The amount of care and patience they find for their passions is staggering and almost always a little contagious.

Not all enthusiasm, however, is born strictly of love, care and nurture. Sometimes, it's born of good ol' fashioned stubbornness—as is the case with one of our staff members and her scale-

Phalaenopsis Orchid

stricken weeping figs. For the last year and a half, she (read: her husband) has been hauling her two 4-m-tall, 68-kg trees outside to be bathed in copious amounts of horticultural oil. Each time, she is hopeful that the oil will get rid of the scale, and each time she is forced to decide whether or not the trees are worth the effort. But in this particular battle of scale versus tenacity, tenacity appears to be gaining ground. It goes to show that, sometimes, the perfect plant isn't perfect at all.

Calathea

So, as you read through the questions and answers that follow in this section, keep in mind that although each person's situation and concern are unique, what everyone has in common is a simple desire to find plants that suit who they are. And what's more satisfying than a perfect fit?

Chinese evergreens are great low-maintenance plants that will take lots of abuse and still look good.

I'm a student living in my first apartment. I'm not much of a gardener, but I'd still like to brighten up my living room with a lush houseplant. The room is small and crowded, but I've saved one corner for a plant. The room faces north. What grows here?

This is a challenging space for a beginner. Unfortunately, dark corners in first apartments are classic spots where many a houseplant has gone to die. However, you can avoid this particular rite of passage by choosing a plant that likes the limited sunlight a north-facing window provides. A corner is often a good out-of-the-way spot for a plant, but if the corner you have in mind is particularly dark, you'll want to consider finding a sunnier location in the room or using mirrors to reflect in light. If neither is an option, don't be discouraged—there are many plants that do well in low-light conditions. In fact, plants that become overgrown in sunny locations often stay neat and compact when grown in lower light. Since your room is crowded, try growing a plant that uses vertical rather than horizontal space. A snake plant, for instance, might be a good plant to start with—besides being attractive, it's also forgiving of both low light and beginners. Remember that it's not necessary to buy a mature plant. Not only are younger plants less expensive, they are also very gratifying to watch grow.

Cast Iron Plant
Aspidistra elatior

This tough plant displays an upright habit with dark-green, sometimes variegated, glossy, leathery foliage that is elliptical to lance shaped. Height: 60cm; Spread: 60cm. Bright indirect light (tolerant of most light levels except direct sun).

Chinese Evergreen
Aglaonema

This plant has a compact habit. Different types are available with attractive, variegated mid-green to dark-green or solid-green, oval leaf blades on stalks. May produce flowers occasionally. Height: 30cm; Spread: 50cm. Indirect light (solid-green types tolerate very low light levels).

Dracaena 'Warneckii'
Dracaena deremensis 'Warnecki'

An upright plant with long, dark-grey-green foliage with lighter streaks and white stripes on leaf edges. Height: 3m; Spread: 60cm. Bright indirect light.

Parlor Palm
Neanthe Bella Palm,
Good Luck Palm
Chamaedorea elegans

A very popular, compact, upright plant with medium-green foliage on arching stems. Height: 1m; Spread: 1m. Bright indirect light.

Snake Plant
Mother-in-Law's Tongue
Sansevieria trifasciata

An excellent plant for beginners that can withstand neglect. Fleshy, rigid foliage is upright, dark green and attractively mottled and striped. The tip of each leaf is slightly barbed, hence the nasty common name mother-in-law's tongue. Height: 1.5m; Spread: 50cm. Bright indirect light.

Snake Plant

Cast Iron Plant

Dracaena 'Warneckii'

A large plant like a weeping fig can make a huge statement in a room, so select one the same way you would choose a perfect piece of furniture or art.

My home has a small but formal living room with a beautifully detailed vaulted ceiling and a large west-facing window. I'd like to introduce some plants to this space. What grows here?

It sounds like you have an ideal location for growing sun-loving plants. West-facing windows are great because they let in the strong afternoon sun that many tropicals thrive in. Because your room is small but your ceiling is high, take full advantage of the generous vertical space and grow a tall feature tree like a weeping fig. Unlike a low-growing bushy plant, an indoor tree takes up little floor space and will create a line that draws attention up toward your vaulted ceiling. Highlighting this feature with a canopy of leaves will add colour and dimension to your vertical space and complement this great architectural feature. Don't be afraid to experiment. Why not consider training some trailing plants to wind their way up an ornate obelisk or trellis? After all, decorative outdoor structures and art often function as beautifully indoors as they do outside.

Golden Pothos
Devil's Ivy
Epipremnum aureus
(syn. Scindapsus aureus)

A popular climbing plant with heart-shaped green foliage marked with yellow. Trails: 2+m. Bright indirect light.

Lipstick Vine
Basket Plant
Aeschynanthus lobbianus

A trailing plant with fleshy, mid-green to dark-green, ovate to lance-shaped foliage. Produces clusters of tubular, orange, red and dark-red blooms in summer. Height: 20–30cm; Spread: 40–60cm. Bright indirect light.

Golden Pothos

Lipstick Vine

Ti-Plant
Cabbage Tree, Palm Lily,
Good Luck Plant
Cordyline fruitcosa

An attractive, upright plant that displays lance-shaped, purple foliage or green foliage striped with purple. Height: 1–2.5m; Spread: 2m. Bright indirect light.

Weeping Fig
Ficus benjamina

Enormously popular in homes, malls and offices, this upright fig is long-lived and tolerant of slightly rootbound conditions. Produces small, ovate, glossy, mid-green leaves. Height: 2–3m; Spread: 1m. Bright indirect light.

Yucca
Spineless Yucca
Yucca elephantipes

An easy, large plant to grow indoors. Light-green to mid-green foliage is narrow and lance shaped, sometimes growing as long as 90cm. Rarely produces single, white to cream blooms in summer when the plant reaches maturity. Height: 3+m; Spread: 1.5m. Direct light.

Yucca

Break up large spaces and create a sound buffer by grouping plants as an interior border, much like you would in a garden.

Our open concept home has the kitchen, dining room and living room in one long space. We like the openness, but one of our kids uses the dining room to do her home-work and finds that the noise from other rooms really carries over. I'm wondering if plants would help. What grows here?

Plants are great sound buffers. Think about how an empty room always sounds more hollow than a room that is full of furniture. Well, plants break up sound the same way furniture does—the more leaves a plant has, the more of a buffer it provides. To create quiet, sectioned-off areas of your living space, divide the room with a border of plants or a trellis covered in vines. Don't limit yourself to creating a border that starts at floor level. Sideboards, bookshelves and sofa tables often provide the perfect spots on which to grow a grouping of plants. On an aesthetic note, creating height with plants will help interrupt the long line of your dining/living space and add visual interest to the open concept design. What you select will, of course, depend upon the amount of light your rooms get, but you will find there are many varieties and sizes of plants from which to choose.

Areca Palm
Butterfly Plant,
Golden Feather Palm
Chrysalidocarpus lutescens
An upright plant with narrow, mid-green foliage on tall, reed-like, arching stems. Height: 2m; Spread: 1m. Bright indirect light.

Buddhist Pine
Kusamaki, Southern Yew
Podocarpus macrophyllus
A very attractive upright plant with dark-green, needle-shaped foliage. Height: 2m; Spread: 1m. Bright indirect light.

Corn Plant 'Massangeana'
Dracaena fragrans
Foliage is held atop a sturdy upright trunk and may be sold with one or more trunks per pot. Wide, strappy, glossy-green leaves with a yellow stripe. Height: 3m; Spread: 1m. Bright indirect light.

Kangaroo Vine
Cissus antarctica
A vigorous vining plant with glossy, ovate, rich-green foliage. Height: 2–3m; Spread: 60cm. Bright indirect light.

Umbrella Tree
Queensland Umbrella Tree,
Octopus Tree
Schefflera actinophylla
An upright plant that is often sold as a bushy plant or trained as a single-stem specimen. Glossy, green foliage is divided to form an umbrella-like appearance. Height: 3m; Spread: 1.5m. Bright indirect light.

Umbrella Tree

Areca Palm

Buddhist Pine

Garden centres are full of topiaries in different forms, so ask for help in selecting the right plant for you.

I've been admiring the topiaries I see in my favourite home decorating magazines. I have a formal living room with a working fireplace, and I'd love to grow topiaries on the marble mantel. What grows here?

A fireplace mantel is an ideal spot to showcase topiaries. One thing to be concerned about, though, is that the heat and dryness from a fire create a stressful environment for plants. Don't let this deter you from creating the look you're after—simply move your topiaries to an alternate spot before you use your fireplace. Caring for topiaries is intensive but rewarding, so choose a type that matches your ambition. Pruned topiaries require regular trimming and often need staking when they are young. For topiaries that are a bit more forgiving of multiple sculpting attempts, choose plants that are young and malleable, or consider growing vines that can be wound around wire forms. When it comes to placing your topiaries, think about whether or not you like symmetry. You can treat each side of your mantle as mirror images or create an asymmetrical look by placing them to one side. However you decide to arrange them, remember that these sculptures will be at eye level, so give as much thought to choosing containers as you do to choosing plants.

English Ivy

Hedera helix

A popular vine displaying flat, 3 to 5-lobed leaves that are green or variegated white or yellow. Height: 2m; Spread: 1m. Bright indirect light.

Myrtle

Myrtus communis

A compact, upright habit makes myrtle an excellent plant for topiary shapes. Displays small, dark-green, oval foliage. Produces double, white blooms in summer. Height: as trained; Spread: as trained. Direct light.

Rosemary

Rosmarinus officinalis

Upright in habit, this plant has hundreds of straight, needle-shaped, succulent, green leaves. Foliage can be harvested for cooking, potpourris and sachets. Height: 30–100cm; Spread: 30–60cm. Direct light.

Rosemary

Myrtle

English Ivy

Topiaries

It's okay to think of plants as temporary accessories that can be changed to suit decorating trends. Pictured here, zebra plant, kalanchoe and other tropicals make a stunning arrangement.

I want a dramatic-looking plant as a centrepiece for the coffee table in my living room. The table is a very modern design and quite low. What grows here?

An important element of drama is surprise, so consider growing something a little unexpected. Why not plant a tray of wheat grass? It has a short window of aesthetic appeal, but it grows quickly and can be kept tall or groomed short. Remember, a centrepiece can have as many or as few elements as you like, so experiment. Choose plants that have interesting variegation or leaf shape. Or, why not create an indoor 'gardenscape?' Start with an attractive container or saucer, and fill it with plants and materials to create a table garden. Choose pebbles, moss and an orchid for an Asian-inspired look, or if your room receives a lot of bright sun, consider growing a water garden in an attractive bowl. Finishing touches are important when creating almost all these looks, so pay attention to details and let your imagination guide you. Whatever you select, don't forget about practicality—a tall coffee-table plant can look impressive but can also block your view of guests or the television.

Air Plant
Tillandsia

Air plants are epiphytes. They have furry scales on their foliage that absorb water and nutrients from the air and airborne dust. *T. ionantha* growing on coral, shells or driftwood is the most popularly sold species at garden centres. Blooms are small and infrequent. Height: 2–25cm. Bright indirect light.

Candelabra Plant
Elkhorn
Euphorbia lactea 'Cristata'

This upright, very odd-looking plant is sometimes referred to as a false cactus. Produces fan-shaped, crested foliage on branches. Height: 60cm; Spread: 40cm. Direct light.

Electric Grass
Isolepis cernua

Becoming popular as a novelty plant, this arching plant displays long, cylindrical, grassy stems with small, white flowers on the ends, appearing in a flush in summer and continually throughout the year. Height: 20–25cm; Spread: 20cm. Bright indirect light.

Kangaroo Paw
Anigozanthos flavidus

A compact plant with spiky, grey-green foliage. Continually produces clusters of unusual, two-lipped, tubular blooms thought to resemble a kangaroo's paw. Height: 30cm; Spread: 30cm. Direct light (but avoid hot summer sun).

Silver Vase Bromeliad
Urn Plant, Living Vase
Aechmea fasciata

Grey-green, spiny foliage is cross-banded with sprinklings of white powder and arches gracefully outward. 3-to 4-year-old plants produce single, pink, inflorescences with small, blue flowers that turn red and may last for up to six months. Height: 40cm; Spread: 50cm. Direct light (but avoid hot summer sun).

Zebra Plant
Saffron Spike
Aphelandra squarrosa

An attractive, upright plant with ovate to elliptical, dark-green foliage with prominent white veins and mid ribs. Produces waxy, yellow blooms on terminal spikes in summer. Height: 45cm; Spread: 30cm. Bright indirect light.

Air Plant

Silver Vase Bromeliad

Cacti are fascinating. There is so much variety in appearance among this large family of plants.

My husband loves cacti, but the sunniest room in our apartment (our living room) is really small. What grows here?

Small room? Grow small cacti. Of course, the answer isn't that simple, but if the brightest room in your home is also your smallest, tiny cacti might be your best option. Too often when we think of cacti, we think of that smiley, Tex-Mex-looking impostor that waves to us from the antennas of cars. In reality, there is a huge family from which to choose, so look for a variety of shapes and sizes, and don't feel that you have to sacrifice attractiveness in order to accommodate space. A cactus bowl might be a great place to start…or to finish—some of the most impressive cacti I've seen have been small collections grown in shallow decorative bowls. During the growing season (spring and summer), keep your room temperature between 18°C and 33°C. Fall/winter, temperatures of 7–11°C are recommended for cacti but because that's not comfortable for us, simply place cacti by a cool window. Although cacti are slow growers that require little maintenance, they are unforgiving of poor drainage so buy a soil mix that has pumice, perlite or small gravel.

Bunny Ears
Opuntia microdasys

This cactus has a bushy habit. Pale-green to mid-green foliage stems are flattened, oblong or almost rounded. Produces single, yellow blooms in spring, followed by red fruits. Height: 40–60cm; Spread: 40–60cm. Direct light.

Golden Barrel
Golden Ball,
Mother-in-Law's Cushion
Echinocactus grusonii

Spherical in habit, this cactus displays spines that are green with golden-yellow tips. Produces single, yellow blooms in summer. Height: 60cm; Spread: 80cm. Direct light.

Old Lady Cactus
Mammillaria hahniana

This is a solitary cactus that forms groups when mature. Mid-green foliage is spherical and coated with long, white hairs, bristles and spines. Produces single, purplish-red blooms in late spring to early summer. Height: 20cm; Spread: 40cm. Direct light.

Pencil Tree
Milkbush, Fingertree,
Rubber Euphorbia
Euphorbia tirucallii

Not a cactus, but often mistaken for one, this interesting upright euphorbia prefers the same environment. It produces pencil-thick, fleshy, green foliage that branches, looking much like a tree with no leaves. Slow-growing—start with a small plant if space is an issue. Height: 60cm; Spread: 1m. Direct light.

Silver Torch
Cleistocactus strausii

This upright cactus is a columnar form with green ribs covered in fine, white spines. Branches freely from the base. Produces single, carmine-red blooms in summer when it reaches 10–15 years of age. Height: 1m; Spread: 1m. Direct light.

Bunny Ears

Pencil Tree

The leathery leaves of a healthy gardenia are as striking and lush as its flowers are beautiful.

I would like to grow a flowering plant in my family room. This space is well used by the entire family. It has large French doors that lead to our sunny deck, and these doors stay open a lot in the summer when we entertain. What grows here?

Because the image of a blooming flower leaves a lasting impression, it's easy to forget that no plant is in constant bloom. So, before you select a plant, consider what you envision for both flower size and bloom period. This will help you determine the plant that will best suit your style. What almost all flowering plants have in common is that they need substantial amounts of light. Just don't forget to filter that light through sheers or, if that's not possible, choose plants that like direct exposure. Generally, rooms that get a lot of use also have a lot of furniture, so you probably have the perfect spot for a plant. Look for space on a coffee table, television stand or cabinet. Another alternative is a flowering tree. Many have elegant blooms that are perfect for adding style and drama to a room. Not only will flowering houseplants help bring in the look of the outdoors, they will also help transition the space between your deck and your family room. Just remember that, in the summer months, gusts of wind might topple over plants that are close to the open French doors.

Flamingo Flower
Anthurium

An upright plant with tall stems bearing ovate, reflexed, glossy, dark-green foliage. Continually produces waxy, colourful, spathe-type blooms in pink, white, red or orange with prominent straight or curly tails. Height: 50–60cm; Spread: 30cm. Bright indirect light.

Gardenia
Gardenia jasminoides

This flowering plant has an upright habit. Dark-green foliage is shiny and leathery. Produces fragrant, semi-double to double, waxy-petalled, white blooms in summer. Fussy about temperature and water when budding. Height: 45cm; Spread: 25–30cm. Direct light (but shade from hot summer sun).

Hibiscus
Hibiscus rosa-sinensis

An upright plant often available in a lollipop-like tree or standard form. Glossy, dark-green foliage highlights the single, semi-double or double, white, yellow, orange, pink or red flowers that bloom continually. Height: 1.5m; Spread: 1m. Direct light.

Kalanchoe
Kalanchoe blossfeldiana

A compact, upright flowering plant with fleshy, glossy, dark-green foliage. Produces clusters of single, tubular-shaped, white, yellow, pink or red blooms primarily in summer (although professional growers can induce blooming throughout the year). Height: 25cm; Spread: 15cm. Direct light.

Reiger Begonia
Begonia x hiemalis

Glossy, dark-green foliage highlights beautiful, double, orange, pink, red, white or yellow blooms from late fall to early spring. Height: 20–25cm; Spread: 20–25cm. Bright indirect light.

Kalanchoe

Flamingo Flower

Hibiscus

Tall plants, like this gorgeous bird of paradise, can double as pretty privacy screens that can block indoor views from the street.

We just moved out of our first home and into a city loft. We have some well-loved plants that we're bringing with us but want to invest in more. Our plan is to break up the large space by creating plant borders. What grows here?

Moving from a house to an open concept loft can be overwhelming. Most people don't think about it when they're in their homes, but it's incredibly easy to take for granted something as simple as your walls. Plant borders will not only help you create interior rooms that feel intimate, they will also help buffer the echo that is so common to open concept spaces. Because you're moving from a house, you're probably bringing lots of furniture, so put bookshelves or a sofa table to work by placing groupings of plants on them. Or why not create a living wall by growing vines on a room screen? In your search for new plants, don't forget to pay some attention to your old ones—like you, they will also need time to adjust to their new environment. To ease them in, place them in areas of your home that receive the same amount and type of light to which they were accustomed. Lofts have beautiful features, so take advantage of high ceilings and choose tall plants to draw attention to open beams and other unique architectural details.

Bird of Paradise
Crane Flowers
Strelitzia reginae

A tall, upright plant prized for its stunning blooms. Large foliage is paddle-shaped and borne on long stalks. Unusual, peachy-orange flowers bloom in spring. A dramatic plant. Height: 2m; Spread: 1m. Direct light.

Boston Fern
Nephrolepis exaltata bostoniensis

A very popular fern with an arching habit. Broad, lance-shaped fronds arch gracefully up and over. Can grow quite large and is attractive on a stand where its fronds can arch freely. Height: 1m; Spread: 2m. Bright indirect light.

Dracaena 'Lemon Lime'
Dracaena deremensis

An upright plant with lance-shaped, striped-yellow foliage. Great for adding contrast to plant groupings. Height: 60–90cm; Spread: 1m. Bright indirect light.

Dracaena 'Lisa Cane'
Dracaena deremensis

An upright plant with dark-green, strap-shaped foliage. Adds height to an indoor border and is easy to care for. Height: 3m; Spread: 60cm. Bright indirect light.

ZZ Plant
Aroid Palm, Fat Boy, Eternity Plant
Zamioculcas zamiifolia

An upright plant with glossy, dark-green foliage displayed on fleshy stems in a prominent pattern. Height: 45–80cm; Spread: 50–95cm. Bright indirect light.

ZZ Plant

Boston Fern 'Dallas'

Dracaena 'Lemon Lime'

Plants with lots of leaves buffer sound and can be used to improve the acoustics in a media room.

My family spends most evenings in our new media room. Although the rest of the family loves its state-of-the-art feel, I want to warm up the space with a few plants. There's a large east-facing window, but the drapes are always drawn shut to keep down the glare on the television. What grows here?

When families go to the movies nowadays, they generally pick up their snacks and walk across the hallway. Media rooms make fabulous additions to homes, but they also tend to be a little dark and can even feel a bit claustrophobic. Fortunately, the answer to warming up this space can be as simple as choosing a few low-light plants and making sure your drapes are open when you're not watching television. Low-light plants will enjoy the morning sun, and your drapes can be closed long before everyone settles in for the evenings. If remembering to open the drapes is a problem, why not look into buying blinds that can be set on a timer? They're a bit of an investment, but if everything else in the room is state of the art, why not 'soup up' your blinds, too? Besides, the promise of another remote to play with might be just enough to entice your family into welcoming a few new plants.

Dragon Tree
Dracaena marginata

An upright plant bearing thin, lance-shaped, red-margined, dark-green foliage. Height: 3m; Spread: 1m. Bright indirect light.

Parlor Palm
Neanthe Bella Palm,
Good Luck Palm
Chamaedorea elegans

A very popular, compact, upright plant with medium-green foliage on arching stems. Height: 1m; Spread: 1m. Bright indirect light.

Peace Lily
Spathiphyllum

A very useful, bushy plant for lower light areas, this upright plant displays glossy, lance-shaped, dark-green foliage.

Produces single, white to cream blooms heavily in spring and sporadically throughout the year. Height: 60–90cm; Spread: 60cm. Bright indirect light.

Rex Begonia
Begonia rex

All varieties of Rex begonia now sold are hybrids that are available in a wonderful range of foliage colours. Leaves are large and ovate and vary in their markings of shades of pink, silver and purple. Height: 25cm; Spread: 30cm. Bright indirect light.

Snake Plant
Mother-in-Law's Tongue
Sansevieria trifasciata

An excellent plant that can withstand neglect—perfect for beginners. Fleshy, rigid foliage is upright, dark green and attractively mottled and striped. The tip of each leaf is slightly barbed, hence the nasty common name mother-in-law's tongue. Height: 1.5m; Spread: 50cm. Bright indirect light.

Rex Begonia

Snake Plant

Peace Lily

An added benefit to using grow lights in a bathroom is that they can double as nightlights.

I've just renovated the bathroom that attaches to my guest bedroom and would like a plant for the dark corner above the medicine cabinet. There's a frosted east-facing window, but I'm worried it might not provide enough light. My neighbour suggested I replace my ceiling pot lights with grow lights. What grows here?

Light probably won't be as big a problem as you're anticipating. The morning sun from your east-facing window is ideal for many low-light plants, including tropicals. What you do need to be concerned about is finding a plant that fits comfortably between the top of your cabinet and the ceiling. Trailers are an attractive option but can sometimes make opening and closing cabinets difficult. As for your neighbour's suggestion, grow lights are an option. These light are great for providing an extra source of light, but know that they can produce a lot of damaging heat. If you use them, be sure there is always at least 45 cm of space between the bulb and the top of your plant. It's also good to note that grow lights cast a bluish-white light that isn't always desirable over a mirror, so having them operate on a separate switch from vanity lights is adviseable.

Baby's Tears
Irish Moss, Mind Your Own Business
Soleirolia soleirolii

This plant's creeping habit is useful for covering soil around tall plants and it is a nice size for small bathrooms. It produces tiny, round leaves. Height: 5cm; Spread: indefinite. Bright indirect light.

Club Moss
Trailing Spike Moss
Selaginella kraussiana

This is a low, spreading plant with bright-green or dark-green, mat-forming foliage. Height: 2.5cm; Spread: indefinite. Bright indirect light.

Grape Ivy
Cissus rhombifolia

An easy-to-care-for and lovely, versatile plant with a climbing habit and tendrils that cling to supports. Adapts well to low light conditions. Foliage is palmate and dark green. Trails: 4m; Spread: 1m. Bright indirect light.

Maidenhair Fern
Delta Maidenhair Fern
Adiantum raddianum

Wiry black stalks that darken with age support pale-green fronds of lacy foliage. Delicate and striking. Height: 60cm; Spread: 80cm. Bright indirect light.

Nerve Plant
Painted Net Leaf
Fittonia albivenis

A creeping plant with oval foliage covered with a fine network of pink or white veins. Lovely on its own or in groupings. Height: 15cm; Spread: indefinite. Indirect light.

Maidenhair Fern

Baby's Tears

Nerve Plant

Fuzzy-leaved plants blemish when they get wet, so avoid using them around tubs and sinks.

My daughter-in-law has taken an interest in houseplants, and I'd like to start her off with a few for her ensuite bathroom. There's quite a bit of space for plants on the granite ledge that surrounds the Jacuzzi, and there's a big glass-block window that lets in lots of light. What grows here?

Ledges around Jacuzzis tend to become catch-alls for soaps, body gels and other 'stuff' designed to make people smell like fruit. So, have a good idea of just how many plants there's room for. When it comes to selecting those plants, pay attention to form. A plant with a cascading habit is fine if it's elevated enough, but avoid trailers that might find their way into the tub. It's also a good idea to invest in some saucers. They will keep your tub ledge free of silt and prevent plants from sitting in puddles of splashed water. If you suspect your containers are more decorative than functional, check to see if their finishes will stand up to getting wet. Candles also pose an issue, so if your daughter-in-law uses them around the tub, remind her to keep them a safe distance away from the plants or, in my opinion, save them for blackouts and birthday cakes.

Caladium
Elephant's Ear, Angel's Wings
Caladium bicolour

Upright in habit, this plant is prized for its striking foliage that lasts only from spring to fall. Leaves are large, colourful, paper-thin and arrow shaped. Height: 60cm; Spread: 60cm. Bright indirect light.

Calathea
Peacock Plant, Zebra Plant, Rattlesnake Plant
Calathea

Grown for their interesting foliage, calathea's long-stalked leaves range from ovate to elliptical, with differing patterns and colour combinations. Height: 45cm; Spread: 23cm. Bright indirect light.

Flamingo Flower
Anthurium

An upright plant with tall stems bearing ovate, reflexed, glossy, dark-green foliage. Continually produces waxy, colourful, spathe-type blooms in orange, pink, red or white with prominent straight or curly tails. Height: 50–60cm; Spread: 30cm. Bright indirect light.

Moth Orchid
Phalaenopsis

A compact, upright plant with oval, fleshy, dark-green foliage and flat-faced, single, pink, purple, red, white or yellow blooms appearing continually. Height: 20–60cm; Spread: 20–30cm. Bright indirect light.

Prayer Plant
Maranta leuconeura

Commonly named prayer plant because the foliage has a habit of folding upwards at night. Produces elliptic to ovate, dark-green foliage with striking bright-red mid ribs and veins. Height: 20cm; Spread: 20cm. Bright indirect light.

Prayer Plant

Calathea

Flamingo Flower

If you want both you and your houseplant to look good in the mirror, aim your hairspray away from plants in the bathroom—hairspray is a pore-blocking agent and will harm your plants.

My three sisters and I share a very busy bathroom but have decided that we'd like to decorate with a plant or two. It's a reasonably large and bright room, but counter space is definitely at a premium. What grows here?

Four girls multiplied by four showers a day equals a lot of humidity. A plant that leaps to mind that will really appreciate this environment is an asparagus fern (pictured above). Not only will it love the humidity, but it can also be grown in a hanging basket that won't infringe on counter space. Another benefit to using hanging planters is that they usually position plants closer to their source of light. But don't limit yourself to hanging your plants from the ceiling. Garden centres carry flat-backed hanging planters, perfect for mounting on a wall or hanging on a towel hook. Since you don't have lots of room on your vanity, try a collection of smaller plants on the back of the toilet tank or on top of a medicine cabinet.

Aluminum Plant
Friendship Plant
Pilea cadierei

Upright in habit, this tough plant's textured oval foliage is green and attractively marked with silver patches. Height: 30cm; Spread: 15–20cm. Bright indirect light.

Asparagus Fern
Emerald Feather
*Asparagus densiflorus
(Sprengeri group)*

An arching fern with glossy, mid-green, needle-like foliage on long stems. Attractive in a hanging basket or displayed on a stand. Height: 30cm; Spread: 60cm. Bright indirect light.

Piggyback Plant
Thousand Mothers, Youth-on-Age
Tolmiea menziesii

A lovely, spreading plant that performs well in a cool, shady environment.

Downy, bright-green, mature foliage supports tiny plantlets in piggyback-fashion. Height: 30cm; Spread: 30cm. Bright indirect light.

Spider Plant
Chlorophytum comosum

An extremely popular plant with lance-shaped or strap-shaped, arching foliage that can be striped with white or cream. Produces single, white, insignificant blooms on long, arching stems throughout the year that develop into plantlets. Very easy to grow provided it's well watered. Height: 15–20cm; Spread: 15–30cm. Bright indirect light.

Wandering Jew
Inch Plant, Luck Plant
Tradescantia zebrina

A trailing plant with fleshy, oval leaves available in many forms of variegation. Produces single, purple blooms in spring and summer. Height: 15cm; Spread: 25cm. Bright indirect light with some direct light.

Aluminum Plant

Spider Plant

Wandering Jew

Some plant containers will be at eye level when you are in a hot tub, so select ones to complement your room and that you'll like looking at.

Our family has just installed an indoor hot tub and would like to place some plants around it. The room has glass sliding doors that lead to the deck, so light isn't a problem, but I am worried that there might be too much humidity. What grows here?

Most houseplants are thirsty for extra humidity and will enjoy a steam bath as much as your family will. A relative humidity of around 60% is preferred (but never seen) by most houseplants, but few will complain unless that number increases to, and stays at, 80%. Quite honestly, those situations are rare. If your room is large, circulation of steamy air shouldn't be a problem, but if humidity does become an issue, simply open a door to an adjoining room or turn on a fan. As for aesthetics, plants can be used to emphasize the rejuvenating feel of the space, or simply as accent colours. Try Boston ferns or bamboo—even a banana— but remember to plant in containers that won't rust or react with cleaning chemicals. Also choose plants that don't mind getting the occasional splash of water—African violets will enjoy the steam but won't tolerate wet leaves.

Bamboo Palm

Chamaedorea erumpens

An upright plant with broad, ovate, dark-green foliage on arching stems. Very tropical looking. Height: 3+m; Spread: 1m. Bright indirect light.

Dwarf Banana

Musa velutina

Prized by the Victorians and today's conservatory owners, this upright plant produces broad, long, ovate leaves. Rarely produces yellow flowers indoors or, for that matter, bananas but are attractive and interesting plants nonetheless. Height: 1.5m; Spread: 90cm. Bright indirect light with some direct light.

Hoya

Wax flower

Hoya carnosa

A vining plant with rigid, fleshy, mid-green foliage. Produces single, fragrant white blooms with red coronas in summer. Trails: 2+m. Direct light.

Kimberly Queen Sword Fern

Australian Sword Fern

Nephrolepis obliterata

'Kimberly Queen'

A large fern with an upright and arching habit. Foliage is dark green and sharply serrated looking. Height: 1m; Spread: 1m. Bright indirect light.

Ponytail Palm

Beaucarnea recurvata

Interesting long, strap-like, dark-green foliage arches up and out of a large, swollen, bulb-like base. Height: 2m; Spread: 1m. Direct light.

Ponytail Palm

Hoya

Goldfish plants are a perfect choice for locations that receive bright indirect light.

We have a large landing in the stairwell between the first and second floors of our home. An overhead skylight makes the space moderately bright, and we'd like to turn it into a reading nook for our daughter. I'd love to let her personalize the space with some plants for the bookshelves. What grows here?

The plants you and your daughter are able to grow will depend largely on the kind of bookshelf you have. It's not as strange as it sounds: traditional wooden bookshelves don't let light filter from shelf to shelf, but both glass and floating shelves do. What all bookshelves do have in common though is a limited amount of space, so you'll want to consider growing small plants. As for adding those personal touches, why not incorporate your daughter's favourite colour into the space? Choosing plants or even containers according to a colour palette might be the perfect way for her to put her signature on the space. African violets, for example, come in many shades of both purple and pink. On a practical note, violets like moderate amounts of light, which makes them a perfect choice for this reading room.

African Violet
Saintpaulia

There are thousands of varieties of standard, miniature and trailing African violets with many different characteristics, but all display a low-growing rosette habit. Height: 5–15cm; Spread: 5–15cm. Bright indirect light.

Button Fern
Pellaea rotundifolia

This compact fern with an arching habit prefers moist but well-drained soil. Foliage is leathery and dark green, and its shape is round when new, changing to narrowly oblong with scalloped margins as it ages. Height: 30cm; Spread: 40cm. Bright indirect light.

Goldfish Plant
Columnea banksii

Best in a hanging basket or in a pot where it can trail freely. Displays smooth or hairy, mid-green to dark-green foliage. Produces tubular, yellow-orange or red blooms in summer. Height: 15cm; Trails: 1–1.5m. Bright indirect light.

Grape Ivy
Cissus rhombifolia

An easy and lovely, versatile plant with a climbing habit and tendrils that cling to supports. Foliage is palmate and dark green. Adaptable to low light conditions. Height: 4m; Spread: 1m. Bright indirect light.

Polka Dot Plant
Freckle Face
Hypoestes phyllostachya

A pretty little plant with oval, green foliage spotted with pink, white or red. Height: 30cm; Spread: 25cm. Bright indirect light.

Button Fern

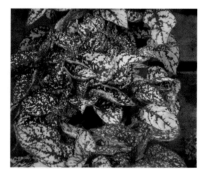

Polka Dot Plant

African Violet

High ledges in foyers are attractive spots to decorate with plants but can be challenging to access for watering and maintenance.

We've just moved into a new home with a spacious foyer. There is a high, moderately wide ledge that wraps around the perimeter of the room, and I'd like to fill the space with plants. It's a great architectural detail but difficult to access for watering. What grows here?

Many plants are sensitive and don't like bursts of cold air or wind, so growing plants in spaces like foyers that open to the outdoors can be challenging. However, having a ledge that's high and hard to reach isn't as bad as it sounds—keeping plants off the floor protects them from unstable air and foot traffic. As for your watering concerns, the solution can be as simple as buying a sturdy stepladder and choosing plants that like dry soil conditions. Of course, proper light is essential to a plant's health, so be sure to gauge how many hours of light the foyer ledge gets. Once that's determined, choose from a variety of upright and trailing plants. Just be sure to buy saucers or a tray to go under those plants—the temptation will be to over-water, so be careful not to turn your ledge into a waterfall. Also, don't feel you have to fill every inch of the space. Grouping plants looks very attractive and might save you a few trips up a ladder.

Golden Pothos
Devil's Ivy
Epipremnum aureus
(syn. *Scindapsus aureus*)

A popular climbing plant with heart-shaped green foliage marked with yellow. Trails: 2+m. Bright indirect light.

Mexican Hat Plant
Devil's Backbone,
Mexican Hat Plant
Kalanchoe daigremontiana

An upright plant often found grouped with succulents at garden centres. Fleshy, lance-shaped foliage produces plantlets on toothed margins. Height: 1m; Spread: 30cm. Direct light.

Mother of Thousands
Strawberry Begonia
Saxifraga stolonifera

A lovely plant that produces plantlets on long, thread-like stolons. Foliage is hairy, deep olive-green with reddish-purple undersides. Produces single, white with yellow-centred blooms in summer. Height: 20cm; Spread: 20cm. Bright indirect light.

Orchid Cactus
Epiphyllum

Closely related to Christmas and Easter cactus, orchid cactus displays fleshy, strap-shaped green stems and branches. Produces semi-double, flaring, trumpet-like blooms in many shades from spring to summer. Height: 30cm; Spread: 1m. Bright indirect light.

Spider Plant
Chlorophytum comosum

An extremely popular plant with lance-shaped or strap-shaped, arching foliage that can be striped with white or cream. Produces single, white, insignificant blooms on long, arching stems throughout the year that develop into plantlets. Height: 15–20cm; Spread: 15–30cm. Bright indirect light.

Orchid Cactus

Golden Pothos

Spider Plant

The shadow a plant casts can be as attractive as the plant itself when it is as artfully lit as this rainbow tree located in a hallway's wall niche.

We have a long hallway with gallery-style track lighting. We want to put in grow lights and display plants in this space. What grows here?

Normally, the biggest issue in this space would be lighting, but since you've solved this problem with grow lights, you can focus your attention on another obstacle: space. Hallways are notoriously narrow, high-traffic areas, so to prevent plants from becoming damaged, keep them off the floor by taking advantage of any high furniture or niches you have in that space. For an alternative solution, why not consider mounting decorative planters or shelves on the walls to create a niche? You could reinforce that gallery feel and showcase your plants and containers as you would art. There are a lot of interesting possibilities to this solution, and a trip to the garden centre is bound to inspire even more. For information on grow lights, see page 8.

Arrowhead Vine
Goosefoot
Syngonium podophyllum
This popular foliage houseplant has a vining habit. Leaves are large, arrow-shaped and veined. Some varieties are variegated. Height: 1–2m. Bright indirect light.

Flamingo Flower
Anthurium
An upright plant with tall stems bearing ovate, reflexed, glossy, dark-green foliage. Continually produces waxy, colourful, spathe-type blooms in pink, white, red or orange with prominent straight or curly tails. Height: 50–60cm; Spread: 30cm. Bright indirect light.

Flamingo Flower

Peperomia

Peperomia Group
Peperomia
An attractive group of plants comprising bushy, trailing and upright types. Foliage varies from textured with prominent veins to thick, fleshy leaves, and includes many shapes and colours. Some produce white spikes of blooms in summer. Height: 20–30cm; Spread: 20–30cm; Trails: 30cm. Bright indirect light.

Pussy Ears
Teddy Bear Vine
Cyanotis somaliensis
A pretty trailing plant with deep olive-green, hairy foliage flushed with purple. Produces single, mauve-blue blooms in summer. Height: 15cm; Spread: 40cm. Bright indirect light.

Rainbow Tree 'Colorama'
Dracaena marginata
An upright plant bearing thin, lance-shaped, reddish-pink banded foliage—dramatic. Height: 60cm; Spread: 1m. Bright indirect light.

Arrowhead Vine

Snipping herbs like curled parsley will keep them from becoming stretched and spindly.

My husband and I enjoy cooking together. The bay window above our kitchen sink is large enough for an indoor herb garden, but it faces east and we're unsure if it will provide enough light. What grows here?

Herbs require at least four or five hours of sunlight a day, so west-facing and south-facing windows are best. However, if the morning sun from your east window isn't blocked by curtains, outdoor trees, an awning, etc., you probably get the minimum light necessary to grow herbs. Just remember that regardless of the intensity of your light source, an indoor herb garden will never be as productive as an outdoor one. To ensure optimum growing conditions, use a soil mixture that is slightly acidic. Acidity is determined by measuring pH and is important because nutrients in the soil are available to plants only when the pH is within an appropriate range. Range of pH is measured from 0–14, with 7.0 being neutral. Herbs generally like a pH of 5.8. You'll also want to select containers that have good drainage—clay pots are a nice choice because they breathe and allow soil to dry out between waterings. A last thing to consider is the environment around your sink. If you use spray cleansers, be sure that the overspray doesn't land on your herb garden.

Bay Tree
Bay Laurel, Sweet Bay
Laurus nobilis

Upright in habit, this plant is best known for its aromatic leaves that are used for flavouring soups, stews and poultry dishes. Leathery foliage is dark green and glossy. Produces single, greenish-yellow blooms in summer. Height: 4m; Spread: 30cm. Direct light.

Curled Parsley
Petroselinum crispum crispum

This lovely herb has bright-green, curled foliage. Snip some to add flavour to all kinds of dishes. Height: 30–45cm; Spread: 15–30cm. Direct light.

Rosemary
Rosmarinus officinalis

Upright in habit, this plant has hundreds of straight, needle-shaped, succulent, green leaves. Foliage can be

harvested for cooking, potpourris and sachets. Height: 30–100cm; Spread: 30–60cm. Direct light.

Sage
Salvia officinalis

Sage is a valuable culinary herb said to aid in digesting fatty foods. Foliage is ovate and can be mid-green to purplish-green. Height: 45–60cm; Spread: 1m. Direct light.

Sweet Basil
Ocimum basilicum

An upright herb useful in cooking. There are many varieties with different coloured leaves and slightly different flavours. Height: 30–60cm; Spread: 30–45cm. Direct light.

Rosemary

Sage

Sweet Basil

Bay Tree

Fragrant flowering plants like this Stephanotis are beautiful, but their scent can be overwhelming. Just move them temporarily away from the table when you are eating.

I usually keep a lightly scented candle in my kitchen, but I think I'd like to replace it with a fragrant plant. What grows here?

Fragrant plants are great but not always the best choice for certain areas of a kitchen. The way food smells has a huge effect on how it tastes, so an overly fragrant plant can actually interfere with how we interpret taste. If this is a concern for you, simply choose a plant that has a mild scent and don't keep it on the kitchen table. Flowering plants generally need four or five hours of direct light to bloom. While you scout out a spot, think about which areas of the kitchen get the most use. If you spend lots of time at the sink or prep food at a particular counter, don't keep flowering plants above those locations—unless you're partial to picking spent blossoms out of your food. When you turn in for the night, don't forget that your plant wants a rest, too. Cooler nighttime temperatures help plants store energy and will encourage blooms to last longer and to hold the intensity of their colour. Since it's fragrance you're after, why not consider a blooming jasmine? The fragrance is wonderful and intensifies in the evenings—but don't take my word for it! What smells great to me might smell putrid to you. My best advice: listen to suggestions and then go with your nose.

Jasmine
Jasminum polyanthum

A climbing and vining plant prized for its lovely, fragrant flowers. Dark-green foliage is oval to lance shaped. Produces pink buds that open to very fragrant, single, white blooms in summer. Height: 3m. Direct light.

Paperwhite
Narcissus

A popular bulb for forcing for indoor floral displays. Be sure to purchase pre-chilled bulbs. Foliage is lance shaped and the single, white blooms held atop stems are very fragrant. Each bulb may produce as many as three or four bloom stalks per bulb. Height: 35cm. Direct light.

Paperwhite

Persian Violet

Persian Violet
Exacum affine

A small, compact and tidy plant, often given as a gift. Displays small, oval, medium-green foliage and produces fragrant, single, violet to blue, pink or white blooms in summer. Height: 25–30cm; Spread: 25–30cm. Bright indirect light.

Polyantha Primrose
Primrose
Primula x *polyantha*

A lovely small, flowering plant with oval, heavily veined, dark-green foliage. Produces fragrant, single, white, yellow, orange, red or purple blooms in spring. Height: 15–20cm; Spread: 15cm. Bright indirect light.

Stephanotis
Floradora, Madagascar Jasmine
Stephanotis floribunda

A large, flowering vine with oval, thick, glossy, mid-green to dark-green foliage. Produces fragrant, single, white blooms in summer. Height: 3–6m; Spread: indefinite. Direct light.

Polyantha Primrose

Herbs are great for making teas. Be sure to grow them close to the brightest, sunniest window in your home.

I'd like to grow some indoor plants that can be used for teas and home remedies. I have space for a collection of them in my moderately sunny family room. What grows here?

People have been taking advantage of the medicinal qualities of plants for, well, as long as there have been plants and people. One great plant that instantly leaps to mind is aloe vera. It has renowned healing properties and will live happily indoors for years. Aloe is usually harvested by cutting off a fleshy section, slicing it open and removing the gel-like centre. A variety of herbs can be grown for homemade teas and salves. Simply place them in front of a south-facing or west-facing window and benefit from both their fragrance and taste. Humans aren't the only mammals to enjoy plants in this manner. Catnip is very popular among the four-legged and one could say it has medicinal qualities.

Lemon Balm
Melissa officinalis

A loosely branched, upright plant. Foliage has a bright, fresh lemon taste. Commonly used for adding flavour and fragrance to culinary products but may also be used in salves and soaps. Young leaves have the best taste and scent. Height: 20–80cm; Spread: 60cm. Direct light.

Lemon Verbena
Aloysia triphylla

An upright plant with stiff, apple-green, willowy leaves and small, pale-lilac flowers in pyramid-shaped clusters. Leaves have a strong lemon fragrance and flavour. Both blossoms and leaves can be harvested for baking, salads, marinades, dressings and syrups. Height: 30–60cm; Spread: 45cm. Direct light.

Medicine Plant
Aloe vera

Best known for the use of the gel contained within its fleshy leaves, there are many types of aloe. All have upright, lance-shaped, semi-rigid foliage. Some have thorns. Some produces small, yellow blooms in summer. Height: 10–60cm; Spread: indefinite. Direct light.

Mint
Mentha

Mint comes in a huge variety of enticing scents and flavours. Harvest the leaves and use fresh for teas, jelly and other culinary delights. The essential oils in mint are best enjoyed fresh, but the leaves are easily dried or frozen for keeping. Height: 15–60cm; Spread: indefinite. Direct light.

Mint

Aloe

Lemon Verbena

A heart leaf philodendron's green foliage looks particularly lush when set against the warm rich tones of dark wood.

I recently inherited a buffet and hutch that is very large and out of scale with my other furniture. I'm hoping big plants will create balance. The room is bright but receives only filtered light through sheers. What grows here?

Introducing large plants to match the scale of your new piece of furniture is definitely an option, but there are other ways to strike balance. In a competition of size, your buffet and hutch will win every time, so why not try a different approach by using something as small and unsuspecting as a flower to change the focus? Beauty almost always trumps brawn, so diverting attention to one area of the hutch (like a shelf) with a striking flower will give you something less jarring to notice. Flowering plants won't last long in those light conditions, but because they're inexpensive, they don't have to. A few upright plants and trailers on the top of the hutch might also help soften the lines and brighten up the dark feel of the wood, and a grouping of tall plants on the other side of the room will create visual weight. Since the windows in your dining room are covered by sheers, choose plants that prefer indirect light. It sounds like you've inherited an heirloom piece—protect it from water stains by using plant saucers so that you can pass it on in pristine condition.

Cineraria
Pericallis

Often given as a gift, this compact flowering plant has an upright habit. Foliage is large, dark green and heart shaped. Produces single, daisy-like blooms in white, pink, blue, red or purple in spring, some with attractive white centres. Height: 30cm; Spread: 25cm. Bright indirect light.

Dracaena 'Michiko Cane'
Dracaena deremensis 'Michiko'

An upright plant with slim, dark-green, strap-shaped foliage. Effectively used in groupings to add height. Height: 3m; Spread: 60–90cm. Bright indirect light.

Heart Leaf Philodendron
Sweetheart Plant
Philodendron scandens

A climbing type of philodendron with a vining habit. Displays heart-shaped, glossy, dark-green foliage. An excellent plant for low light areas. Can be grown in a hanging basket, on a moss pole or frame, or displayed on a stand. Height: 3m; Spread: 3m. Bright indirect light.

Pot Mum
Chrysanthemum morifolium

A compact, upright flowering plant. Foliage is mid to dark green and deeply lobed. Produces single or double, white, pink, purple or yellow blooms usually only once indoors. Height: 30–45cm; Spread: 30cm. Bright indirect light.

Satin Pothos
Satin Pothos 'Argyraeus'
Scindapsus pictus

Bearing smaller leaves than other pothos, this plant is also slower growing and only requires repotting biennially. Produces olive-green, satin-textured foliage marked with silver. Trails: 45–90cm. Bright indirect light.

Chrysanthemum 'Gaiety'

Cineraria

Dracaena 'Michiko Cane'

Grouping a collection of African violets in an attractive saucer makes watering them from the bottom an easy task.

My grandmother kept a beautiful collection of African violets that I always admired (in spite of always being warned never to touch them). Sentimentality has gotten the better of me, and I'd like to start a collection in my own dining room. What grows here?

As you probably figured out, it's those easily blemished, yet irresistibly fuzzy leaves that inspire scoldings of, "Don't touch!" Luckily, everything else about African violets makes them ideal houseplants. Not only are they one of the few plants that will flower in low light conditions, they are also easy to keep flowering. In fact, African violets are often described as liking 'bright shade.' The other key to keeping these plants healthy is never to let them sit in water. Keep saucers under your plants and water from the bottom, being careful to use room temperature water to moisten rather than soak the soil. On the subject of soil, choose a slightly acidic mix that has equal parts peat moss and vermiculite. There are commercially blended African Violet mixes that allow air to reach the shallow roots and aid drainage, too. There are many flower forms and colours from which to choose, so take a look at as many of the single, semi-double and double varieties as you can and then let preference and sentimentality guide you.

African Violet
Saintpaulia

There are thousands of varieties of standard, miniature and trailing African violets with many different characteristics, but all display a low-growing rosette habit. Fuzzy foliage may be serrated, plain edged or spoon, holly or lance shaped and range in colour from dark-green to variegated cream and green. Flower forms are as variable as the foliage, including single, semi-double, double, frilled and star forms. Bloom colours are solid shades to bicolour, multicolour and even white edged. No wonder they are prized by collectors. Experts maintain blooms all year long; however, novices can still enjoy several flushes of flowers by using a fertilizer specifically formulated for these plants. Height: 5–15cm; Spread: 5–15cm. Bright indirect light.

African Violet 'Colorado'
Interesting quilted, glossy, mid-green to dark-green foliage. Produces single magenta flowers with frilled edges continually. Height: 15cm; Spread: 15cm.

African Violet 'Delft'
Foliage is mid green. Produces huge, semi-double, cornflower-blue blooms continually. Height: 15cm; Spread: 15cm.

African Violet 'Virginia'
Foliage is variegated green and cream. Produces single, pink blooms continually. Height: 15cm; Spread: 15cm.

African Violet 'Wonderland'
Foliage is olive green and wavy. Produces semi-double, light blue-violet blooms continually. Height: 15cm; Spread: 15cm.

African Violet 'Colorado'

Assorted African Violets

African Violet 'Delft'

Keep plants like this zebra plant away from lamps that stay on while you read at night. Incandescent bulbs put out enough heat to damage leaves and blossoms if plants are located too close to the bulbs.

My large bed and dresser take up most of the space in my bedroom, but I would still like to try growing a tall, thin plant in one of the corners. I'm a little apprehensive because the room isn't particularly sunny. What grows here?

Focusing too hard on one answer is often the best way to come up with no solution. There are tall, thin plants that will grow in the corner of your room on a plant stand or on the floor, but why not give yourself a few more options? There are containers that can be mounted onto walls, and they come in a variety of colours and materials to suit every decorating style. Besides being attractive, they free up floor space and can be positioned close to your light source. Another option is to rotate plants in and out of your bedroom. All you'd have to do is find a sunny space in another room and use it as a recovery area. Start with three small plants and establish them in the recovery space. Then, move one to your bedroom dresser or nightstand and keep an eye on it. When it starts showing signs of stress, swap it out with another plant. A third option is to try a hanging planter. Not only are they not the macramé monstrosities of yesteryear, but they also offer the perfect solution for small spaces.

Corn Plant 'Massangeana'
Dracaena fragrans

Foliage is held atop a sturdy upright trunk and may be sold with one or more trunks per pot. Wide, strappy, glossy-green leaves with a yellow stripe. Height: 3m; Spread: 1m. Bright indirect light.

Dracaena 'Janet Craig'
Draceana deremensis

A very popular, slower-growing, upright plant. Produces wide, dark-green, strappy foliage. Height: 2m; Spread: 60cm. Bright indirect light.

False Aralia
Dizygotheca elegantissima

A delicate-looking, upright plant with dark green-black, lacy, divided foliage. Height: 2m; Spread: 60cm. Bright indirect light.

Rex Begonia
Begonia rex

All varieties of Rex begonia now sold are hybrids that are available in a wonderful range of foliage colours. Leaves are large and ovate and vary in their markings of shades of pink, silver and purple. Height: 25cm; Spread: 30cm. Bright indirect light.

Swedish Ivy
Candle Plant
Plectranthus

Typically grown in a hanging basket where the attractive foliage spills over the sides freely. Foliage is heart shaped to ovate with scalloped edges and may be green with white veins, green with white edges or just solid green. Height: 25cm; Spread: 1m. Bright indirect light.

Zebra Plant
Saffron Spike
Aphelandra squarrosa

An attractive, upright plant with ovate to elliptical, dark-green foliage with prominent white veins and mid ribs. Produces waxy, yellow blooms on spikes in summer. Height: 45cm; Spread: 30cm. Bright indirect light.

Swedish Ivy

Corn Plant

False Aralia

Dish gardens are a tidy way for young gardeners to grow a variety of small plants with similar needs.

My kids have set their hearts on growing their own plants in their bedrooms. Generally, they are quite responsible—but kid-proof plants wouldn't hurt. What grows here?

Kids and gardening are a natural fit—but not a perfect one. However, with a little careful tailoring, the experience can be rewarding for the entire family. Start by choosing non-toxic plants that suit the ages of your children. Unfortunately, no plant is kid proof, so if your kids play in their rooms, avoid plants with leaves that easily break or bruise. Finding spots that are off the floor and away from high-traffic play space will also prevent plants from getting knocked over or run into. To figure out your light requirements, why not involve your kids in the process? Have them track the sunlight in their rooms over the course of a day. Then, together, determine what kind of plants to grow. It will give your children a sense of ownership and give you the opportunity to steer the selection process. Remember, kids have a tendency either to love their plants a bit too much or a lot too little. We've heard many a story about thoughtful kids who treated plants to a nibble of macaroni and cheese and a glass or two of juice. So, when you've made your selections, be sure to set up a watering schedule—and keep an eye out for disappearing leftovers.

Echeveria
Echeveria

Echeverias are pretty plants with fleshy leaves arranged in a rosette pattern. Foliage can be greenish blue, red, purple or burgundy pink. Single blooms that appear in summer range from yellow to red. Height: 5–30cm; Spread: 10–50cm. Direct light.

Peperomia Group
Peperomia

An attractive group of plants comprising bushy, trailing and upright types. Foliage varies from textured with prominent veins to thick, fleshy leaves, and includes many shapes and colours. Some produce white spikes of blooms in summer. Height: 20–30cm; Spread: 20–30cm; Trails: 30cm. Bright indirect light.

Starfish Plant
Earth Star
Cryptanthus

The common name of this plant matches its interesting appearance. Rigid, strap-shaped foliage comes in solid or striped forms. Produces small, single, white, slightly fragrant blooms in summer. Height: 10cm; Spread: 10cm. Direct light.

Venus Fly Trap
Dionaea muscipula

A fascinating insectivore. Two-lobed foliage is hinged and has spines along the outer edge, giving the appearance of teeth (called traps). Insects are trapped and ingested between the hinged leaves. Produces single, white blooms in summer. Height: 15cm; Spread: 15cm. Bright indirect light.

Starfish Plant

Peperomia

Venus Fly Trap

Peace lilies are happy to grow almost anywhere in the house. Although they prefer bright indirect light, they will tolerate low-light conditions.

I'd like to green up our walkout basement rec. room. The room opens to the south side of the yard but is slightly shaded in the summer by one of our large crabapple trees. What grows here?

Rec. rooms used to be the damp neglected areas in homes that accumulated everything but plants. When you did find something growing in them, it was usually fuzzy and unwanted. Today, no space is wasted, and rec. rooms are welcoming spaces that function as family rooms and are used for activities from watching television to playing pool. Because you have a walkout basement, you probably have enough sunlight to grow a variety of plants that like low to moderate light. So start by bringing down one or two plants and see how they do. Just watch out for problem spots in the room—if you have heat registers in the ceiling, don't place plants directly beneath them. Also, make sure that large plants don't block access to electronic equipment or interfere with games. The tree outside your window could be carefully pruned to allow just a bit more light into your rec. room if you find it too dark in the summer months.

Chinese Evergreen
Aglaonema

Different types are available with attractive, variegated mid-green to dark-green or solid-green, oval leaf blades on stalks. Occasionally produces flowers. Height: 30cm; Spread: 50cm. Indirect light (solid green types tolerate very low light levels).

Kentia Palm
Sentry Palm, Thatch Leaf Palm
Howea forsteriana

A wide-spreading palm with foliage displayed on large fronds up to 3m long. Very dramatic. Height: 3m; Spread: 3m. Bright indirect light.

Peace Lily
Spathiphyllum

A very useful, upright and bushy plant for lower light areas. Displays glossy, lance-shaped, dark-green foliage. Produces single, white to cream blooms heavily in spring and sporadically throughout the year. Height: 60–90cm; Spread: 60cm. Bright indirect light.

Philodendron 'Prince Albert'
Philodendron

An upright, bushy plant with large burgundy-coloured leaves. Makes an excellent contrast plant in groupings. Height: 60cm; Spread: 1m. Bright indirect light.

Snake Plant
Mother-in-Law's Tongue
Sansevieria trifasciata

Fleshy, rigid foliage is upright, dark green and attractively mottled and striped. The tip of each leaf is slightly barbed, hence the nasty common name mother-in-law's tongue. Height: 1.5m; Spread: 50cm. Bright indirect light.

Chinese Evergreen

Philodendron 'Prince Albert'

Kentia Palm

When space is restricted (as it is in a basement suite) look up—a high shelf or hanging basket may be just the ticket.

A buddy of mine is moving away for a year and has asked friends to 'adopt' a few plants from his collection. I agreed to take a few, but I live in a basement suite and don't know what plants are best for this space. I'd prefer not to welcome him home to dead plants. What grows here?

Basement suites, generally, rely on light from small windows. Adding to this challenge is that shrubs are often planted close to these windows, which reduces the already limited light source. So, when it's time for your friend to start divvying up his plants, offer to take only those that aren't fussy and that will tolerate low light—as in, don't offer to take his prized orchids! Keep in mind that fluorescents provide a source of energy that plants can use. So, if you have this type of lighting, think about position-ing your plants on the tops of bookcases or other tall furniture. This will keep your plants close to the light source, allowing them to maximize the energy. The actual transporting of the plants is a whole other beast. Not a lot fits in the back of a vehicle, so plan ahead and figure out what you can accommodate. If it is at all possible, plan the exchange for a day when the weather is mild. And unless you're fond of back pain, don't water large plants on the day they need to be moved.

Lipstick Vine
Basket Plant
Aeschynanthus lobbianus

A trailing plant with fleshy, mid-green to dark-green, ovate to lance-shaped foliage. Produces clusters of tubular, orange, red and dark-red blooms from summer to winter. Height: 20–30cm; Spread: 40–60cm. Bright indirect light.

Pothos 'Marble Queen'
Epipremnum aureum pinnatum (syn. *Scindapsus aureus*)

A pothos with heart-shaped foliage that is more white than green, giving the appearance that the leaves have been splashed. Trails: 2m. Bright indirect light.

Ribbon Plant
Dracaena sanderiana

An upright plant with lance-shaped, mid-green foliage with white or cream stripes. Height: 1.5m; Spread: 40–80cm. Bright indirect light.

Rubber Tree
India Rubber Fig, India Rubber Tree
Ficus elastica

A number of varieties of this popular plant are available. Fleshy foliage varies from deep green, black green to variegated and tri-colour. Height: 2–3m; Spread: 1+m. Bright indirect light.

Spider Plant
Chlorophytum comosum

An extremely popular plant with lance- or strap-shaped, arching foliage that can be striped with white or cream. Produces single, white, insignificant blooms on long, arching stems throughout the year that develop into plantlets. Height: 15–20cm; Spread: 15–30cm. Bright indirect light.

Spider Plant

Rubber Tree

Lipstick Vine

If you do keep your home cool at night, make sure you pull plants away from the windows during winter months.

I prefer the temperature quite cool when I sleep, so we turn our thermostat down to 12°C at night. I'm afraid it might be too cold for plants. What grows here?

You're right to be concerned—12°C is too cold for most plants. Cool temperatures are important for allowing plants to store energy rather than burn it, but temperatures that dip below 14°C can inhibit plant growth. Watch for the signs—they aren't as blatant as shivering or teeth chattering, but they are definitely noticeable. When temperatures drop too low, leaves may turn limp or discolour. In this environment, buds are also likely to fall off before they bloom. Don't forget that room temperatures fluctuate with the seasons. If you have draperies, keep them closed at night—windows let heat escape, and in winter months, frosty windowsills become dangerous real estate for plants. When it comes to misting your plants, do so in the early morning so that excess moisture can dry before the temperature drops. A basic rule is to err on the side of caution and to know your plants: plants like cyclamen and orchids don't mind cool nights but Chinese evergreens hate them.

Aloe
Medicine Plant
Aloe vera

Best known for the gel contained within its fleshy leaves, there are many types of aloe. All have upright, lance-shaped, semi-rigid foliage. Some have thorns. Some produce small, yellow blooms in summer. Height: 10–60cm; Spread: indefinite. Direct light.

Chinese Fan Palm
Livistona chinensis

This large, upright plant displays its long foliage in a fan shape on toothed stalks. Height: 2m; Spread: 1m. Bright indirect light.

Christmas Cactus
Schlumberga x *buckleyi*

Branching, arching fleshy stems are divided into flat segments. Produces

Christmas Cactus

Aloe

white, yellow, salmon, pink or red blooms in early winter. Height: 30–60cm; Spread: 1m. Bright indirect light.

Moth Orchid
Phalaenopsis

A compact, upright plant, with oval, fleshy, dark-green foliage and flat-faced, single, white, yellow, pink, purple or red blooms appearing continually. Height: 20–60cm; Spread: 20–30cm. Bright indirect light.

Norfolk Island Pine
Araucaria heterophylla

A beautiful upright plant that is not a pine as its common name suggests (it is a conifer). Soft needles are displayed on long, outward spreading branches. Height: 2–3+m; Spread: 1–2m. Bright indirect light.

Moth Orchid

Norfolk Island Pine

Window coverings are great for helping you control the light and the heat during summer months.

We just added a sunroom to our house last year, and find that while it's quite a comfortable temperature in the winter, it gets very hot in the summer. What grows here?

Houseplants are quite forgiving of seasonal changes as long as they aren't sudden or extreme. So, chances are most of your plants will acclimatize nicely to the temperature change if the process is gradual. Plants will tolerate less than ideal environments, but they won't appreciate extended periods of stress, so during hot summer months, you'll have to change your watering schedule—once a week won't be frequent enough. I find ceiling fans and blinds on the windows to be invaluable tools in controlling temperature in these kind of rooms. Although your sunroom maintains a comfortable temperature during the winter, it's still a good idea to take a few precautions. Moving plants away from the windows is a small job and one that removes any risk of your plants becoming frost bitten if the outside temperature takes a plunge.

Desert Rose
Impala Lily
Adenium obesum

A compact plant with an upright habit. Glossy, green foliage in spiral, terminal clusters. Produces single, most commonly pink, and rarely red and white blooms, in summer. Height: 25–30cm; Spread: 20cm. Direct light (but avoid hot summer sun).

Hibiscus
Hibiscus rosa-sinensis

An upright plant often available in a lollipop-like tree or standard form. Glossy, dark-green foliage highlights the single, semi-double or double, white, yellow, orange, pink or red flowers that bloom continually. Height: 1.5m; Spread: 1m. Direct light.

Hibiscus

Desert Rose

Kafir Lily
Clivia miniata

An upright plant with strap-shaped, dark-green foliage. Produces tubular, orange-yellow blooms in clusters in early spring. Height: 45cm; Spread: 30cm. Bright indirect light.

Lemon Tree 'Meyer'
Improved Meyer Lemon Tree
Citrus meyeri

A dwarf, upright variety. Foliage is narrow, ovate, finely toothed and light green. Produces fragrant, single, white blooms in spring or summer. May produce pale-yellow fruit up to 7.5cm in diameter. Height: 1.5m; Spread: 1m. Direct light.

Madagascar Palm
Pachypodium lamerei

An upright plant with dark-green, lance-shaped foliage held atop a spiny columnar stem. Grown indoors, this plant rarely produces its single, creamy-white blooms in summer. Height: 2m; spread: 1.5m. Direct light.

Kafir Lily

My bougainvillea and cannas spend the summers outside and love it. I just make sure to keep them indoors until there is no risk of frost.

We have a large furnished deck that the entire family gravitates to in the summer. We're thinking about taking some plants from our sunroom and moving them outside with us. What grows here?

Many indoor plants will enjoy a summer on the deck as much as your family will, but you'll have to do a little work to acclimatize them to the outdoors and again when you bring them back indoors as summer ends. You don't want to shock or sunburn your plants, so simply find a place on the deck that receives some dappled shade and move the plants outside in the day and back in at night for about a week. Don't put them out until all risk of frost has passed. Another factor to consider is how exposed your deck is to the elements. A gentle rain is wonderful for plants, but a summer storm can do some damage. Strong winds can break leaves and branches, and heavy rains can saturate and/or wash away soil, disrupting root systems. Even in the absence of extreme weather, a moderate wind is enough to start drying out leaves, so adjust the watering schedule accordingly. It's not that difficult of a process. Just remember to bring in tropicals before temperatures dip below 10°C, and check your plants thoroughly for bugs before the plant move back to the sunroom.

Bay Tree
Bay Laurel, Sweet Bay
Laurus nobilis

Upright in habit, this plant is best known for its aromatic leaves that are used for flavouring soups, stews and poultry dishes. Leathery foliage is dark green and glossy. Produces single, greenish-yellow blooms in summer. Height: 4m; Spread: 30cm. Direct light.

Bougainvillea
Paper Flowers
Bougainvillea

Usually grown out of doors but many enthusiasts in northern climates over-winter this plant in bright rooms. Bougainvillea displays a vining habit with small, medium-green, ovate foliage. Produces profuse single, white, pink, red or carmine blooms in summer. Height: up to 4m. Direct light.

Bougainvillea

Oxalis or Shamrock Plant

Cardamom
Elettaria cardamomum

An upright plant with mid-green, lance-shaped foliage. Seeds and seed pods are used as an aromatic spice in baking and cooking. Rarely flowers as a houseplant. Height: 1.5m; Spread: 1.5m. Bright indirect light.

Pygmy Date Palm
Miniature Date Palm
Phoenix roebelenii

This upright plant displays very narrow, arching, mid-green foliage on long stems. Height: 1m; Spread: 1.5m. Bright indirect light.

Shamrock
Good Luck Plant
Oxalis regnelli

This little, upright plant produces clover-like foliage on top of slender stalks. Single, white blooms appear in spring and summer and sporadically throughout the year. Height: 25cm; Spread: 15cm. Bright indirect light.

Pygmy Date Palm

Always buy orchids from a reliable grower so that you're not starting with a plant that is infested with scale, mealy bugs or aphids.

My sister-in-law's gorgeous collection of orchids has inspired me to start my own collection. The room I have in mind isn't quite a sunroom or an atrium, but it gets a lot of bright direct light. What grows here?

Most orchids prefer at least six hours of light a day, so a bright room is great. Your obstacle, however, is direct light. Orchids are hardier than one would think, but too much direct sunlight will cause their leaves to sunburn or bleach out. It's not a science, but the colour of an orchid's leaves will reveal a lot about its health. As a general rule, orchids that receive ideal light will have light-green to medium-green coloured leaves that are cool to the touch. Fortunately, you can easily correct your light problem by hanging sheer draperies on your window. A second thing to remember is that orchids will bloom longer if you treat them to cool nighttime temperatures (no lower than 14°C). Don't forget to take your time selecting varieties. Orchids are the largest family of flowering plants, and there are many that are suitable for novice collectors.

Brassia Orchid
Spider Orchid
Brassia

A compact plant with an arching habit. Displays large, spherical pseudobulbs, each with long, strap-shaped leaves. Produces spider-like, fragrant, yellow-green blooms on 1–1.5m-long spikes in May, lasting 4–8 weeks. Height: 45cm; Spread: 45cm. Bright indirect light.

Cattleya Orchid
Corsage Orchid
Cattleya

An upright plant with semi-rigid, leathery, oblong to ovate, medium-green foliage. Small varieties grow well in terrariums. Produces large, showy, waxy, single, white, yellow, green or pink blooms between spring and fall. Some varieties are fragrant. Height: 30cm–1.5m; Spread: 30–60cm. Direct light (but protect from hot sun).

Cymbidium Orchid
Cymbidium

An upright plant with mid-green, strap-shaped foliage and single, white, yellow, pink or red blooms in late winter or spring. Height: 30–90cm; Spread: 30–90cm. Bright indirect light.

Oncidium Orchid
Golden Shower Orchid, Dancing Ladies Orchid
Oncidium

A compact, upright plant with lance-shaped foliage. Produces single, yellow, pink, maroon, yellow and brown blooms in summer. Some may bloom year-round. Height: 15–60cm; Spread: 30cm. Bright indirect light.

Slipper Orchid
Paphiopedilum

A compact, upright plant with green or mottled, ovate to lance-shaped foliage and single blooms that display yellow, rose, green, white and mahogany colours between spring and fall. Height: 30cm; Spread: 15cm. Bright indirect light.

Paphiopedilum Orchid 'P. Claire del Lune x Alba'

Oncidium Orchid 'Riverwood'

Cymbidium Orchid

Who says you can't have an indoor water garden? Lisa and Ted Smith's is the centrepiece of their sunroom.

I was recently at a garden centre and saw a small but beautiful container full of water plants. I have a similar sized and shaped container and would love to use it to grow a water garden in my sunroom. What grows here?

Most water plants need a dormant season and, therefore, can't be kept indoors permanently. Fortunately, there are species (like *Cyperus involucratus*) that are content to grow year-round inside your home, so give them a try. It might seem obvious, but make sure to start with a container that has no drainage holes—a pot that isn't properly sealed or that is cracked will prove disastrous. How much water you keep in that container can vary—as long as you cover the soil with 2.5 cm of water, you're good to grow. Bright light is essential, and with enough of it, a *Cyperus* plant will grow quite vigorously and even sprout new heads. One staff member knows a woman who started with a *Cyperus* in a 10-cm pot that grew to over 1.5 m tall. If that feels a little ambitious, try a dwarf papyrus. It's smaller but in the same family. Be sure to keep an eye on the water level—the woman with the 1.5-m tall *Cyperus* also has a dog that thinks he has two water dishes.

Canna Lily 'Pretoria'
Variegated Water Canna
Canna

This plant grown from a tender bulb has striking zebra-striped foliage with alternating bands of creamy yellow and green. Produces single, tall spikes of melon-orange blooms in midsummer to fall. Height: 2m. Direct light.

Dwarf Papyrus
Paper Reed 'Nanus'
Cyperus papyrus

An upright plant that bears wispy leaf clusters at tips of thin stems. Flowers are inconspicuous. A shorter plant than *C. involucratus*, making it suitable for smaller water bowls. Height: 30–60 cm; Spread: 45–60 cm. Direct light.

Parrot Feather
Diamond Millfoil
Myriophyllum aquaticum

Trailing stems of feathery green, needle-like leaves highlight this floating plant. Height: 60 cm; Spread: indefinite. Direct light.

Umbrella Plant 'Gracilis'
Cyperus involucratus

An upright plant with interesting foliage radiating like umbrella spokes from the top of tall, thin stems. Height: 60cm–1.5m; Spread: 25cm (determined by pot size). Direct light.

Water Lettuce
Shell Flower
Pistia stratiotes

This plant looks like a small, open-faced cabbage floating on the water's surface. Foliage is furry and ribbed. Spreads by producing plantlets that can be cut off to produce more plants. Height: 15 cm; Spread: indefinite. Direct light.

Parrot Feather

Umbrella Plant

Canna Lily 'Pretoria'

Water Lettuce

Foyers of apartment or condo buildings can be wonderful indoor community gardens.

Our condominium board recently converted our foyer to an atrium and would like to fill the built-in planters with a variety of interesting plants. The ceilings are high and the space is quite large and bright. What grows here?

A bright atrium can be a great selling point, but it needs to be full of healthy, beautiful plants to convince tenants that it's of extra value to them. This means investing in the right plants and, more importantly, maintaining them. Sometimes the easiest way to do that is by using a professional plant service. It eliminates any worry about watering schedules and increases the chances of plant problems being caught early. Since you have the luxury of both bright light and high ceilings, take advantage of these features and grow a few tall trees—just be sure to space them properly so they have room to grow. Keep in mind that plants living in the same planter can receive completely different amounts of light. Think of a forest: anything growing under a canopy of leaves will receive less light than will taller plants. My best advice is to start with a great quality potting mix—it's the number one thing you can do to avoid problems with pests and diseases.

Chinese Fan Palm
Livistona chinensis

This large, upright plant displays its long foliage in a fan shape on toothed stalks. Height: 2m; Spread: 1m. Bright indirect light.

Oleander
Nerium oleander

A large, upright plant with lance-shaped, leathery foliage. Can be purchased in tree or shrub form. Produces single, white, pink or red blooms in summer. Height: 2–6m; Spread: 1–3m. Direct light.

Plumbago
Cape Leadwort
Plumbago auriculata

A vigorous climber with bright matte-green, oblong to spoon-shaped foliage and single, sky-blue or white blooms in summer. Height: 3m; Spread: 1m. Direct light.

Plush Vine
Mikania dentata (syn. *M. ternata*)

A very pretty trailing plant with hairy, greenish-purple, palmate foliage with purple veins and purple undersides. Can be grown in a hanging basket or in a pot placed on a stand. Trails: 20–25cm; Spread: 30cm. Bright indirect light.

Yucca
Spineless Yucca
Yucca elephantipes

An undemanding, large plant to grow indoors. Light-green to mid-green foliage is narrow and lance shaped, sometimes growing as long as 90cm. Rarely produces single, white to cream blooms in summer when the plant reaches maturity. Height: 3+m; Spread: 1.5m. Direct light.

Plumbago

Plush Vine

Oleander

Plants at Work

Have you ever wondered why certain stereotypes about office environments are engrained in our minds? You know which ones I'm talking about. There's the image of the maniacal corporate raider who sits all day at his magnificent desk wringing his hands and plotting takeovers. But that's only one. Let's not forget about the tragic hero— the wrongfully dismissed employee who can be found cleaning out his or her desk, painstakingly placing a few significant possessions into a small cardboard box. Nine times out of ten, those clichéd, box-destined belongings include a picture

Norfolk Pine

Cyclamen

of a loved one, an oversized coffee mug and, usually, the pathetic-looking plant that sat on the desk. The significance of the photograph and the mug are obvious, but why the scrawny plant? Well, the answer is quite simple: our plants, like our photographs and our favourite mugs, bring us a unique brand of comfort that we don't bother questioning. Simply put, the plant represents individuality and, in a small but significant way, helps us carve out who we are in an environment where individuality can feel trampled by the pursuit of the big picture.

Symbolic significance and beauty aside, plants are practical additions to many work environments. Whether they are used to create plant borders, to buffer sound, to welcome guests or to clean the air, plants contribute a lot to our work spaces. And oddly enough, their contribution is one that's often made before we have a chance to make ours. Think about it. When you walk into a doctor's office or a reception area, your first impression is sealed by the time you're through the door. Within seconds, it's decided that how a person decorates is a reflection of what kind of a person he or she is: friendly, organized, smart, aloof—even untrustworthy.

Regardless of the impression you want to make with plants, there is always the issue of how to care for them once they are in your office. Even here at Hole's, a place filled with employees who think about plants for a living, there are occasions when we forget to haul watering cans to our offices. It just happens. Fortunately, we remember more times than we forget, and we were smart enough to choose plants that would tolerate brief stints of neglect. Really, that's all there is to it—a little planning and a lot of return. So as you read the questions and answers that follow, think about all the beautiful and practical ways you could incorporate plants into your work environment. After all, to most people, plants are a kind of unacknowledged staple, so it just makes sense that we'd want to be surrounded by them in our professional lives.

Reception areas see a lot of traffic, so choose plants like this Dieffenbachia that can take being brushed up against occasionally.

The reception area of our accounting office is quite uninviting. We'd like to add plants to make the space warmer and more interesting, but the front doors open directly outside and allow in cold drafts. What grows here?

The function of a reception room may be, literally, to receive and welcome visitors, but a welcoming reception room is more than an attractive distraction; it's also a signal to visitors that the proprietor and the staff care. Cold drafts are definitely a concern in many reception areas, so strategically place plants where drafts are blocked by bookcases, screens and other furniture. Drafts will be strongest along the floor, so keep plants off the ground by using stands and hanging planters. To add visual interest, choose plants that have colourful variegation. And don't forget to dress up the room with seasonal displays: poinsettias for Christmas, violets in the spring and chrysanthemums during the fall. Like us, reception areas only get one chance to make a first impression, so make it a good one!

Cast Iron Plant
Aspidistra elatior

This tough plant displays an upright habit with dark-green, sometimes variegated, glossy, leathery foliage that is elliptical to lance shaped. Height: 60cm; Spread: 60cm. Bright indirect light (tolerant of most light levels except direct sun).

Corn Plant 'Massangeana'
Happy Plant
Dracaena fragrans

Foliage is held atop a sturdy trunk and may be sold with one or more trunks per pot. Wide, strappy, glossy-green leaves with a yellow stripe. Height: 3m; Spread: 1m. Bright indirect light.

Dieffenbachia
Dumb Cane
Dieffenbachia

An upright plant with large, oblong, paddle- or ovate-shaped foliage that varies from cream, yellow and green patterns to solid green. Height: 1–3m; Spread: 60cm. Bright indirect light.

Dracaena 'Janet Craig'
Draceana deremensis

A very popular, slow-growing, upright plant. Produces wide, dark-green, strappy foliage. Height: 2m; Spread: 60cm. Bright indirect light.

Pothos 'Lemon Lime'
Epipremnum aureum
(syn. *Scindapsus aureus*)

A great plant for adding contrast to a grouping. Produces heart-shaped, lime-coloured foliage with lemon markings. Trails: 2+m. Bright indirect light.

Corn Plant 'Massangeana'

Dracaena 'Janet Craig'

Cast Iron Plant

For some people, working next to a fragrant plant all day can be as enjoyable as sitting next to someone who's overly fond of perfume, so before you buy plants, ask your employees if any of them have allergies or are sensitive to fragrance.

We'd like to get small plants to brighten up each of our employees' cubicles. The perimeter cubicles get light from the windows, but the central ones receive light primarily from fluorescent fixtures. What grows here?

Light is the key to growing all plants, so determining how many hours of sunlight the perimeter cubicles get and noting whether or not that light is direct or diffused is key to selecting the right plants. If your windows have any type of coverings, you'll probably be restricted to growing medium-light to low-light plants. As for the area that relies on fluorescent lights, it will sustain only low-light plants. Just remember that light is a food source that fuels flower production, so flowering plants (with the exception of African violets) will probably require more light than you have. Variegated plants might also be hard to grow because they require light to maintain their vibrant colour. As for the size of the plants, pick ones that won't take over the desks—practicality is key. And don't forget about maintenance. Decide who's responsible for watering and remind employees to turn plants that start leaning toward the sun.

African Violet
Saintpaulia

There are thousands of varieties of standard, miniature and trailing African violets with many different characteristics, but all display a low-growing rosette habit. Height: 5–15cm; Spread: 5–15cm. Bright indirect light.

Christmas Cactus
Schlumberga x *buckleyi*

Branching, arching, fleshy stems are divided into flat segments. Produces white, yellow, salmon, pink or red blooms in early winter. Height: 30–60cm; Spread: 1m. Bright indirect light.

Nerve Plant
Painted Net Leaf
Fittonia albivenis

A creeping plant with oval foliage covered with a fine network of pink or white veins. Height: 15cm; Spread: indefinite. Indirect light.

Peperomia Group
Peperomia

An attractive group of plants comprising bushy, trailing and upright types. Foliage varies from textured with prominent veins to thick, fleshy leaves, and includes many shapes and colours. Some produce white spikes of blooms in summer. Height: 20–30cm; Spread: 20–30cm; Trails: 30cm. Bright indirect light.

Rex Begonia
Begonia rex

All varieties of Rex begonia now sold are hybrids that are available in a wonderful range of foliage colours. Leaves are large and ovate and vary in their markings of shades of pink, silver and purple. Height: 25cm; Spread: 30cm. Bright indirect light.

Nerve Plant

Peperomia

Christmas Cactus

Minds are ususally focused on business in a conference room, so be sure to designate someone to think about the plants that live there.

I'd like a few plants for our conference room. The ceilings are reasonably high (about 3.5 metres tall), but there are no outside windows. We do leave the fluorescent fixtures on all day. What grows here?

Conference rooms often become multi-purpose spaces where chairs and tables are constantly rearranged, so don't overcrowd the room with too many plants. For practical purposes, choose a few that are large enough to anchor the room but small enough to move when necessary. Think about the layout of your space. If you have a side table where hot coffee urns are often set up, don't add a plant to that area. Most importantly, choose plants that perform well under artificial light—this means buying low-light plants. Fluorescents will help, but you'll need to keep them on for most of the day to get maximum benefits from them. Placing plants on the tops of shelves, counters or stands will bring them closer to the light source. There are many low-light plants that will survive in this space, but you may have to replace them every year or so. Choose plants that will also take a little manhandling. Don't forget about maintenance— this is a temporary space and one that's easy to forget about.

Asparagus Fern
Emerald Feather
Asparagus densiflorus (Sprengeri group)

An arching fern with glossy, mid-green, needle-like foliage on long stems. Height: 30cm; Spread: 60cm. Bright indirect light.

Cast Iron Plant
Aspidistra elatior

This tough plant displays an upright habit with dark-green, sometimes variegated, glossy, leathery foliage that is elliptical to lance shaped. Height: 60cm; Spread: 60cm. Bright indirect light (tolerant of most light levels except direct sun).

Chinese Evergreen
Aglaonema

This plant has a compact habit. Different types are available with attractive, variegated mid-green to dark-green or solid-green, oval leaf blades on stalks. May produce flowers occasionally. Height: 30cm; Spread: 50cm. Indirect light (solid green types tolerate very low light levels).

Dracaena 'Warneckii'
Dracaena deremensis warnecki

An upright plant with long, dark grey-green foliage with lighter streaks and white stripes on leaf edges. Height: 3m; Spread: 60cm. Bright indirect light.

Snake Plant
Mother-in-Law's Tongue
Sansevieria trifasciata

An excellent plant that can withstand neglect—perfect for beginners. Fleshy, rigid foliage is upright, dark green and attractively mottled and striped. The tip of each leaf is slightly barbed, hence the nasty common name mother-in-law's tongue. Height: 1.5m; Spread: 50cm. Bright indirect light.

Snake Plant

Chinese Evergreen

Dracaena 'Warneckii'

Plants can help transform a sterile office into an inviting work space and divide work areas.

We work in a high-rise downtown and would like to create dividers in our large, open office by using tall plants between the desks. What grows here?

Borders of plants are not only beautiful in an office space, they also help clean the air and buffer sound. When it comes to planning your borders, be sure not to limit yourself to tall plants—vines are a great alternative and can be trained to crawl up a row of trellises. And why not make your borders mobile? Simply adding caster wheels to window-box containers with attached trellises takes borders from functional to convenient. Whatever you decide on, space plants according to your needs: close together if the border is for privacy or farther apart if the border is aesthetic. If budget is not an issue, buy plants that have reached their mature size. It's a bit more of an investment but will give you the instant atmosphere you're looking for. If you really want to treat yourself, use a professional plant service. It eliminates all maintenance concerns and frees you of extra responsibilities.

Corn Plant 'Massangeana'
Dracaena fragrans

Foliage is held atop a sturdy upright trunk and it may be sold with one or more trunks per pot. Wide, strappy, glossy-green leaves with a yellow stripe. Height: 3m; Spread: 1m. Bright indirect light.

Croton
Codiaeum

A popular, upright plant prized for its stunning foliage. Strikingly veined leaves vary greatly in colour and shape. Height: 1m; Spread: 65cm. Direct light.

Fishtail Palm
Caryota mitis

This big palm has long arching stems covered in mid-green, fishtail-shaped foliage, divided herring bone fashion, with tattered edges. Height: 3m; Spread: 2m. Bright indirect light.

Umbrella Tree
Schefflera actinophylla

An upright plant that is often sold as a bushy plant or trained as a single-stem specimen. Glossy, green foliage is divided and forms an umbrella-like appearance. Height: 3m; Spread: 1.5m. Bright indirect light.

Weeping Fig
Ficus benjamina

Enormously popular in homes, malls and offices, this upright fig is long-lived and tolerant of slightly rootbound conditions. Produces small, ovate, glossy, mid-green leaves. Height: 2–3m; Spread: 1m. Bright indirect light.

Fishtail Palm

Corn Plant 'Massangeana'

Umbrella Tree

Succulents are capable of storing large amounts of water, which is why they can tolerate long dry periods.

I have a daycare centre and would like to set up a child-height plant station that the kids could take turns watering and maintaining. The space we rent has lots of windows, but we don't have an excessive amount of space. What grows here?

Kids love bright colours and interesting shapes, and a plant that delivers both is a succulent. You will, of course, want to stay away from the ones that are sharp and pointy, but you won't have any trouble finding nice varieties that are perfect for your plant station. Besides coming in interesting shapes and colours, succulents flower and are easy to propagate. A once-a-week watering is more than enough for succulents, but you'll still want to set up a proper watering schedule and supervise the maintenance. Best of all, these plants are quite forgiving of imaginative kids, so if they become 'pets' that occasionally get patted or bumped, they won't be any worse for wear.

Burro's Tail
Donkey's, Horse's or Lamb's Tail
Sedum morganianum

A trailing sedum with stems that are covered in small, overlapping, cylindrical, fleshy leaves. These stems hang over the edges of pots looking like tails or ropes. Produces single, pink blooms in early spring. Height: 30cm; Spread: 30cm. Direct light.

Echeveria
Echeveria

Echeverias are pretty plants with fleshy leaves arranged in a rosette pattern. Their succulent foliage can be greenish-blue, red, purple or burgundy-pink. Single blooms that appear in summer range from yellow to red. Height: 5–30cm; Spread: 10–50cm. Direct light.

Jade Plant
Crassula ovata

Just one of many *Crassula*, jade plants are popular, long-lived plants with fleshy, mid-green foliage distributed along upright, fleshy stems. When grown indoors they rarely produce single, white to pale-pink blooms in summer. Height: 80+cm; Spread: 80+cm. Direct light.

Living Stones
Lithops

Fascinating succulent plants that resemble stones. Foliage consists of a pair of very thick, fleshy leaves fused together. Produces daisy-like, single, pink, white or yellow blooms in fall. Height: 3–4cm; Spread: 8–15cm. Direct light.

Rosary Vine
Hearts on a String,
Sweetheart Vine
Ceropegia linearis ssp. *woodii*

A pretty trailing plant with sparsely spaced, heart-shaped, fleshy, green foliage with purple markings and purple undersides on wiry stems. Produces insignificant, tubular, lantern-like, purplish-brown blooms in summer. Trails: indefinitely. Direct light.

String of Pearls
String of Beads
Senecio rowleyanus

A trailing plant with spherical, mid-green foliage on pendant thread-like stems. Produces single, white blooms in summer. Height: 8cm. Trails: 30+cm. Direct light.

Burro's Tail

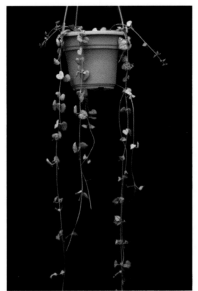

Rosary Vine

Lithops

Ctenanthe is a beautiful plant with a spreading, upright habit. Its long green leaves are accented with yellow markings.

Our modern-designed clothing store has very dark walls and soft lighting—almost a gallery feel. We usually brighten up the space with bouquets of fresh flowers, but I think I'd like to try some brightly coloured plants instead. I suspect artificial light will be required. What grows here?

Sometimes, in a space like this, it helps to think about how you define *houseplants*. It may sound a little harsh, but it's okay to think of them as you would cutflowers—cutflowers that last 40 days, that is. Moderate-sized tropicals are both colourful and often inexpensive, and even in low light, they will outperform a cutflower. Just remember to buy a few attractive containers that can conceal the plastic pots most plants come in. When your tropicals begin to show signs of stress (and they will), replace them with new ones, and let employees take the old ones home to sunny windows. If you think your customers would enjoy them, have a draw at the end of each month and send a tropical home with a lucky shopper. Buying low-light plants is another option to consider. Peace lilies, for example, are reasonably tolerant of poor light and can also be replaced inexpensively.

Ctenanthe 'Tricolour'
Never Never Plant
Ctenanthe lubbersiana

An attractive foliage plant with a spreading, upright habit. Long, dark-green leaves, with irregular yellow streaks, have reddish-purple undersides. Height: 2m; Spread: 1m. Bright indirect light.

Peace Lily
Spathiphyllum

A very useful, bushy plant for lower light areas, this upright plant displays glossy, lance-shaped, dark-green foliage. Produces single, white to cream blooms heavily in spring and sporadically throughout the year. Height: 60–90cm; Spread: 60cm. Bright indirect light.

Peace Lily 'Domino'
Spathiphyllum

A very useful, bushy plant for lower light areas, this upright plant displays glossy, lance-shaped, mottled green and white foliage. Produces single, white to cream blooms heavily in spring and sporadically throughout year. Height: 60cm; Spread: 45cm. Bright indirect light.

Prayer Plant
Maranta leuconeura

Commonly named prayer plant because the foliage has a habit of folding upwards at night. Produces elliptic to ovate, dark-green foliage with striking bright-red mid ribs and veins. Height: 20cm; Spread: 20cm. Bright indirect light.

Spider Plant
Chlorophytum comosum

An extremely popular plant with lance-shaped or strap-shaped, arching foliage that can be striped with white or cream. Produces single, white, insignificant blooms on long, arching stems throughout the year that develop into plantlets. Height: 15–20cm; Spread: 15–30cm. Bright indirect light.

Prayer Plant

Peace Lily 'Domino'

Spider Plant

Raised planters can accommodate both tall upright plants and low-growing types that cover the soil, giving a lush effect.

The food court in the mall where I work has beautiful waist-high planters and large skylights. Most of the planters are used as borders to break up the space into 'rooms.' What grows here?

An inviting green space in a mall is a perfect resting spot for a weary shopper. Besides looking attractive, plants in a mall help filter noise and clean the air. Malls have a lot to offer, including vertical space, so take advantage of high ceilings and skylights by incorporating a few taller features into your planters. Why not consider growing vines up an obelisk or some other decorative structure? Just keep in mind that the edges of planters are sometimes used as creative seating, so cascading plants occasionally become damaged. Flowering plants are always a nice option, but their blooms often get picked, so as an alternative, consider selecting plants that have colourful and shapely leaves rather than flowers. Unfortunately, you'll also have to consider the issue of litter. Many people still do it, so check low-spreading plants to see if they are concealing trash.

English Ivy
Hedera helix
A popular vine displaying flat, 3 to 5-lobed leaves that are green or variegated white or yellow. Height: 2m; Spread: 1m. Bright indirect light.

Golden Pothos
Devil's Ivy
Epipremnum aureus
(syn. Scindapsus aureus)
A popular climbing plant with heart-shaped green foliage marked with yellow. Trails: 2+m. Bright indirect light.

Kimberly Queen Sword Fern
Australian Sword Fern
Nephrolepis obliterata
A large fern with an upright and arching habit. Foliage is dark green and fronds are pointed. Height: 1m; Spread: 1m. Bright indirect light.

Moses in a Cradle
Boat Lily, Three Men in a Boat
Tradescantia spathacea (syn. Rhoeo)
A compact plant with long, lance-shaped, dark-green foliage with purple undersides. Single, white blooms appear sporadically. Height: 20–30cm; Spread: 20–30cm. Bright indirect light.

Purple Heart
Purple Queen
Tradescantia pallida 'purpurea'
A trailing plant with dark-purple, pointed and oblong leaves. Produces single, pink blooms in summer. Height: 60cm; Spread: 40cm. Bright indirect light.

English Ivy (top) and Golden Pothos (bottom)

Kimberly Queen Sword Fern

Purple Heart

Lady Palm

Public Spaces

Everyone knows that living in the public eye is difficult. There's the pressure to perform to a certain standard, to contribute to what can feel like an intangible goal, to follow rules, to set examples and—of course—to look good while doing it. Well, for plants that live and grow in public spaces like schools, hospitals and nursing homes, there is a similar type of expectation placed on them.

Public spaces are shared, and, as we all know, there are *always* rules for sharing. In fact, there are rules for everything that goes on in public. What makes these spaces particularly challenging is that they have to accommodate diverse needs while appealing to the tastes of the general public—not an easy task. Fortunately, one way to make public spaces more welcoming is to bring nature in. And when it is done well, people take notice.

Because plants create atmosphere, they can reflect or de-emphasize what goes on in indoor environments. A hospital, for example, might decorate its reception area with brightly coloured tropical plants to provide a much-needed distraction for nervous patients; whereas, a law courts building may want to present a more tailored look—one that might emphasize a modern or contemporary style. It doesn't take a lot of effort, but it's how establishments become known as "the building with all the plants," or "the food court with the skylights and waist-high planters." There's just no denying that plants make an impression and offer personality to a space.

Plants in Schools

One of my favourite things to do is watch my daughter discover the world of plants. Much to Marcia's dismay and amusement, our daughter has inherited my penchant for plant science, specifically, an interest in what kind of bugs live on plants. In fact, to Emma, plants and flowers are nothing more than structures that harbour interesting creatures. So, as much as my wife needs an ally in her campaign to select houseplants based on their beauty— not their interesting mutations— she's just not going to find it in Emma.

For many kids, science is a subject that tends to be learned about rather than marvelled at. We all study photosynthesis and the water cycle, but it seems that we too often get caught up looking at science through books and not enough time testing theories through experimentation and play. As a result, science becomes this 'thing' we define and memorize rather than question and touch. Well, introducing plants to a learning environment is a great way to turn that around and to nurture curiosity, understanding and respect for nature.

Whenever I have the opportunity, I always encourage teachers to bring plants into their schools. It just makes sense. Think about it: you wouldn't teach kids the alphabet without also intending for them to hold books and to think about what they've read. Well, why then would you teach kids about photosynthesis without also providing a physical example? Science is intimidating for many kids, so understanding the theory behind something like the water cycle becomes easier when it's demonstrated by showing how a terrarium makes its own version of rain.

For the most part, selecting plants for a school environment isn't that difficult. As always, issues relating to light and humidity need to be addressed, but the real obstacle tends to be maintenance. A school spotted with tropical plants is a fantastic thing, but there has to be someone available to water those plants during summer months when kids and teachers are enjoying a well-deserved break. So, my advice is to be extremely practical and to take a little time to plan ahead. As you will learn from the questions and answers that follow, success is very attainable, and what better place to nurture success than at school—just one more lesson learned.

Coleus is a beautiful plant that may capture students' interests. As an added bonus, it is easy to take cuttings from so that students can start their own plants.

The bank of west-facing windows in my classroom runs above a bookshelf that doubles as a ledge where I want to grow plants. Air from vents blows up in front of the shelf. What grows here?

This is a challenging space. The trick will be to keep your plants away from the vents without crowding them against the windows. This becomes especially important in the winter when temperatures drop and windows become cold. The constant air flow will dry out soil and foliage at an alarming rate, so select plant varieties that will tolerate dry conditions, don't use clay pots (they breathe and will dry out too quickly) and be vigilant about watering. Grouping plants together is one way to encourage transpiration, but why not consider a creative alternative? If your ledge is wide enough, think about turning an empty fish tank into a greenhouse. The glass would protect your plants from the vent and insulate against the cold. In essence, you'd be creating a type of terrarium. If none of these options work for you, cover the vents with deflectors and experiment with a single grouping of inexpensive 'sacrificial' plants. A last option is to ask students to move plants to their desks at the end of each day. This will give the plants a break from the vent and might even pique a student's interest in botany.

Button Fern
Pellaea rotundifolia

This compact fern with an arching habit prefers dry surroundings. Foliage is leathery and dark green, and its shape is round when new, changing to narrowly oblong with scalloped margins. Height: 30cm; Spread: 40cm. Bright indirect light.

Coleus
Flame Nettle
Solenostemon (syn. *Coleus*)

Prized for its stunning foliage, this upright plant produces tooth-edged, pointed, oval leaves in many colours and patterns. Flowers are borne on stalks from spring to summer and are fairly insignificant. Height: 30cm; Spread: 25cm. Direct light.

Neoregelia
Blushing Bromeliad
Neoregelia

Grown for its foliage that blushes at the plant's centre when it is ready to bloom. Displays shiny, medium-green foliage with yellow stripes and produces single, blue or white blooms sporadically. Height: 20–30cm; Spread: 40–60cm. Direct light (but avoid hot summer sun).

Nerve Plant
Painted Net Leaf
Fittonia albivenis

A creeping plant with oval foliage covered with a fine network of pink or white veins. Height: 15cm; Spread: indefinite. Indirect light.

Pilea
Friendship Plant
Pilea

This group of plants has an upright and spreading to trailing habit. Produces textured oval foliage that is attractively marked. Height: 3–30cm; Spread: 15–30cm. Bright indirect light.

Neoregelia

Pilea

Button Fern

Bringing plants into a classroom can help to clean the air, foster a sense of responsibility and maybe even inspire a lifelong love of horticulture.

I'm a junior-high teacher, and I want to set up an indoor garden to clean the air in my homeroom. I have plenty of space but no windows. What grows here?

Everyone knows that, through the process of photosynthesis, plants absorb carbon dioxide and release oxygen. But what is less known is that many plants also absorb the benzene, formaldehyde and trichloroethylene gases released from synthetic materials—a process referred to as *outgassing*. Unfortunately, sick building syndrome is not a figment of a hypochondriac's imagination. Although the actual causes are uncertain, the remedy often includes introducing plants that 'scrub' the air of chemical contaminants. It doesn't take many either: 2–3 plants per 17–21 m² of living space are all that's needed to improve air quality. It's not just a plant's leaves that combat air pollution; soil and roots also help rid the air of toxins. So, to increase the amount of contact that the soil has with the air, remove lower leaves that cover the surface of the soil. As for lighting, choose low-light plants and consider grow lights. The plants may not live as long but by adding an extra light source, you'll still be able to grow plants and, essentially, more fresh air.

Boston Fern
Nephrolepis exaltata bostoniensis

A very popular fern with an arching habit. Broad, lance-shaped fronds arch gracefully up and over. Height: 1m; Spread: 2m. Bright indirect light.

Chinese Evergreen
Aglaonema

This plant has a compact habit. Different types are available with attractive, variegated mid-green to dark-green or solid-green, oval leaf blades on stalks. May produce flowers occasionally. Height: 30cm; Spread: 50cm. Indirect light (solid green types tolerate very low light levels).

Dracaena 'Lemon Lime'
Dracaena deremensis

An upright plant with lance-shaped, yellow-striped foliage. Height: 60–90cm; Spread: 1m. Bright indirect light.

Heart Leaf Philodendron
Sweetheart Plant
Philodendron scandens

A climbing type with a vining habit. Displays heart-shaped, glossy, dark-green foliage. An excellent plant for low-light areas. Trails: 3m; Spread: 3m. Bright indirect light.

Peace Lily
Spathiphyllum

A very useful, bushy plant for lower light areas. Displays glossy, lance-shaped, dark-green foliage. Produces single, white to cream blooms heavily in spring and sporadically throughout the year. Height: 60–90cm; Spread: 60cm. Bright indirect light.

Chinese Evergreen

Boston Fern

Peace Lily

Polka dot plants readily illustrate what happens when plants don't receive adequate light.

I'm a Grade 5 science teacher with a group of students who are more interested in the life expectancy of my hairline than they are in my lesson plans. To recapture their attention, I've decided to have them try an experiment that teaches them about how light (or the lack of it) affects plants. What grows here?

Your experiment is a great idea and the perfect tool for reinforcing the science curriculum. As you know, light is essential for photosynthesis, but it doesn't have to be a bright source—as proven by plants that live and thrive in dark forests. Since your students seem to have a penchant for observing biological change, have them introduce a few pairs of identical plants to two different growing environments (one with light and one without). Students can make predictions about how they think certain leaf shapes and forms will respond in comparison to others. Ask them to keep a log that documents the weekly changes. Defining light, something that can't be held or seen, becomes a lot easier when you have a visual, so include a pair of plants that have variegated or coloured leaves to demonstrate how some plants will resort back to green when they don't receive adequate light. When all the data is collected and the experiment is over, let students draw names to decide who gets to take the plants home.

Calla Lily
Zantedeschia

This bulbous plant displays an upright habit with mid-green, arrow-shaped or lance-shaped foliage, sometimes spotted white. Produces single, white, yellow, pink or purple spathes in summer. Height: 30–55cm; Spread: 25cm. Direct light.

Gerbera Daisy
Barberton Daisy
Gerbera jamesonii

Compact in habit, gerberas display toothed, lance-shaped foliage. Produces big, daisy-like, double, yellow, orange, red, pink or white blooms in summer with prominent centres. Height: 25–60cm; Spread: 25cm. Direct light (but shade from hot summer sun).

Kalanchoe
Kalanchoe blossfeldiana

A compact, upright flowering plant with fleshy, glossy, dark-green foliage. Produces clusters of single, tubular-shaped, white, yellow, pink or red blooms primarily in summer (although commercial growers induce blooming throughout the year). Height: 25cm; Spread: 15cm. Direct light.

Ornamental Pepper
Chili pepper
Capsicum anuum

This upright plant displays lance-shaped, slightly hairy, dark-green foliage. Produces single, white, insignificant blooms followed by small, brightly coloured fruit. Height: up to 45cm; Spread: up to 45cm. Direct light.

Polka Dot Plant
Freckle Face
Hypoestes phyllostachya

A pretty little plant with oval, green foliage spotted with pink, white or red. Height: 30cm; Spread: 25cm. Bright indirect light.

Gerbera Daisy

Calla Lily

Ornamental Pepper

African violets are excellent plants for teaching simple propagation techniques.

I've noticed that a lot of my elementary students talk about gardening at home with their parents or grandparents. So, as part of their studies, I'd like to teach them about propagation and plants. What grows here?

Many plants are simple to propagate. African violets, for example, take only six to nine months to go from a cutting to a flowering plant. If you want to try propagating this plant with your students, simply snap off an entire leaf (including the stem) from an existing plant, and cut the end at a 45° angle. Stick the end of the leaf in a small pot containing a moistened mixture of vermiculite and sand. Place a clear plastic baggie loosely over both the plant and the container, and place it in indirect light. When roots form in two to three weeks, repot the leaf in a small container filled with a high-quality soil mix. Other plants like pothos and spider plants can also be easily propagated by rooting cuttings and plantlets in water. It's a great way to teach kids about science, and if they start their projects in September, they can give them as gifts for either Mother's Day or Father's Day. The plants on the following page are all easy to propagate.

African Violet
Saintpaulia

There are thousands of varieties of standard, miniature and trailing African violets with many different characteristics, but all display a low-growing rosette habit. Height: 5–15cm; Spread: 5–15cm. Bright indirect light.

Echeveria
Echeveria

Echeverias are pretty plants with fleshy leaves arranged in a rosette pattern. Their succulent foliage can be greenish-blue, red, purple or burgundy-pink. Single blooms that appear in summer range from yellow to red. Leaves and stems root quickly where they touch the soil. Height: 5–30cm; Spread: 10–50cm. Direct light.

Golden Pothos
Devil's Ivy
Epipremnum aureus
(syn. *Scindapsus aureus*)

A popular climbing plant with heart-shaped green foliage marked with yellow. Trails: 2+m. Bright indirect light.

Jade Plant
Crassula ovata

Just one of many *Crassula*, jade plants are popular, long-lived plants with fleshy, mid-green foliage distributed along upright, fleshy stems. When grown indoors they rarely produce single, white to pale-pink blooms in summer. Leaves and stems root quickly where they touch the soil. Height: 80+cm; Spread: 80+cm. Direct light.

Strawberry Begonia
Saxifraga stolonifera

A lovely plant that produces plantlets on long, thread-like stolons. Foliage is hairy, deep olive-green with reddish-purple undersides. Produces single, white with yellow centred blooms in summer. Height: 20cm; Spread: 20cm. Bright indirect light.

Golden Pothos

African Violet

Jade Plant

Skylights provide a great source of bright indirect light. Just remember that leaf debris and snow can compromise the amount of light that reaches your plants.

The foyer in our school has a large planter situated below a skylight. My Grade 6 class wants to remove the silk plants and replace them with tropicals. I think it's a great idea and would like some low–maintenance plants. What grows here?

The air in schools tends to be quite dry, so it might be hard to grow tropical plants that crave high levels of humidity. Grouping the plants together in a planter and watering them regularly will help alleviate the dryness in the air. Before you start selecting plants, prepare the soil in your planter. Invest in a professional mix that will allow for good drainage and proper root development. Most tropicals prefer diffused light, so the skylight should offer an ideal exposure. This is a great learning opportunity, so insist that your students dig in, so to speak, and figure out how many plants they need and where the tallest ones must go. Tropicals don't like to dry out, so once your planting is done, set up a watering schedule and make sure that someone maintains it when the school is closed for vacations. And don't forget to take a picture of your entire class around their new garden. It's a great keepsake and a way to measure the growth of your students and your plants.

Parlor Palm
Neanthe Bella Palm,
Good Luck Palm
Chamaedorea elegans

A very popular, compact, upright and small palm with medium-green foliage on arching stems. Height: 1m; Spread: 1m. Bright indirect light.

Ribbon Plant
Dracaena sanderiana

An upright plant with lance-shaped, mid-green foliage with white or cream stripes. Height: 1.5m; Spread: 40–80cm. Bright indirect light.

Snake Plant
Mother-in-Law's Tongue
Sansevieria trifasciata

An excellent plant that can withstand neglect—perfect for beginners. Fleshy, rigid foliage is upright, dark green and attractively mottled and striped. The tip of each leaf is slightly barbed, hence the nasty common name mother-in-law's tongue. Height: 1.5m; Spread: 50cm. Bright indirect light.

Umbrella Plant 'Gracilis'
Cyperus involucratus

An upright plant with interesting grassy foliage radiating like umbrella spokes from the top of tall stems. Height: 30cm; Spread: 25cm. Bright indirect light.

ZZ Plant
Aroid Palm, Fat Boy, Eternity Plant
Zamioculcas zamiifolia

An upright plant with glossy, dark-green foliage displayed on fleshy stems in a prominent pattern. Height: 45–80cm; Spread: 50–95cm. Bright indirect light.

Snake Plant

Parlor Palm

ZZ Plant

Terrariums make wonderful self-contained ecosystems that students can personalize with rock collections or fun figurines.

I'd like each of my students to make a terrarium at the start of the school year. If all goes well, I'd love for them to take the terrariums home before summer holidays. What grows here?

Terrariums are miniature worlds, perfect for capturing a child's imagination. In fact, encourage your students to think of their terrariums that way—as self-sustaining environments, complete with weather! Of course, it doesn't actually rain inside a terrarium, but when plants transpire moisture through their leaves, that moisture condenses on the glass and runs back into the soil. You'll need to start with a clear container, like a fish bowl or a mason jar. Almost any glass container can be turned into a terrarium; just be sure that the mouth is wide enough to fit a small hand. Proper drainage is essential, so start with layers of gravel, high-quality potting mix and, later, moss. Then, to create the look of a landscape, select appropriate plants of varying heights, and accent with stones and driftwood. Once students have created their miniature landscapes, have them place the terrariums in indirect light and care for them with loving amounts of neglect. Should you decide to cover the containers with lids, remember never to put them in direct sunlight—too much heat will 'cook' your plants. See page 26 for detailed instructions on how to build a terrarium.

Baby's Tears
Irish Moss, Mind Your Own Business
Soleirolia soleirolii

This plant's creeping habit is useful for covering soil around tall plants. Produces tiny, round leaves. Height: 5cm; Spread: indefinite. Bright indirect light.

Club Moss
Trailing Spike Moss
Selaginella kraussiana

This is a low, spreading plant with bright-green or dark-green, mat-forming foliage. Height: 2.5cm; Spread: indefinite. Bright indirect light.

Creeping Fig
Climbing Fig
Ficus pumila

Displays a spreading habit with small, green or variegated foliage. Height: 1m; Spread: 30cm. Bright indirect light.

Pilea
Friendship Plant
Pilea

This group of plants has an upright and spreading to trailing habit. Produces textured oval foliage that is attractively marked. Height: 3–30cm; Spread: 15–30cm. Bright indirect light.

Venus Fly Trap
Dionaea muscipula

A fascinating insectivore with a compact habit of growth. Two-lobed foliage is hinged and has spines along the outer edge, giving the appearance of teeth (called traps). Insects are trapped and ingested between the hinged leaves. Produces single, white blooms in summer. Height: 15cm; Spread: 15cm. Bright indirect light.

Pilea

Baby's Tears

Venus Fly Trap

Plants for Hospitals and Nursing Homes

Plants have always been vital to people. We've looked to them for shelter, food, medicine and even art. Our entire history, in fact, is littered with social and religious references to the symbolic importance of plants and nature. Because the past has a way of being pregnant with the future, it comes as no surprise that plants continue to influence our lives. What our generation has discovered through science and research is that plants contribute to more than aesthetics and symbolism—they contribute to a sense of well-being.

Kalanchoe

Persian Violet

Lady Palm

As someone who studies plant science, I know there is no shortage of research being done on the effects plants have on quality of life. And although I'm always interested in reading about the new discoveries, I'm often just as content to examine what I already know—that there's just something about plants that make us feel better. It's one of the reasons why we offer plants and flowers as gifts to people in the hospital, why we look to them to make our holidays merry, why we ask of them the impossible task of easing grief.

Anyone who's visited someone in a hospital knows the feeling of preparing to walk into that high-stress environment. Well, imagine what it's like functioning in that environment every day. Because many people deal constantly with this reality, it's important to provide comfort wherever possible. So whether it's a matter of introducing plants as part of a recreational therapy program or into a visitor's lounge, there are many ways to use plants to promote healthy living and to improve quality of life. After all, when circumstances take us away from the people and surroundings we love most—love best—we instinctually look for comfort in anything that feels familiar. For many of us, that thing we instinctually connect to is nature.

Nina Reshauge finds, whether it's indoors or outdoors, gardening can benefit both mind and body.

As part of our recreational therapy program, we'd like to set up an indoor garden for the residents of our long-term care centre. There's a wall of east-facing windows along one of our activity rooms. What grows here?

Our ability to be active may diminish over time, but our desire to feel physically purposeful never goes away. Incorporating gardening into your residents' daily activities can contribute to reducing stress and to creating a restorative environment. When planning your indoor gardening beds, give special consideration to their height. Some residents will be gardening from a sitting position, so create raised planters that are easy to access. This means being able to comfortably reach the centre of each from any point around the perimeter. Why not try a variety of gardens? Technically, a container garden is anything that's grown in a pot. Just think about the different benefits each garden could provide. Pruning a topiary garden, for example, is a great way to increase dexterity and hand strength. Herb gardens are satisfying because touching them releases their stimulating aromatics. Perhaps the residents can offer plant suggestions based on what they have grown in their own homes. Even if a resident is unable to physically participate, there are many emotional benefits to be derived from sitting in front of a sunny window and being surrounded by nature.

African Violet
Saintpaulia

There are thousands of varieties of standard, miniature and trailing African violets with many different characteristics, but all display a low-growing rosette habit. This plant has been favoured for many, many years and bridges the generations in the enjoyment it provides. Height: 5–15cm; Spread: 5–15cm. Bright indirect light.

Dieffenbachia
Dumb Cane
Dieffenbachia

Often used as an upright specimen. Large, fleshy, oblong, ovate or paddle-shaped foliage varies from cream, yellow and green patterns to solid green. Height: 1–3m; Spread: 60cm. Bright indirect light.

African Violet

Dieffenbachia

Lemon Geranium
Pelargonium crispum

An upright plant with rough, crinkled, serrated, rounded or lobed leaves about 1cm in length. The leaves may be used for teas, sauces, sorbets and vinegars. Height: 30cm–1m; Spread: 30–45cm. Direct light.

Myrtle
Myrtus communis

A compact, upright habit makes myrtle an excellent plant for topiary shapes. Displays small, dark-green, oval foliage. Produces double, white blooms in summer. Height: as trained; Spread: as trained. Direct light.

Reiger Begonia
Begonia x *hiemalis*

Glossy, dark-green foliage highlights beautiful, double, white, yellow, pink, orange or red blooms from late fall to early spring. Height: 20–25cm; Spread: 20–25cm. Bright indirect light.

Reiger Begonia

Low-maintenance corn plants have an upright growing habit that makes them suitable for small spaces.

The visitor's lounge on our hospital ward has large south/west-facing windows and enough space for one large plant...with perhaps two smaller ones at its base. What grows here?

A visitor's lounge is often the place where tired family members escape to, so the ultimate goal is to make it feel as removed as possible from the rest of the hospital. A feature plant is a great choice for this small space because it will give this bright room a focal point, but the choices should be fairly low maintenance. To create that sense of escape, consider choosing a tall plant with attractive foliage or an interesting shape. To add more visual impact, create a grouping of plants that complement each other. If your feature plant has dark foliage, for example, select smaller plants in contrasting colours. Conserving square footage becomes an issue in a small space, so make sure that your accent plants are compact and upright—and don't forget about the containers. Matching or complementary pots that vary in size will help unify the space and make the lounge feel more inviting.

Areca Palm
Butterfly Plant,
Golden Feather Palm
Chrysalidocarpus lutescens

An upright plant with narrow, mid-green foliage on tall, reed-like, arching stems. Height: 2m; Spread: 1m. Bright indirect light.

Corn Plant 'Massangeana'
Dracaena fragrans

Foliage is held atop a sturdy upright trunk and may be sold with one or more trunks per pot. Wide, strappy, glossy-green leaves with a yellow stripe. Height: 3m; Spread: 1m. Bright indirect light.

English Ivy
Hedera helix

A popular vine displaying flat, 3 to 5-lobed leaves that are green or variegated white or yellow. Trails: 2m; Spread: 1m. Bright indirect light.

Silver Shield
King of Hearts
Homalomena wallisii

Displaying a compact, upright habit, this plant has dark-green, heart-shaped leaves on long stalks. Height: 65cm; Spread: 45cm. Bright indirect light.

Spider Plant
Chlorophytum orchidastrum

An upright plant displaying broad, lance-shaped, dark-green foliage with a prominent orange centre stripe and stem. Height: 35cm; Spread: 35cm. Bright indirect light.

English Ivy

Areca Palm

Silver Shield

Fertilizing flowering plants like this chenille plant will help extend their bloom period. These plants won't bloom forever so you'll have to replace them as needed.

My mother has just moved to a senior's lodge, and she's really missing her garden. I'd like to buy her some small plants to bloom constantly in her small room. She has a large mostly east-facing window that gets some afternoon light. What grows here?

Before you even begin to select plants, check if your mother is allowed to have them in her room and whether or not the facility has a policy regarding fragrance. If all is a go, take advantage of that window!—it's a wonderful source of morning light. If it catches some afternoon sun as well, growing a variety of flowering plants shouldn't be a problem. It might sound like stating the obvious, but to increase the amount of light that comes through your window, keep drapes open in the mornings and make sure windows are clean. Don't forget, however, that although flowering plants require a lot of light to flower, they also need cooler nighttime temperatures to prolong the life of those blooms. If possible, perhaps you and your mother can make trips to the garden centre together as enjoyable outings. If growing the plants she chooses for her room is still not enough to satisfy her itch to garden, ask the staff if your mother can tend to a few plants in one of the common areas. It's a great activity and a great way to meet other residents who may share her interests.

Calla Lily
Zantedeschia

This bulbous plant displays an upright habit with mid-green, arrow-shaped or lance-shaped foliage, sometimes spotted white. Produces single, white, yellow, pink or purple spathes in summer. Height: 30–55cm; Spread: 25cm. Direct light.

Chenille Plant
Red-hot Catstail, Philippine Medusa, Foxtail
Acalypha hispida

This pretty, upright plant has rich-green, oval, hairy foliage. Prized for its dark-pink, pendant, chenille-like blooms in summer. Height: 1–2m. Bright indirect light.

Easter Cactus
Hatior gaertneri

Branching, arching, fleshy stems are divided into flat segments. Produces pink or red blooms in spring. Height: 30cm; Spread: 30cm. Bright indirect light.

Moth Orchid
Phalaenopsis

A compact plant with oval, fleshy, medium-green foliage and flat-faced, single, white, yellow, pink, purple or red blooms that may appear continually. Height: 20–60cm; Spread: 20–30cm. Bright indirect light.

Persian Violet
Exacum affine

A small, compact and tidy plant, often given as a gift. Displays small, oval, medium-green foliage and produces fragrant, single, violet to blue, pink or white blooms in summer. Height: 25–30cm; Spread: 25–30cm. Bright indirect light.

Polyantha Primrose
Primrose
Primula x *polyantha*

A lovely small, flowering plant with oval, heavily veined, dark-green foliage. Produces fragrant, single, white, yellow, orange, red or purple blooms in spring. Height: 15–20cm; Spread: 15cm. Bright indirect light.

Polyantha Primrose

Persian Violet

Moth Orchid

A wicker basket filled with cape primrose, kalanchoe and a button fern makes a beautiful presentation and the basket can be reused.

Instead of giving the usual cutflower arrangements to friends in the hospital, I prefer to give flowering plants. What grows here?

Plants are a nice alternative to cutflowers. Besides being practical and economical, there is almost always something seasonal to choose from, so look for favourites that match the calendar. Although plants can be lovely gifts, they can also be work, so have a good idea of your friend's aptitude for keeping houseplants. If he or she doesn't have a green thumb, include a note with some information regarding care of the plant (watering and light conditions). If you are familiar with the layout of your friend's home, you might even suggest the spot in which you think the plant would thrive once they leave the hospital. In winter months, offer helpful advice on how to transport the plant without freezing or damaging it. Paper bags or sleeves, for example, will provide more insulation than plastic ones will. As an additional show of thoughtfulness, I really like the idea of sending friends welcome-home plants to celebrate their recovery!

Azalea
Rhododendron simsii

Compact and upright in habit, this flowering plant's foliage is small, dark-green, leathery and egg shaped. Produces semi-double, white, pink or magenta blooms in spring, summer and fall. Height: 45cm; Spread: 30cm. Bright indirect light.

Cape Primrose
Streptocarpus

This compact, upright plant has strap-shaped, hairy foliage. Produces single, white, pink or purple blooms with veined throats in spring to fall. Height: 20–30cm; Spread: 20–30cm. Bright indirect light.

Christmas Cactus
Schlumberga x *buckleyi*

Branching, arching fleshy stems are divided into flat segments. Produces white, yellow, salmon, pink or red blooms in early winter. Height: 30–60cm; Spread: 1m. Bright indirect light.

Kalanchoe
Kalanchoe blossfeldiana

A compact, upright flowering plant with fleshy, glossy, dark-green foliage. Produces clusters of single, tubular-shaped, white, yellow, pink or red blooms primarily in summer (although growers induce blooming throughout the year). Height: 25cm; Spread: 15cm. Direct light.

Pineapple Lily
Eucomis

Grown from a true bulb, this unusual plant has an upright habit with lance-shaped, light-green foliage. Produces masses of tiny, star-like, green, white or pink blooms in summer borne on a thick stalk tipped with a rosette of small green leaves. Height: 30–60cm. Direct light.

Poinsettia
Euphorbia pulcherrima

An upright plant, traditionally grown for the Christmas season. Foliage is a deep green with colourful bracts available in shades of white, pink, red, burgundy and other variations. Height: 60cm; Spread: 60cm. Direct light.

Pineapple Lily

Azalea

Kalanchoe

A few plants can transform a sterile public area into a lush interior landscape where the building's inhabitants can escape—even on cold, intemperate days.

We've created a café-eating area on the mezzanine level of our municipal building. We'd like to use plants around the perimeter to give the area a patio feel. What grows here?

To create a patio feel, put as much thought into selecting your con-tainers as you do into selecting your plants. Outdoor-looking con-tainers, such as cast iron urns and terracotta planters, will instantly trans-form your space and give it that café feel. To bring in the allusion of the outdoors, consider potting masses of one type of plant. The visual empha-sis will make the space seem unified and lush. To add a bit of variety, trail ivy in hanging baskets, or grow climbers on trellises. You might also want to consider growing a wall of plants. Garden centres are full of pots and hangers perfect for mounting on walls, and individual terracotta pots hung in a checkerboard pattern can look spectacular when brimming over with plants that can be changed for pretty seasonal displays.

Arrowhead Vine
Goosefoot
Syngonium podophyllum
This popular foliage houseplant has a vining habit. Leaves are large, arrow-shaped and veined. Some varieties are variegated. Trails: 1–2m. Bright indirect light.

Fiddleleaf Fig
Banjo Fig
Ficus lyrata
An upright fig with broad, fiddle-shaped, leathery, foliage that is glossy and dark green. This is a large plant for open spaces. Height: 3+m; Spread: 1+m. Bright indirect light.

Hibiscus
Hibiscus rosa-sinensis
Upright habit. Foliage is dark-green and glossy. Single, semi-double white, yellow, orange, pink, red blooms. Flowers continually. Height: 1.5m; Spread: 1m. Direct light.

Philodendron Monstera
Monstera, Splitleaf Philodendron, Swiss Cheese Plant
Monstera deliciosa
A large, fast-growing, upright plant with gigantic, dark-green leaves that are perforated and deeply cut. Requires sturdy support (grow on a moss stick and push aerial roots into the moss or tuck into soil). Height: 3m. Bright indirect light.

Swedish Ivy
Candle Plant
Plectranthus
Typically grown in a hanging basket where foliage spills over freely. Foliage is heart-shaped to ovate with scalloped edges and may be green with white veins, green with white edges or just solid green. Trails: 25cm; Spread: 1m. Bright indirect light.

Swedish Ivy

Arrowhead Vine

Fiddleleaf Fig

Indoor Plant Favourites

This section provides an indepth look at many plants that are grown indoors today. Some are very popular, easy to grow and readily available; others are lesser known, more challenging to grow and difficult to find, but worth the search. This is by no means a finite list of houseplants. Rather, it is a selection of our favourites, which you can expand on as opportunity and experience allow. Remember that there are always new varieties being released as plant enthusiasts continue breeding work and new discoveries are made. Be adventurous!

Where applicable, the plants here are presented by group (for example, palms, dracaenas and philodendrons), and some are divided even further based on how they are grouped for sale at many garden centres. All other plants are listed alphabetically by their common name with the Latin name following. There is an index on page 278 should you have any difficulty finding a particular plant.

African Milk Bush 'Rubrum'
Synadenium compactum

Upright in habit, this plant has dark-reddish foliage that is oval to round in shape. Height: 2m; Spread: 1m. Bright indirect light.

Ease of Care: moderate

Water: medium (allow 1cm of the soil to dry out)

Fertilizer: moderate (10-6-16 full strength once per month, February to October)

Propagation: cutting

Common Plant Problems: spider mites

Growth Rate: fast

Repot: annually

Cleaning Tips: wipe with a soft cloth or gently shower

Origins: tropical Africa to Madagascar Islands

Notes: All parts of this plant are toxic if ingested, and sap may cause skin irritation. Sought after by collectors.

African Violet
Saintpaulia

There are thousands of varieties of standard, miniature and trailing African violets with many different characteristics, but all display a low-growing rosette habit. Fuzzy foliage may be serrated, plain edged, spoon, holly or lance shaped and range in colour from dark-green to variegated cream and green. Flower forms are as variable as the foliage, including single, semi-double, double, frilled and star forms. Bloom colours arc solid shades to bicolour, multi-colour and even white edged. Experts maintain blooms all year long; however, novices can still enjoy several flushes of flowers. Height: 5–15cm; Spread: 5–15cm. Bright indirect light.

Ease of Care: easy

Water: medium (allow 1cm of the soil to dry out)

Fertilizer: heavy (African violet fertilizer once every 2 weeks, February to October)

Propagation: seed, leaf cutting

Common Plant Problems: thrips, crown rot, powdery mildew

Growth Rate: slow

Repot: biennially

Cleaning Tips: dust by gently blowing on leaves, remove spent flowers and dead foliage

Origins: tropical East Africa

Notes: Plants have a small root system; do not over pot. African violets dislike being wet; water from the bottom. Sought after by collectors.

Standard Varieties

African Violet 'Concord'
Saintpaulia

Foliage is mid green. Produces single, white and dark blue-purple blooms continually. Height: 15cm; Spread: 15cm. Bright indirect light.

African Violet

African Violet 'Delft'
Saintpaulia

Foliage is mid green. Produces huge, semi-double, cornflower-blue blooms continually. Height: 15cm; Spread: 15cm. Bright indirect light.

African Violet 'Fancy Pants'
Saintpaulia

Foliage is mid green. Produces single, white blooms with frilled red margins continually. Bright indirect light.

African Violet 'Wonderland'
Saintpaulia 'Granger's Wonderland'

Foliage is olive-green and wavy. Produces semi-double, light blue-violet blooms continually. Height: 15cm; Spread: 15cm. Bright indirect light.

African Violet 'Alabama'
Saintpaulia optimara

Foliage is medium green with light-green undersides. Produces single, white blooms with a blue edge continually. Height: 15cm; Spread: 15cm. Bright indirect light.

African Violet 'Colorado'
Saintpaulia optimara

Interesting quilted, glossy, mid- to dark-green foliage. Produces single, magenta flowers with a frilled edge continually. Height: 15cm; Spread: 15cm. Bright indirect light.

African Violet 'Nevada'
Saintpaulia optimara

Foliage is mid green and bright green underneath. Produces single, white with red purple-edged blooms continually. Height: 15cm; Spread: 15cm. Bright indirect light.

African Violet 'Virginia'
Saintpaulia optimara

Foliage is variegated green and cream. Produces single, pink blooms continually. Height: 15cm; Spread: 15cm. Bright indirect light.

Air Plant

Air Plant
Tillandsia

Air plants are epiphytes. They have furry scales on their foliage that absorb water and nutrients from the air and airborne dust. *T. ionantha,* which grows on coral, shells or driftwood, is the most popularly sold species at garden centres. Blooms are small and infrequent. Height: 2–25cm. Bright indirect light.

Ease of Care: easy

Water: lightly mist daily in summer, twice weekly in winter

Fertilizer: light (mist with 10-6-16 at half-strength once per month, February to October)

Propagation: division

Common Plant Problems: mealy bugs

Growth Rate: slow

Repot: grow on stones, coral or bark

Cleaning Tips: wipe with a soft paintbrush or swab

Origins: southern United States, West Indies, Central and South America

Notes: Often sold with a magnet attached to the coral or bark that the plant is mounted on so that it can be placed on a refrigerator as a novelty. Group plants on a large piece of driftwood for an interesting effect. Sought after by collectors.

Amaryllis

Amaryllis

Hippeastrum

Usually for sale in fall, amaryllis is a tender bulb that produces upright, strap-shaped, light- to mid-green foliage. It is not unusual for *Hippeastrum* hybrids to produce up to six blooms per stem. Colours range from orange, pink, purple, red or white and may be edged or striped. Blooms in winter to spring annually. Height: 30–60cm. Direct light.

Ease of Care: easy

Water: moist (keep soil consistently moist but not soggy; see Notes)

Fertilizer: heavy (10-6-16 once every 2 weeks, February to October; see Notes)

Propagation: offsets

Growth Rate: medium

Repot: biennially

Cleaning Tips: wipe leaves with a soft cloth

Origins: Central and South America

Notes: Plant bulbs with neck and shoulders above the soil. Water sparingly when newly planted and increase water when growth is established. Turn regularly to promote straight growth (flowers may require support). Remove dead flower stalks. Water and fertilize every 2 weeks in summer, and grow outdoors in sun. Quit watering mid fall, and once leaves dry up, store in a cool, dry place until new shoots emerge. Bring into light and resume watering.

Amazon Lily

Eucharis amazonica
(syn. *E. grandiflora*)

This bulbous plant has an upright habit. Foliage is dark green and lance shaped. Produces single, white, fragrant, trumpet- or daffodil-like blooms in summer. Flowers annually and on occasion biennially. Height: 40–60cm; Spread: 30cm. Bright indirect light.

Ease of Care: moderate

Water: moist (keep soil consistently moist but not soggy)

Fertilizer: heavy (10-6-16 once every 2 weeks, February to October)

Propagation: offsets

Common Plant Problems: infrequent

Growth Rate: medium

Repot: biennially

Cleaning Tips: wipe leaves with a soft cloth

Origins: Central and South America

Notes: Dislikes cold night temperatures and drafts. Sought after by collectors.

Amazon Lily

Aralia, Balfour
Dinner Plate Aralia
Polyscias scutellaria 'Balfourii'
A striking specimen plant with an upright habit. Foliage is large, rounded and green or green with white edges. Height: 1m; Spread: 45cm. Bright indirect light.

Ease of Care: moderate

Water: medium (allow 1cm of the soil to dry out)

Fertilizer: heavy (10-6-16 once every 2 weeks, February to October)

Propagation: cutting

Common Plant Problems: mealy bugs, spider mites

Growth Rate: medium

Cleaning Tips: wipe leaves with a soft cloth or gently shower

Origins: Africa, Asia and the Pacific regions

Notes: This plant drops its leaves if environment is wrong. Dislikes dry air—mist frequently. Sought after by collectors.

Aralia, Ming
Fern Leaf Aralia
Polyscias fruticosa
An upright plant with attractive feathery, dark-green foliage. Height: 2m; Spread: 1m. Bright indirect light.

Ease of Care: difficult

Water: medium (allow 1cm of the soil to dry out)

Fertilizer: heavy (10-6-16 once every 2 weeks, February to October)

Propagation: cutting

Common Plant Problems: spider mites, mealy bugs

Growth Rate: medium

Repot: annually

Cleaning Tips: gently shower

Origins: south Malaysia and the Pacific regions

Notes: Unhappy in a dry atmosphere; mist regularly. Water sparingly in winter. Will quickly shed leaves if too wet. Sought after by collectors.

Arrowhead Vine

Arrowhead Vine
Goosefoot
Syngonium podophyllum
This popular foliage houseplant has a vining habit. Leaves are large, arrow shaped and veined. Some varieties are variegated. Trails: 1–2m. Bright indirect light.

Ease of Care: easy

Water: medium (allow 1cm of the soil to dry out)

Fertilizer: heavy (10-6-16 once every 2 weeks, February to October)

Propagation: cutting

Common Plant Problems: aphids, mealy bugs, spider mites, fungal diseases, bacterial leaf spot

Growth Rate: medium

Repot: annually

Cleaning Tips: wipe leaves with a soft cloth or gently shower

Origins: Central and South America

Notes: Juvenile leaves are ovate to triangular in shape, changing to arrow shaped as plant matures.

Azalea

Azalea
Rhododendron simsii

Compact and upright in habit, this flowering plant has small, dark-green, leathery and egg-shaped foliage. Produces semi-double, white, pink or magenta blooms in spring, summer and fall. Height: 45cm; Spread: 30cm. Bright indirect light.

Ease of Care: moderate

Water: moist (keep soil consistently moist but not soggy)

Fertilizer: heavy (30-10-10 once every 2 weeks, February to October)

Propagation: cutting

Common Plant Problems: rare

Growth Rate: medium

Repot: annually

Cleaning Tips: remove spent blooms

Origins: Europe, Japan

Notes: Can be grown as tree or topiary shapes. Prefers cool location. Do not allow to dry out.

Baby's Tears
Irish Moss, Mind Your Own Business
Soleirolia soleirolii

This pretty plant's creeping habit is useful for covering soil around tall plants. Produces tiny, round leaves. Height: 5cm; Spread: indefinite. Bright indirect light.

Ease of Care: easy

Baby's Tears

Water: moist (keep soil consistently moist but not soggy)

Fertilizer: heavy (10-6-16 once every 2 weeks, February to October)

Propagation: division

Common Plant Problems: infrequent

Growth Rate: medium

Repot: annually

Cleaning Tips: gently shower

Origins: west Mediterranean islands

Notes: Good plant for terrariums. Very easy to propagate by potting small clumps.

Bat Plant

Bat Plant
Devil Flower, Cat's Whiskers
Tacca chantrieri

An unusual plant with an upright habit. Lance-shaped foliage is dark green. Produces purple blooms in summer with long green tendrils. Height: 60cm; Spread: 1m. Bright indirect light.

Ease of Care: difficult

Water: moist (keep soil consistently moist but not soggy)

Fertilizer: light (10-6-16 at half-strength once per month, February to October)

Propagation: division, rhizomes, seed

Common Plant Problems: spider mites, grey mould

Growth Rate: medium

Repot: every 2–3 years

Notes: Requires good air circulation and very high humidity. A challenging plant to grow. Mist regularly. Keep drier in winter. Sought after by collectors.

Bay Tree
Bay Laurel, Sweet Bay
Laurus nobilis

Upright in habit, this plant is best known for its aromatic leaves that are used for flavouring soups, stews and poultry dishes. Leathery foliage is dark-green and glossy. Produces single, greenish-yellow blooms in summer. Height: 4m; Spread: 30cm. Direct light.

Ease of Care: easy

Water: medium (allow 1cm of the soil to dry out)

Fertilizer: heavy (10-6-16 once every 2 weeks, February to October)

Propagation: cutting

Common Plant Problems: mealy bugs, scale insects, powdery mildew

Growth Rate: slow

Repot: annually

Cleaning Tips: wipe leaves with a soft cloth or gently shower

Origins: Mediterranean

Notes: Harvest leaves as needed and use fresh or dried. Sought after by collectors.

Bay Tree

Begonia

Begonia

We have found it useful to divide begonias that are bred to be grown as houseplants into two major groups: foliage begonias (grown primarily for their attractive leaves) and flowering houseplant begonias.

Foliage Begonias

Generally bushy or trailing in habit. Foliage is highly variable in shape, texture and colour. Insignificant blooms are usually removed. Height: 25cm–2m; Spread: 30–50cm. Bright indirect light.

Ease of Care: easy

Water: medium (allow 1cm of the soil to dry out)

Fertilizer: heavy (10-6-16 once every 2 weeks, February to October)

Propagation: cutting, division

Common Plant Problems: aphids, mealy bugs, spider mites, thrips, grey mould, powdery mildew, stem rot

Growth Rate: slow

Repot: annually

Cleaning Tips: gently blow on leaves or brush with a soft paintbrush

Angel Wing Begonia

Origins: China, India, the Mediterranean and New Guinea

Notes: Short-lived plants, so take cuttings frequently. Dislike overwatering. Remove dying leaves promptly. Sought after by collectors.

Iron Cross Begonia

Begonia masoniana

A striking begonia with ovate, sharply pointed, warty, apple-green foliage with black-brown cross markings. Height: 50cm; Spread: 50cm. Bright indirect light.

Rex Begonia

Begonia rex

All varieties of Rex begonia now sold are hybrids that are available in a wonderful range of foliage colours. Leaves are large and ovate and vary in their markings in shades of pink, silver and purple. Height: 25cm; Spread: 30cm. Bright indirect light.

Shrub Begonia

Begonia serratipetala

A bushy begonia with a shrub-like habit. Produces long, pointed, wavy-margined foliage in bronze green with red veins. Height: 45cm; Spread: 45cm. Bright indirect light.

Flowering Begonias

Grown for their beautiful blooms that are single or double and available in a wide range of bright colours. Height: 20cm–2m; Spread: 20–35cm. Bright indirect light.

Ease of Care: easy

Water: medium (allow 1cm of the soil to dry out)

Fertilizer: heavy (15-30-15 once every 2 weeks, February to October)

Propagation: cutting, division

Common Plant Problems: aphids, spider mites, thrips, grey mould, powdery mildew, stem rot

Growth Rate: fast

Repot: annually

Cleaning Tips: gently blow on leaves or brush with a soft paintbrush

Origins: China, India, the Mediterranean and New Guinea

Notes: Short-lived plants, so take cuttings frequently. Dislike over-watering. Remove dying leaves promptly. Sought after by collectors.

Angel Wing Begonia
Begonia 'Corallina de Lucerna'

A tall, upright begonia with interesting ovate, olive-green foliage with silver-white spots. Continuously produces single, deep-pink to bright-red blooms. Height: 2m; Spread: 35cm. Bright indirect light.

Reiger Begonia
Begonia x *hiemalis*

Glossy, dark-green foliage highlights beautiful, double, white, yellow, pink, orange or red blooms from late fall to early spring. Height: 20–25cm; Spread: 20–25cm. Bright indirect light.

Rex Begonia

Reiger Begonia

Bird of Paradise
Crane Flowers
Strelitzia reginae

A tall, upright plant prized for its stunning blooms. Large foliage is paddle shaped and borne on long stalks. Unusual, peachy-orange flowers bloom in spring. Height: 2m; Spread: 1m. Direct light.

Ease of Care: easy

Water: medium (allow 1cm of the soil to dry out)

Fertilizer: heavy (15-30-15 once every 2 weeks, February to October)

Propagation: division

Common Plant Problems: scale insects, spider mites, leaf spot, fungal and bacterial diseases

Growth Rate: medium

Repot: every 3–5 years

Cleaning Tips: wipe leaves with a soft cloth or gently shower

Origins: South Africa

Notes: This large plant requires plenty of space. New plants take 4–6 years to bloom.

Bird of Paradise

Blue Flowering Torch
Tillandsia cyanea

Compact in habit, this interesting plant's grassy-type foliage is mid green. Produces an unusual compact flowerhead resembling a torch with single, purple-blue blooms. Blooms appear once but last up to 10 weeks before dying and producing offsets. Height: 30cm; Spread: 20cm. Bright indirect light.

Ease of Care: easy

Water: medium (allow 1cm of the soil to dry out)

Fertilizer: heavy (10-6-16 once every 2 weeks, February to October)

Propagation: offsets

Common Plant Problems: mealy bugs, scale insects

Growth Rate: slow

Repot: biennially

Cleaning Tips: wipe leaves with a soft cloth or gently shower

Origins: Ecuador

Notes: A very interesting and unique plant. Sought after by collectors.

Bougainvillea
Paper Flowers
Bougainvillea

Usually grown out of doors but many enthusiasts overwinter this plant in a very bright room. Bougainvillea displays a vining habit with small, medium-green, ovate foliage. Produces profuse, single, white, pink, red or carmine blooms in summer. Height: up to 12m. Direct light.

Ease of Care: moderate

Water: moist (keep soil consistently moist but not soggy)

Fertilizer: heavy (15-30-15 once every 2 weeks, February to October)

Propagation: cutting

Common Plant Problems: aphids, spider mites, whiteflies

Growth Rate: fast

Repot: annually

Origins: South America

Notes: Needs at least 4 hours of direct light everyday during the active growth period in order to produce blooms. Keep cooler and drier during the winter rest period. Prune $\frac{1}{3}$rd of the season's growth in early spring. Bougainvilleas will lose their leaves for a short period in winter. Sought after by collectors.

Bouvardia

Bouvardia
Bouvardia x *domestica*

A compact, upright plant with ovate or lance-shaped foliage and white, pink or red tubular blooms in clusters in summer. Height: 60–90cm; Spread: 60cm. Direct light.

Ease of Care: moderate

Water: medium (allow 1cm of the soil to dry out)

Fertilizer: heavy (15-30-15 once every 2 weeks, February to October)

Propagation: seed, division

Common Plant Problems: mealy bugs, spider mites, whiteflies

Growth Rate: slow

Repot: annually

Cleaning Tips: remove spent blooms

Origins: subtropical southern United States to South America

Notes: Prune after flowering. Sought after by collectors.

Blue Flowering Torch

Bromeliads

Bromeliads are interesting plants grown for their striking, unusual foliage or distinct flowers, or both. Foliage is generally leathery and strap-like in form. Flowers appear at the centre of the foliage and are quite varied in appearance. Each rosette of foliage produces one bloom in its lifetime, then offsets produce the next bloom. Bromeliads are epiphytes and can be grown and displayed on tree branches. Height: 5cm–1+m; Spread 5–50+cm. Direct light (but avoid hot summer sun).

Silver Vase Bromeliad
Urn Plant, Living Vase
Aechmea fasciata

Grey-green, spiny foliage is cross-banded with sprinklings of white powder and arches gracefully outward. Mature 3 to 4-year-old plants produce single, pink, inflorescences with small blue flowers that turn red and last up to 6 months. Height: 40cm; Spread: 50cm. Direct light (but avoid hot summer sun).

Ease of Care: easy

Water: medium (allow 1cm of the soil to dry out, see Notes)

Fertilizer: light (10-6-16 at half-strength once per month, February to October)

Propagation: offsets

Common Plant Problems: over-watering and overpotting can kill plants

Growth Rate: slow

Repot: annually when necessary

Cleaning Tips: do not wipe the powdery coating from the leaves; remove spent blooms

Origins: southern United States to Central and South America and West Indies

Notes: Keep 'centre vase' of foliage filled with water (empty and refill vase every 1–2 months to avoid water becoming stagnant). Has a small root system. Can become top heavy, so plant in heavy clay pots. Sought after by collectors.

Guzmania

Guzmania
Guzmania

A bromeliad primarily prized for its blooms. Lance-shaped, mid-green foliage highlights flowerheads of tubular white or yellow blooms, often surrounded by colourful bracts borne on bright-yellow, orange or red stems in summer Blooms last many months. Height: 30–45cm; Spread: 30–45cm. Bright indirect light.

Ease of Care: easy

Water: medium (allow 1cm of the soil to dry out; see Notes below)

Fertilizer: moderate (10-6-16 full strength once per month, February to October)

Propagation: seed, offsets

Common Plant Problems: mealy bugs

Growth Rate: medium

Repot: annually when necessary

Cleaning Tips: remove spent blooms

Origins: south Florida, Central America, West Indies, South America

Notes: Mist frequently in the growing season. Keep barely moist and do not mist in winter. Keep 'centre vase' of foliage filled with water (empty and refill vase every 1–2 months to avoid water becoming stagnant). Sought after by collectors.

Neoregelia
Blushing Bromeliad
Neoregelia

Grown for its foliage that blushes at the plant's centre when it is ready to bloom. Displays shiny, medium-green foliage with yellow stripes and produces single, blue or white blooms sporadically. Height: 20–30cm; Spread: 40–60cm. Direct light (but avoid hot summer sun).

Ease of Care: easy

Water: medium (allow 1cm of the soil to dry out; see Notes below)

Fertilizer: moderate (10-6-16 full strength once per month, February to October)

Propagation: offsets

Growth Rate: slow

Repot: annually if necessary

Cleaning Tips: remove spent blooms

Origins: southern United States to Central and South America, West Indies

Notes: Keep 'centre vase' of foliage filled with water (empty and refill vase every 1–2 months to avoid water becoming stagnant). Sought after by collectors.

Silver Vase Bromeliad

Vriesea
Flaming Sword
Vriesea splendens

Prized for its sword-like blooms and arching, smooth-edged, dark-green foliage with purple-black cross banding. When mature can produce long, red flowerheads at any time of the year. Blooms last many months. Height: 1m; Spread: 30cm. Direct light (protect from midday sun).

Ease of Care: easy

Water: medium (allow 1cm of the soil to dry out; see Notes below)

Fertilizer: moderate (10-6-16 full strength once per month, February to October)

Propagation: seed, offsets

Common Plant Problems: mealy bugs, scale insects, leaf spots (caused by drying)

Growth Rate: medium

Repot: annually if needed

Cleaning Tips: remove spent blooms

Origins: Mexico, Central America, West Indies, South America

Notes: Mist frequently in growing season. Keep 'centre vase' of foliage filled with water (empty and refill vase every 1–2 months to avoid water becoming stagnant). Sought after by collectors.

Starfish Plant
Earth Star
Cryptanthus

The common name of this plant matches its interesting appearance. Rigid, strap-shaped foliage varies from solid green to striped olive-green and white with deep-pink mid ribs. Produces small, single, white, slightly fragrant blooms in summer. Height: 10cm; Spread: 10cm. Direct light.

Ease of Care: easy

Water: dry (allow 3cm of soil to dry out thoroughly before watering)

Fertilizer: light (10-6-16 at half-strength once per month, February to October)

Propagation: seed, offsets

Common Plant Problems: mealy bugs, scale insects

Growth Rate: slow

Repot: biennially

Cleaning Tips: wipe with a soft paintbrush or swab, or gently shower

Origins: east Brazil

Notes: Reduce water slightly in winter. Sought after by collectors.

Starfish Plant

Buddhist Pine

Buddhist Pine
Kusamaki, Southern Yew
Podocarpus macrophyllus

A very attractive upright plant with dark-green, needle-shaped foliage. Height: 2m; Spread: 1m. Bright indirect light.

Ease of Care: moderate

Water: medium (allow 1cm of the soil to dry out)

Fertilizer: heavy (10-6-16 once every 2 weeks, February to October)

Propagation: cutting

Common Plant Problems: mealy bugs

Growth Rate: medium

Repot: annually

Cleaning Tips: gently shower

Origins: east China, Japan

Notes: Do not overpot as it dislikes having waterlogged roots. May be sold as multiple plants trained to a tepee shape in a pot. Sought after by collectors.

Cacti Group
Cactus

A very diverse and fascinating group of plants often divided by garden centres into desert and forest types. Plants range in form, size, colour, flower, bloom time and frequency. Height: 5cm–2+m; Spread: 5–60+cm (most cacti grown as houseplants fall in this range). Desert types require direct light; forest types require bright indirect light.

Desert Type Favourites

Ease of Care: easy

Water: medium in spring and summer (allow 1cm of the soil to dry out), sparingly in fall and winter—just enough to prevent shrivelling)

Fertilizer: heavy (cactus fertilizer once every 2 weeks, February to October)

Propagation: seed, cuttings

Common Plant Problems: mealy bugs, scale insects, spider mites, basal stem rot, soft rot

Growth Rate: species vary from slow to fast

Repot: annually when young; as necessary when mature (when plant fills the pot)

Cleaning Tips: use tweezers to remove debris

Origins: worldwide

Notes: Take care when handling; see page 33 for repotting tips. Sought after by collectors.

Assorted Cacti

Bunny Ears
Opuntia microdasys

This plant has a bushy habit. Pale- to mid-green foliage stems are flattened, oblong or almost rounded. Produces single, yellow blooms in spring, followed by red fruits. Height: 40–60cm; Spread: 40–60cm. Direct light.

Origins: North and Central Mexico
Notes: Sought after by collectors.

Golden Barrel
Golden Ball, Mother-in-Law's Cushion
Echinocactus grusonii

Spherical in habit, this cactus displays spines that are green with golden-yellow tips. Produces single, yellow blooms in summer. Height: 60cm; Spread: 80cm. Direct light.

Origins: Central Mexico
Notes: Sought after by collectors.

Lady of the Night Cactus
Cereus hexagonus

This tall, columnar and upright cactus has a multi-stemmed habit and is fast growing. Mid green and ridged, it produces single, white blooms in summer (that open at night), followed by

pale-red fruit. Difficult to find. Height: up to 9m (most home specimens no higher than 2m). Direct light.

Origins: Guyana, Venezuela
Notes: Sought after by collectors.

Old Lady Cactus
Mammillaria hahniana

This is a solitary cactus that forms groups when mature. Mid-green foliage is spherical and coated with long, white hairs, bristles and spines. Produces single, purplish-red blooms in late spring to early summer. Height: 20cm; Spread: 40cm. Direct light.

Origins: Central Mexico
Notes: Sought after by collectors.

Silver Torch Cactus
Cleistocactus strausii

This upright cactus is a columnar form with green ribs covered in fine, white spines. Branches freely from the base. Produces single, carmine-red blooms in summer when it reaches 10–15 years of age. Height: 1m; Spread: 1m. Direct light.

Origins: Bolivia
Notes: Sought after by collectors.

Queen of the Night Cactus
Cereus hildmannianus

A tall, columnar, upright and fast-growing cactus. Foliage is blue-green and ridged. Produces huge, single, white blooms in summer that open at night. Difficult to find. Height: up to 9m (most home specimens no higher than 2m). Direct light.

Origins: south-east Brazil, northern Argentina
Notes: Sought after by collectors.

Lady of the Night Cactus

Christmas Cactus

Forest Type Favourites
Christmas Cactus
Schlumberga x buckleyi

Branching, arching fleshy stems are divided into flat segments. Produces white, yellow, salmon, pink or red blooms in early winter. Height: 30–60cm; Spread: 1m. Bright indirect light.

Ease of Care: easy

Water: medium in fall and winter (allow 1cm of the soil to dry out), drier in spring and summer

Fertilizer: moderate (10-6-16 full strength once per month, February to October)

Propagation: cutting

Common Plant Problems: mealy bugs

Growth Rate: medium

Repot: biennially

Cleaning Tips: wipe with a soft cloth or swab, or gently shower

Origins: tropical rainforests, south-east Brazil

Notes: A dry and cool resting period in very early spring and a stint outdoors in shade, followed by a gradual increase in watering, will promote annual reblooming. Once buds have formed, don't turn the plants (buds turn towards the light and repeated turning weakens their necks causing the buds to fall off). Sought after by collectors.

Easter Cactus
Hatior gaertneri

Branching, arching, fleshy stems are divided into flat segments. Produces pink or red blooms in spring. Height: 30cm; Spread: 30cm. Bright indirect light.

Ease of Care: easy

Water: medium in early spring and summer (allow 1cm of the soil to dry out), drier in fall and winter

Fertilizer: moderate (10-6-16 full strength once per month, February to October)

Propagation: cutting

Common Plant Problems: mealy bugs

Growth Rate: medium

Repot: annually

Cleaning Tips: wipe with a soft cloth or swab, or gently shower

Origins: Brazil

Notes: After blooming, plants can be placed outdoors in shade and brought indoors in fall to begin a dry and cool resting period, with a gradual increase in water as buds form, to promote annual reblooming. Once buds have formed don't turn the plants (buds turn towards the light and repeated turning weakens their necks causing the buds to fall off). Sought after by collectors.

Orchid Cactus
Epiphyllum

Closely related to Christmas and Easter cacti, orchid cactus displays fleshy, strap-shaped, green stems and branches. Produces semi-double, flaring, trumpet-like blooms in many shades in spring to summer. Height: 30cm; Spread: 1m. Bright indirect light.

Ease of Care: easy

Water: medium in early spring and summer (allow 1cm of the soil to dry out), drier in fall and winter

Fertilizer: heavy (15-30-15 once every 2 weeks, February to October)

Propagation: cutting

Common Plant Problems: mealy bugs, scale insects, stem spots

Growth Rate: medium

Repot: biennially

Cleaning Tips: wipe with a soft cloth or swab, or gently shower

Origins: Argentina, south Mexico, West Indies

Notes: After blooming, plants can be placed outdoors in shade and brought indoors in fall to begin a dry and cool resting period, with a gradual increase in water as buds form, to promote annual reblooming. Orchid cactus flowers well only if potbound. Sought after by collectors.

Rat's Tail Cactus
Aporocactus flagelliformis

Although this cactus is a forest type, its needs match those of the desert types listed on page 187. This fast-growing cactus displays a trailing habit with pencil-like, pendant, fleshy stems and fine spines. Produces double, crimson-pink blooms in spring or summer. Difficult to find. Height: 10cm; Spread: 1.5m. Direct light.

Origins: Mexico

Notes: Sought after by collectors.

Caladium
Elephant's Ear, Angel's Wings
Caladium bicolour

Upright in habit, this plant is prized for its striking foliage that lasts only from spring to fall. Leaves are large colourful, paper-thin and arrow shaped. Height: 60cm; Spread: 60cm. Bright indirect light.

Ease of Care: easy

Water: moist during growing season (keep soil consistently moist but not soggy)

Fertilizer: heavy (10-6-16 once every 2 weeks, February to October)

Propagation: divide tubers in spring

Common Plant Problems: spider mites, bacterial and fungal leaf spot

Growth Rate: medium

Repot: annually

Origins: tropical South America

Notes: Caladiums need a rest period of 5 months from early fall to early spring. When foliage dies down in fall, reduce watering. Store tubers in their pot in a cool, dry place. Gradually increase warmth and water in early spring.

Caladium

Calathea

Calathea
Peacock Plant, Zebra Plant,
Rattlesnake Plant
Calathea

Grown for their interesting foliage,
calathea's long-stalked leaves range from
ovate to elliptical, with differing patterns
and colour combinations. Height: 45cm;
Spread: 23cm. Bright indirect light.

Ease of Care: moderate

Water: moist (keep soil consistently
moist but not soggy)

Fertilizer: heavy (10-6-16 once every
2 weeks, February to October)

Propagation: division

Common Plant Problems: mealy bugs,
spider mites, fungal and bacterial leaf
spots

Growth Rate: medium

Repot: annually

Cleaning Tips: wipe leaves with a soft
cloth or gently shower, remove dead
foliage

Origins: tropical Central and South
America, West Indies

Notes: Sensitive to excessive fluoride.

Calla Lily
Zantedeschia

This bulbous plant displays an upright
habit with mid-green, arrow-shaped
or lance-shaped foliage, sometimes
spotted white. Produces single, white,
yellow, pink or purple spathes in summer. Height: 30–55cm; Spread: 25cm.
Direct light.

Ease of Care: moderate

Water: moist (keep soil consistently
moist but not soggy)

Fertilizer: heavy (15-30-15 once every
2 weeks, February to October)

Propagation: seed, division

Common Plant Problems: bacterial
soft rot, rhizome rot, grey mould, rust,
viral diseases

Growth Rate: medium

Repot: annually

Cleaning Tips: wipe leaves with
a soft cloth or gently shower

Origins: South and East Africa

Notes: May cause mild stomach upset
if ingested. Contact with sap can
irritate skin. Needs a rest period where
it should be stored in a cool, frost-free
spot. Sought after by collectors.

Camellia
Camellia

Upright in habit, this plant's glossy,
mid-green to dark-green foliage is
lance shaped to elliptical. Conditions
must be cool to flower. Produces single,
semi-double or double, white, pink
or red blooms in spring. Height: 2m;
Spread: 1m. Bright indirect light.

Ease of Care: moderate

Water: moist (keep soil consistently
moist but not soggy)

Calla Lily

Fertilizer: heavy (30-10-10 once every 2 weeks, February to October)

Propagation: cutting, air layering

Common Plant Problems: bud mites, scale insects, spider mites

Growth Rate: medium

Repot: annually

Cleaning Tips: wipe leaves with a soft cloth or gently shower

Origins: north India, Himalayas

Notes: Camellias tolerate hard pruning. Remove dead flowers. Sought after by collectors.

Campanula
Italian Bellflower, Star of Bethlehem
Campanula isophylla

A very pretty flowering plant with small, heart-shaped, toothed leaves. Produces single, white, pink or blue blooms in summer. Height: 15–20cm; Spread: up to 30cm. Bright indirect light.

Ease of Care: easy

Water: moist (keep soil consistently moist but not soggy)

Fertilizer: heavy (15-30-15 once every 2 weeks, February to October)

Propagation: seed, division

Common Plant Problems: aphids, spider mites, powdery mildew

Growth Rate: medium

Repot: annually

Cleaning Tips: gently shower, remove spent blooms

Origins: southern Europe, Turkey

Notes: Discard or plant in garden after flowering.

Canna Lily
Indian Shot Plant, Indian Reed Flower
Canna

This tender bulb produces large, exotic blooms and their large banana-like leaves are just gorgeous. Height: 75cm–2+m. Direct light.

Ease of Care: moderate

Water: moist (keep soil consistently moist but not soggy)

Fertilizer: heavy (15-30-15 once every 2 weeks, February to October)

Propagation: divide rhizomes

Common Plant Problems: spider mites

Growth Rate: fast

Repot: annually

Cleaning Tips: wipe with a soft cloth or gently shower, remove spent blooms

Notes: Deadheading will greatly improve the number and quality of flowers produced. Prefers a warm location.

Cape Primrose

Cape Primrose
Streptocarpus

This compact, upright plant has strap-shaped, hairy foliage. Produces single, white, pink or purple blooms with veined throats in spring to fall. Height: 20–30cm; Spread: 20–30cm. Bright indirect light.

Ease of Care: moderate

Water: medium (allow 1cm of the soil to dry out)

Fertilizer: heavy (15-30-15 once every 2 weeks, February to October)

Propagation: division, leaf cuttings

Common Plant Problems: aphids, mealy bugs, leaf spot

Growth Rate: medium

Repot: annually

Cleaning Tips: remove spent flowers

Origins: South Africa, Madagascar, China, south-east Asia

Notes: A lovely plant that will flower non-stop spring to fall. Protect from cold drafts and reduce watering in winter. Sought after by collectors.

Cardamom
Elettaria cardamomum

An upright plant with mid–green, lance-shaped foliage. Seeds and seed-pods are used as an aromatic spice in baking and cooking. Rarely flowers as a houseplant. Height: 1.5m; Spread: 1.5m. Bright indirect light.

Ease of Care: easy

Water: medium (allow 1cm of the soil to dry out)

Fertilizer: heavy (10-6-16 once every 2 weeks, February to October)

Propagation: seed, division

Common Plant Problems: thrips, root rot

Growth Rate: medium

Repot: annually

Cleaning Tips: wipe leaves with a soft cloth or gently shower

Origins: India, Sri Lanka, Malaysia, Sumatra

Notes: Harvest seeds and seedpods for storing. Sought after by collectors.

Carpet Plant
Flame Violet, Lace Flower Vine
Episcia

This vining plant has attractive, oval, hairy foliage with a puckered surface. Produces single, white, yellow, red or orange blooms in spring to fall. Height: 5–10cm; Spread: indefinite. Bright indirect light.

Ease of Care: moderate

Water: moist (keep soil consistently moist but not soggy)

Fertilizer: heavy (15-30-15 once every 2 weeks, February to October)

Propagation: seed, cutting, plantlets

Common Plant Problems: aphids, mealy bugs, fungal spots

Growth Rate: medium

Repot: annually

Cleaning Tips: clean leaves with a soft paint brush

Origins: Mexico to South America

Notes: Episcia requires high humidity and is a creeping plant that sends down roots when leaves touch the soil. Sought after by collectors.

Cast Iron Plant
Aspidistra elatior

This tough plant displays an upright habit with dark–green, sometimes var-iegated, glossy, leathery foliage that is elliptical to lance shaped. Height: 60cm; Spread: 60cm. Bright indirect light (tolerant of most light levels except direct sun).

Ease of Care: easy

Water: medium (allow 1cm of the soil to dry out)

Fertilizer: heavy (10-6-16 once every 2 weeks, February to October)

Propagation: division

Common Plant Problems: mealy bugs, spider mites

Growth Rate: medium

Repot: annually

Cleaning Tips: wipe leaves with a soft cloth or gently shower

Origins: Himalayas, China, Japan

Notes: Relatively disease free, but does suffer if soil remains saturated. A great plant for low light locations.

Cast Iron Plant

Chenille Plant
Red-hot Catstail, Philippine
Medusa, Foxtail
Acalypha hispida

This pretty, upright plant has rich–
green, oval, hairy foliage. Prized for
its dark-pink, pendant, chenille-like
blooms in summer. Height: 1–2m.
Bright indirect light.

Ease of Care: moderate

Water: moist (keep soil consistently
moist but not soggy)

Fertilizer: heavy (15-30-15 once every
2 weeks, February to October)

Propagation: cutting

Common Plant Problems: mites
(if the air is too dry)

Growth Rate: fast

Repot: annually

Cleaning Tips: wipe with a soft
paintbrush, remove spent blooms

Origins: subtropical regions

Notes: Needs high humidity (mist
frequently). Plant is difficult to over-
winter so take cuttings and discard
in second year. Sought after by
collectors.

Chenille Plant

Chestnut Vine
Chestnut Vine
Tetrastigma voinierianum

A large-leaved, fast-growing vine that
requires strong support. Displays 3 to
5-lobed, dark-green leaves with furry
undersides. Height: 2m; Spread: 2m.
Bright indirect light.

Ease of Care: easy

Water: medium (allow 1cm of the soil
to dry out)

Fertilizer: heavy (10-6-16 once every
2 weeks, February to October)

Propagation: cutting

Common Plant Problems: spider mites

Growth Rate: fast

Repot: annually

Cleaning Tips: wipe leaves with a soft
cloth or gently shower

Origins: Indonesia and Malaysia to
North Australia

Notes: Grow indoors in a cool place—
dislikes warm, dry air. Sought after by
collectors.

China Doll
Radermachera sinica

A foliage houseplant with an upright
habit. Displays compound leaves with
shiny, deeply veined leaflets with taper-
ing points. Height: 2m; Spread: 1m.
Bright indirect light.

Ease of Care: moderate

Water: moist (keep soil consistently
moist but not soggy)

Fertilizer: heavy (10-6-16 once every
2 weeks, February to October)

Propagation: cutting

Common Plant Problems: mealy bugs,
spider mites

Growth Rate: medium

Repot: no

Cleaning Tips: gently shower

Origins: Taiwan

Notes: Tolerant of dry air.

Chinese Evergreen

Chinese Evergreen
Aglaonema

This plant has a compact habit. Different types are available with attractive, variegated mid-green to dark-green or solid-green, oval leaf blades on stalks. May produce flowers occasionally. Height: 30cm; Spread: 50cm. Indirect light (solid-green types tolerate very low light levels).

Ease of Care: moderate

Water: medium (allow 1cm of the soil to dry out)

Fertilizer: heavy (10-6-16 once every 2 weeks, February to October)

Propagation: cutting, divide in spring

Common Plant Problems: yellowing leaves (caused by over-watering)

Growth Rate: medium

Repot: annually

Cleaning Tips: wipe leaves with a soft cloth or gently shower, remove dead foliage

Origins: Asia

Notes: Reduce watering in winter. Sensitive to drafts.

Chinese Lantern Lily
Sandersonia aurantica

An upright, climbing plant with lance-shaped, mid-green leaves. Produces single, lantern-shaped, orange blooms in summer. Height: 75cm; Spread: indefinite. Direct light.

Ease of Care: moderate

Water: moist (keep soil consistently moist but not soggy)

Fertilizer: heavy (15-30-15 once every 2 weeks, February to October)

Propagation: seed, division

Common Plant Problems: infrequent

Growth Rate: medium

Repot: annually

Cleaning Tips: wipe leaves with a soft cloth or gently shower

Origins: South Africa

Notes: Store tubers in a dry, frost-free place over winter. Only grown in summer. Sought after by collectors.

Cineraria
Pericallis

Often given as a gift, this compact flowering plant has an upright habit. Foliage is large, dark green and heart shaped. Produces single, daisy-like blooms in white, pink, blue, red or purple in spring, some with attractive white centres. Height: 30cm; Spread: 25cm. Bright indirect light.

Ease of Care: moderate

Water: moist (keep soil consistently moist but not soggy)

Fertilizer: no

Propagation: seed

Common Plant Problems: limp, yellow leaves (caused by over-watering and drying out)

Growth Rate: medium

Repot: no

Origins: Canary Islands, Madeira, the Azores

Notes: Prefers a cool, bright location. Buy plants with unopened buds for longer flower display. Usually discarded after flowering.

China Doll

Citrus Group

Citrus sold as houseplants are dwarf species of shrubby trees that will produce fruit on young plants. All benefit from a summer outside and protection from cold drafts when brought indoors to over-winter. Most produce flowers in late spring or early summer. Flowers can be pollinated with a swab. Height: 1.5m; Spread: 1m. Direct light.

Calamondin Orange
Panama Orange
Citrofortunella microcarpa
(syn. *Citrus mitis*)

A compact, upright, shrubby tree. Small, leathery, ovate foliage is dark green. Usually produces fragrant, single, white blooms in spring or summer but may flower sporadically throughout the year. Produces small oranges. Height: 1.5m; Spread: 1m. Direct light.

Ease of Care: moderate

Water: medium (allow 1cm of the soil to dry out)

Fertilizer: heavy (10-6-16 once every 2 weeks, February to October)

Propagation: cutting

Common Plant Problems: scale insects, spider mites

Growth Rate: medium

Repot: annually if necessary

Lemon Tree 'Meyer'

Cleaning Tips: wipe leaves with
a soft cloth or gently shower

Origins: hybrid

Notes: Small oranges are bitter
but very attractive. Sought after
by collectors.

Lemon Tree 'Meyer'
Improved Meyer Lemon Tree
Citrus meyeri

A dwarf, upright variety. Foliage is
narrow, ovate, finely toothed and light
green. Produces fragrant, single, white
blooms in spring or summer. Produces
pale-yellow fruit up to 7.5cm in diameter. Height: 1.5m; Spread: 1m. Direct
light.

Ease of Care: moderate

Water: medium (allow 1cm of the soil
to dry out)

Fertilizer: heavy (10-6-16 once every
2 weeks, alternating with 30-10-10 at
half strength, February to October)

Propagation: cutting

Common Plant Problems: scale
insects, spider mites

Growth Rate: medium

Repot: annually

Cleaning Tips: wipe leaves with
a soft cloth or gently shower

Origins: Asia

Notes: Grows easily from cuttings and
makes an attractive container plant.
Sought after by collectors.

Orange Tree 'Washington'
Sweet Orange
Citrus sinensis

A spiny, small tree that displays elliptical, dark-green foliage. Produces fragrant, single, white blooms in spring or
summer. Bears smooth-skinned, bright-
orange fruit about 7cm in diameter.
Height: 1.5m; Spread: 1m. Direct light.

Ease of Care: moderate

Water: medium (allow 1cm of the soil
to dry out)

Fertilizer: heavy (10-6-16 once every
2 weeks, alternating with 30-10-10 at
half strength, February to October)

Propagation: cutting

Common Plant Problems: scale
insects, spider mites

Growth Rate: medium

Repot: annually

Cleaning Tips: wipe leaves with
a soft cloth or gently shower

Origins: Asia

Notes: Fruit is seedless.
Sought after by collectors.

Club Moss
Trailing Spike Moss
Selaginella kraussiana

This is a low, spreading plant with bright-green or dark-green, mat-forming foliage. Height: 2.5cm; Spread: indefinite. Bright indirect light.

Ease of Care: moderate

Water: moist (keep soil consistently moist but not soggy)

Fertilizer: heavy (10-6-16 once every 2 weeks, February to October)

Propagation: cutting, division, spores

Growth Rate: medium

Repot: annually

Cleaning Tips: gently shower

Origins: rainforests in tropical regions

Notes: Good plant for a terrarium.

Coffee Plant
Coffea arabica

This upright plant doesn't produce coffee beans; rather it's grown for its glossy, dark-green foliage. May produce fragrant, single, white blooms in midsummer or early fall when plant reaches 3–4 years of age. Height: 1.5m; Spread: 30cm. Bright indirect light.

Ease of Care: easy

Water: moist (keep soil consistently moist but not soggy)

Fertilizer: heavy (10-6-16 once every 2 weeks, February to October)

Propagation: seed

Coffee Plant

Coleus

Common Plant Problems: scale insects

Growth Rate: medium

Repot: annually

Cleaning Tips: wipe leaves with a soft cloth or gently shower

Notes: Plants can be raised from unroasted coffee beans. Sensitive to drafts and to drying out. Sought after by collectors.

Coleus
Flame Nettle
Solenostemon (syn. *Coleus*)

Prized for its stunning foliage, this upright plant produces tooth-edged, pointed oval leaves in many colours and patterns. Flowers are borne on stalks in spring or summer and are fairly insignificant. Height: 30cm; Spread: 25cm. Direct light.

Ease of Care: easy

Water: moist (keep soil consistently moist but not soggy)

Fertilizer: heavy (10-6-16 once every 2 weeks, February to October)

Propagation: cutting, seed

Common Plant Problems: spider mites, leggy (caused by insufficient light or age)

Growth Rate: medium

Repot: annually

Cleaning Tips: wipe leaves with a soft cloth or gently shower

Crown of Thorns

Origins: tropical Africa and Asia
Notes: Sensitive to hard water. Keep
evenly moist at all times. Pinch back
growing tips regularly to keep bushy
and take cuttings as needed.

Croton
Codiaeum

A popular, upright plant prized for
its stunning foliage. Strikingly veined
leaves vary greatly in colour and shape.
Height: 1m; Spread: 65cm. Direct light.

Ease of Care: moderate
Water: medium (allow 1cm of the soil
to dry out)
Fertilizer: heavy (10-6-16 once every
2 weeks, February to October)
Propagation: cutting, air layering
Common Plant Problems: spider
mites, bacterial and fungal leaf spots
Growth Rate: medium
Repot: annually
Cleaning Tips: wipe leaves with
a soft cloth or gently shower
Origins: Malaysia
Notes: Sensitive to drafts and over-
watering. Prefers high humidity.

Crown of Thorns
Euphorbia milii

This upright plant sports small, bright-
green leaves on fleshy, thorny stems.
Produces single, white, cream or red
blooms continually if light is consistent.
Height: 1m; Spread: 45cm. Direct light
(but protect from hot summer sun).

Ease of Care: easy
Water: medium (allow 1cm of the soil
to dry out)
Fertilizer: heavy (cactus fertilizer once
every 2 weeks, February to October)
Propagation: seed
Common Plant Problems: mealy bugs,
spider mites
Growth Rate: medium
Repot: biennially
Cleaning Tips: swab carefully or gently
shower
Origins: Madagascar
Notes: Sap may irritate skin. Leaves
may drop in winter but recovery is
rapid. Water sparingly in winter.
Sought after by collectors.

Croton

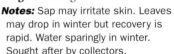

Ctenanthe

Ctenanthe 'Tricolour'
Never Never Plant
Ctenanthe lubbersiana

An attractive foliage plant with a spreading, upright habit. Long, dark-green leaves with irregular yellow streaks have reddish–purple undersides. Height: 2m; Spread: 1m. Bright indirect light.

Ease of Care: moderate

Water: moist (keep soil consistently moist but not soggy)

Fertilizer: heavy (10-6-16 once every 2 weeks, February to October)

Propagation: seed, division

Common Plant Problems: mealy bugs, spider mites

Growth Rate: fast

Repot: annually

Cleaning Tips: wipe leaves with a soft cloth or gently shower

Origins: Costa Rica, Brazil

Notes: Dislikes direct sunlight, cold temperatures and drafts, and cold or hard water. Do not allow to dry out. Sought after by collectors.

Cyclamen
Cyclamen persicum

A popular, long-flowering plant with a compact, upright habit. Heart-shaped foliage is dark green and patterned. Unusual, single, pink, red or white blooms on long flower stalks. Flowers continually in adequate light. Height: 25cm; Spread: 15cm. Bright indirect light.

Ease of Care: moderate

Water: moist (keep soil consistently moist but not soggy)

Fertilizer: heavy (15-30-15 once every 2 weeks, February to October)

Propagation: seed

Common Plant Problems: cyclamen mite

Growth Rate: medium

Repot: annually

Cleaning Tips: wipe leaves with a soft cloth or gently shower, remove dead foliage and spent flowers

Origins: south east Mediterranean, North Africa

Notes: Water from the bottom. Prefers a cool location. Sought after by collectors.

Cyclamen

Cypress
Monterey Cypress
Cupressus macrocarpa

An upright plant with feathery, yellow foliage that is lemon scented. Height: 2m; Spread: 14–20cm. Bright indirect light.

Ease of Care: moderate

Water: moist (keep soil consistently moist but not soggy)

Fertilizer: heavy (10-6-16 once every 2 weeks, February to October)

Propagation: seed, cutting

Common Plant Problems: scale insects, spider mites

Growth Rate: medium

Repot: annually

Cleaning Tips: gently shower

Origins: Northern Hemisphere

Notes: Needs a cool location in winter months. Sought after by collectors.

Desert Rose
Impala Lily
Adenium obesum

A compact plant with an upright habit. Glossy, green foliage in spiral, terminal clusters. Produces single, most commonly pink and rarely red and white blooms in summer. Height: 25–30cm; Spread: 20cm. Direct light (but avoid hot summer sun).

Ease of Care: moderate

Water: dry (allow 3cm of the soil to dry out thoroughly before watering)

Fertilizer: light (10-6-16 at half-strength once per month, February to October)

Propagation: seed, root cuttings from non-flowering shoots in summer

Common Plant Problems: aphids

Growth Rate: slow

Repot: biennially if necessary

Cleaning Tips: remove spent blooms

Origins: Arabian Peninsula and east to south west Africa

Notes: Milky sap from broken branches can irritate skin. Sought after by collectors.

Dieffenbachia
Dumb Cane
Dieffenbachia

Often used as an upright specimen. Large, fleshy, oblong, ovate or paddle-shaped foliage varies from cream, yellow and green patterns to solid green. Height: 1–3m; Spread: 60cm. Bright indirect light.

Water: medium (allow 1cm of the soil to dry out)

Fertilizer: heavy (10-6-16 once every 2 weeks, February to October)

Propagation: cutting, air layering

Common Plant Problems: aphids, mealy bugs, spider mites, fungal spot, stem rot

Desert Rose

Growth Rate: medium

Repot: annually

Cleaning Tips: wipe leaves with a soft cloth or gently shower

Origins: North and South America, West Indies

Notes: Sap is poisonous and can irritate skin. Foliage is poisonous if ingested. Senstive to drafts and cold temperatures.

Dieffenbachia 'Exotica'
Dieffenbachia seguine

Large, variegated-creamy-white foliage is edged with green. Height: 90cm; Spread: 90cm. Bright indirect light.

Dieffenbachia 'Marianne'
Dieffenbachia picta

Large, oval foliage is cream with a green edge. Height: 60cm; Spread: 90cm. Bright indirect light.

Dieffenbachia 'Tropic Snow'
Dieffenbachia

Large, green leaves are marked with pale-green and cream variegation. Height: 1m; Spread: 1m. Bright indirect light.

Dieffenbachia 'Marianne'

Dracaena Group

A large group of popular plants that make attractive specimens or features in the home or office environment. Foliage may be narrow and strap-like or wide and elliptical. Foliage colours range from solid green to multi-coloured. Dracaenas will shed their lower leaves as they age, leaving an exposed cane. Height: 60cm–3+m; Spread: 30cm–1.5+m. Bright indirect light.

Corn Plant 'Massangeana'
Happy Plant
Dracaena fragrans

Foliage is held atop a sturdy, upright trunk and may be sold with one or more trunks per pot. Displays strap-shaped, glossy, green leaves with a yellow stripe. Height: 3m; Spread: 1m. Bright indirect light.

Ease of Care: moderate

Water: medium (allow 1cm of the soil to dry out)

Fertilizer: heavy (10-6-16 once every 2 weeks, February to October)

Propagation: stem cuttings

Common Plant Problems: fungal leaf spot

Growth Rate: medium

Repot: annually

Cleaning Tips: wipe leaves with a soft cloth or gently shower

Origins: East Africa

Notes: Sensitive to excessive fluoride.

Dracaena 'Janet Craig'
Dracaena deremensis

A very popular, slower-growing, up-right plant. Produces wide, dark-green, strappy foliage. Height: 2m; Spread: 60cm. Bright indirect light.

Ease of Care: moderate

Water: medium (allow 1cm of the soil to dry out)

Fertilizer: heavy (10-6-16 once every 2 weeks, February to October)

Propagation: stem cuttings

Common Plant Problems: fungal leaf spot

Growth Rate: slow to medium

Repot: annually

Cleaning Tips: wipe leaves with a soft cloth or gently shower

Origins: East Africa

Notes: Sensitive to excessive fluoride. Tolerant of low light levels.

Dracaena 'Michiko Cane'

Dracaena 'Lemon Lime'
Dracaena deremensis

An upright plant with lance-shaped, striped-yellow foliage. Height: 60–90cm; Spread: 1m. Bright indirect light.

Ease of Care: easy

Water: medium (allow 1cm of the soil to dry out)

Fertilizer: heavy (10-6-16 once every 2 weeks, February to October)

Propagation: cutting

Common Plant Problems: spider mites

Growth Rate: medium

Repot: annually

Cleaning Tips: wipe leaves with a soft cloth or gently shower

Origins: Canary Islands, West Africa

Notes: Sensitive to excessive fluoride.

Dracaena 'Lemon Lime'

Draceana 'Lisa Cane'
Dracaena deremensis

An upright plant with dark-green, strap-shaped foliage. Height: 3m; Spread: 60cm. Bright indirect light.

Ease of Care: moderate

Water: medium (allow 1cm of the soil to dry out)

Fertilizer: heavy (10-6-16 once every 2 weeks, February to October)

Propagation: stem cuttings

Common Plant Problems: spider mites

Growth Rate: medium

Repot: annually

Cleaning Tips: wipe leaves with a soft cloth or gently shower

Origins: Canary Islands, tropical Africa, West Africa

Notes: Direct sun can scorch leaves. Sensitive to excessive fluoride. Sought after by collectors.

Dracaena 'Michiko Cane'
Dracaena deremensis 'Michiko'

An upright plant with slim, dark-green, strap-shaped foliage. Height: 3m; Spread: 60–90cm. Bright indirect light.

Ease of Care: moderate

Water: medium (allow 1cm of the soil to dry out)

Fertilizer: heavy (10-6-16 once every 2 weeks, February to October)

Propagation: stem cuttings

Common Plant Problems: spider mites

Growth Rate: medium

Repot: annually

Cleaning Tips: wipe leaves with a soft cloth or gently shower

Origins: Canary Islands, West Africa

Notes: Direct sun can scorch leaves. Sensitive to excessive fluoride. Sought after by collectors.

Dracaena 'Janet Craig'

Dracaena 'Warneckii'

Dracaena 'Rikki'
Dracaena deremensis

An upright plant with rich-green leaves with yellow bands. Height: 1.5m; Spread: 60cm. Bright indirect light.

Ease of Care: moderate

Water: medium (allow 1cm of the soil to dry out)

Fertilizer: heavy (10-6-16 once every 2 weeks, February to October)

Propagation: cutting

Common Plant Problems: mealy bugs, scale insects

Growth Rate: medium

Repot: annually

Cleaning Tips: wipe leaves with a soft cloth or gently shower

Origins: Canary Islands, West Africa

Notes: Maintains colour under low-light conditions. Sensitive to excessive fluoride. Sought after by collectors.

Dracaena 'Warneckii'
Dracaena deremensis warnecki

An upright plant with long, dark grey-green foliage with lighter streaks and white stripes on leaf edge. Height: 3m; Spread: 60cm. Bright indirect light.

Ease of Care: easy

Water: medium (allow 1cm of the soil to dry out)

Fertilizer: heavy (10-6-16 once every 2 weeks, February to October)

Propagation: stem cuttings

Common Plant Problems: spider mites

Growth Rate: medium

Repot: annually

Cleaning Tips: wipe leaves with a soft cloth or gently shower

Origins: Canary Islands, tropical Africa, West Africa

Notes: Easy care plants for offices and restaurants. Sensitive to excessive fluoride.

Dragon Tree
Dracaena marginata

An upright plant bearing thin, lance-shaped, red-margined, dark-green foliage. Height: 3m; Spread: 1m. Bright indirect light.

Ease of Care: easy

Water: medium (allow 1cm of the soil to dry out)

Fertilizer: heavy (10-6-16 once every 2 weeks, February to October)

Propagation: stem cuttings

Common Plant Problems: spider mites

Growth Rate: medium

Repot: annually

Cleaning Tips: wipe leaves with a soft cloth or gently shower

Dragon Tree

Origins: Reunion Island
Notes: Lower leaves generally fall
to leave exposed cane. Sensitive
to excessive fluoride.

Rainbow Tree 'Colorama'
Dracaena marginata

An upright plant bearing thin, lance-
shaped, reddish-pink banded foliage.
Height: 60cm; Spread: 1m. Bright indirect light.

Ease of Care: easy
Water: medium (allow 1cm of the soil
to dry out)
Fertilizer: heavy (10-6-16 once every
2 weeks, February to October)
Propagation: cutting
Common Plant Problems: spider mites
Growth Rate: medium
Repot: annually
Cleaning Tips: wipe leaves with
a soft cloth or gently shower
Origins: Madagascar
Notes: Lower leaves generally fall
to leave exposed cane. Sensitive
to excessive fluoride.

Ribbon Plant
Dracaena sanderiana

An upright plant with lance-shaped,
mid-green foliage with white or cream
stripes. Height: 1.5m; Spread: 40–80cm.
Bright indirect light.

Ease of Care: easy
Water: medium (allow 1cm of the soil
to dry out)
Fertilizer: heavy (10-6-16 once every
2 weeks, February to October)
Propagation: stem cuttings
Common Plant Problems: spider mites
Growth Rate: medium
Repot: annually

Cleaning Tips: wipe leaves with
a soft cloth or gently shower
Origins: Cameroon
Notes: Good accent plant. Sensitive
to excessive fluoride.

Rainbow Tree 'Colorama'

Easter Lily

Dwarf Banana
Musa velutina

Prized by the Victorians and today's conservatory owners, this upright plant produces broad, long, ovate leaves. Rarely produces yellow flowers indoors or, for that matter, bananas. Height: 1.5m; Spread: 90cm. Bright indirect light with some direct light.

Ease of Care: easy

Water: moist (keep soil consistently moist but not soggy)

Fertilizer: heavy (10-6-16 once every 2 weeks, February to October)

Propagation: seed, suckers

Common Plant Problems: aphids, mealy bugs, spider mites

Growth Rate: fast

Repot: annually

Cleaning Tips: wipe leaves with a soft cloth or gently shower

Origins: north-east India

Notes: Dislikes dry air—mist frequently. Sought after by collectors.

Easter Lily
Lilium longiflorum

Traditionally grown and given for Easter as its name implies. This plant is grown from a bulb and produces lance-shaped, dark-green leaves and fragrant, trumpet-shaped, single, white blooms in spring. Height: 1m; Spread: 30cm. Bright indirect light.

Ease of Care: easy

Water: medium (allow 1cm of the soil to dry out)

Fertilizer: heavy (10-6-16 once every 2 weeks, February to October)

Propagation: bulblets

Growth Rate: medium

Repot: no

Cleaning Tips: remove spent blooms

Origins: south Japan, Taiwan

Notes: Remove yellow pollen to prolong the life of the flower. Discard after flowering. Can be planted outdoors in a very sheltered spot but not reliably hardy.

Electric Grass
Isolepsis cernua

Becoming popular as a novelty plant, this arching plant displays long, cylindrical, grassy stems with small, white flowers on the end appearing in a flush in summer and continually throughout the year. Height: 20–25cm; Spread: 20cm. Bright indirect light.

Ease of Care: easy

Water: moist (keep soil consistently moist but not soggy)

Fertilizer: moderate (10-6-16 full strength once per month, February to October)

Propagation: division

Common Plant Problems: infrequent

Growth Rate: medium

Repot: biennially

Cleaning Tips: gently shower

Origins: western and southern Europe

Notes: New leaves stand erect at first then arch down with age. Best planted in a hanging basket. Do not allow to dry out. Sought after by collectors.

Elephant's Ear
Elephants Ear, Kris Plant
Alocasia sanderiana

Grown from a bulb, this large, upright plant is unrivalled in leaf size. Displays huge, arrow-shaped, dark-green leaves with a purplish undersides and wavy or deeply lobed, silver margins. Height: 1–2m; Spread: 1–2m. Bright indirect light.

Ease of Care: moderate

Water: moist (keep soil consistently moist but not soggy)

Fertilizer: heavy (10-6-16 once every 2 weeks, February to October)

Propagation: seed, divide rhizomes or separate offsets in spring and summer

Common Plant Problems: mealy bugs, scale insects, bacterial leaf diseases

Growth Rate: medium

Repot: annually

Cleaning Tips: wipe with a soft cloth or gently shower

Origins: south and south-east Asia

Notes: Prefers organically rich soil. Mist frequently during dry periods. Sought after by collectors.

Dwarf Banana

Eucalyptus
Gum Tree, Ironbark
Eucalyptus
An upright plant with aromatic, round, silvery-grey foliage. Height: 3m; Spread: 1m. Direct light.

Ease of Care: easy
Water: medium (allow 1cm of the soil to dry out)
Fertilizer: heavy (10-6-16 once every 2 weeks, February to October)
Propagation: seed
Common Plant Problems: aphids, mites, scale insects
Growth Rate: medium to fast
Repot: annually
Cleaning Tips: wipe with a soft cloth or gently shower
Origins: Australia
Notes: Prefers cool to average room temperatures. Oil from eucalyptus leaves is used in perfumes and medicines. Usually discarded after 2 years. Sought after by collectors.

False Aralia
Dizygotheca elegantissima
A delicate-looking, upright plant with dark green-black, lacy, divided foliage. Height: 2m; Spread: 60cm. Bright indirect light.

Ease of Care: moderate
Water: medium (allow 1cm of the soil to dry out)
Fertilizer: heavy (10-6-16 once every 2 weeks, February to October)
Propagation: seed, cutting, air layering
Common Plant Problems: scale insects, mealy bugs, mites
Growth Rate: slow
Repot: biennially
Cleaning Tips: gently shower, remove dead foliage
Origins: south-east Asia to Pacific Islands, Central and South America
Notes: Do not overpot. Dislikes sudden temperature changes. Sought after by collectors.

False Aralia

Asparagus Fern

Water: medium (allow 1cm of the soil
  to dry out)
Fertilizer: heavy (10-6-16 once every
  2 weeks, February to October)
Propagation: seed, division
Common Plant Problems: mealy bugs,
  mites
Growth Rate: fast
Repot: annually
Cleaning Tips: gently shower
Origins: Europe, Asia, Africa
Notes: Very pretty grown in mixed
  plantings.

Asparagus Fern
Asparagus setaceus (syn. *A. plumosus*)
This fern displays a lovely arching
habit. Produces soft, feathery, deep-
green foliage. Height: 60–90cm; Spread:
1–2m. Bright indirect light.

Ease of Care: easy
Water: medium (allow 1cm of the soil
  to dry out)
Fertilizer: heavy (10-6-16 once every
  2 weeks, February to October)
Propagation: seed, division
Common Plant Problems: aphids,
  spider mites
Growth Rate: medium
Repot: annually
Cleaning Tips: gently shower
Origins: Europe, Asia, Africa
Notes: Looks very attractive in
  a hanging basket or displayed on
  a stand.

Autumn Fern
Japanese Shield Fern
Dryopteris erythrosora

Attractive, stiff fronds are coppery-
red when young, turning dark green
with age. Height: 60cm; Spread: 38cm.
Bright indirect light.

Ease of Care: easy
Water: moist (keep soil consistently
  moist but not soggy)
Fertilizer: heavy (10-6-16 once every
  2 weeks, February to October)
Propagation: division, spores

Fern Group
There are many ferns that can be
grown indoors as houseplants—some
easier to grow than others. Leaf shape
varies, as does size, but most prefer
high levels of humidity when grown in
homes with centralized heating (keep
soil consistently moist but not soggy).
Remove dry, dead foliage to maintain
appearance. Height: 5cm–1m; Spread:
15cm–2m. Bright indirect light.

Asparagus Fern
Emerald Feather
Asparagus densiflorus (Sprengeri
group)
An arching fern with glossy, mid-green,
needle-like foliage on long stems.
Trails: 30cm; Spread: 60cm. Bright
indirect light.

Ease of Care: easy

Common Plant Problems: rust, leaf gall, fungal spots

Growth Rate: medium

Repot: annually

Cleaning Tips: gently shower

Origins: Japan

Notes: Although this fern can be drought tolerant, it is happier with consistent moisture.

Bird's Nest Fern
Asplenium nidus

An interesting, upright plant with broad, lance-shaped, glossy, bright-green foliage. A very tropical-looking fern. Height: 45cm; Spread: 1m. Bright indirect light.

Ease of Care: moderate

Water: moist (keep soil consistently moist but not soggy)

Fertilizer: heavy (10-6-16 once every 2 weeks, February to October)

Propagation: spores

Common Plant Problems: mealy bugs, scale insects

Growth Rate: slow

Repot: annually

Cleaning Tips: gently shower

Origins: all continents except Antartica

Notes: New leaves are easily damaged. Sought after by collectors.

Boston Fern
Nephrolepis exaltata bostoniensis

A very popular fern with an arching habit. Broad, lance-shaped fronds arch gracefully up and over. Height: 1m; Spread: 2m. Bright indirect light.

Ease of Care: moderate

Water: moist (keep soil consistently moist but not soggy)

Fertilizer: heavy (10-6-16 once every 2 weeks, February to October)

Propagation: rooted runners, spores

Common Plant Problems: mealy bugs, scale insects

Growth Rate: medium

Repot: annually

Cleaning Tips: gently shower

Boston Fern 'Dallas'

Origins: rain forests in tropical and subtropical regions

Notes: Take care to position this plant away from heat registers and to place on stands that allow the foliage to arch freely.

Boston Fern 'Dallas'
Nephrolepis exaltata

A trailing fern with glossy, dark-green fronds. Height: 30cm; Spread: 30cm. Bright indirect light.

Ease of Care: easy

Water: moist (keep soil consistently moist but not soggy)

Fertilizer: heavy (10-6-16 once every 2 weeks, February to October)

Propagation: division, spores

Common Plant Problems: mealy bugs, scale insects

Growth Rate: medium

Repot: annually

Cleaning Tips: gently shower

Origins: rainforests, tropical and subtropical regions

Notes: Related to the Boston fern, but much smaller more compact and tolerant of lower humidity and light.

Boston Fern 'Fluffy Ruffles'
Nephrolepis exaltata

Attractive, triangular-shaped fronds have pretty ruffled appearance. Height: 30cm; Spread: 45cm. Bright indirect light.

Ease of Care: moderate

Water: moist (keep soil consistently moist but not soggy)

Fertilizer: heavy (10-6-16 once every 2 weeks, February to October)

Propagation: division

Common Plant Problems: mealy bugs, scale insects

Growth Rate: medium

Repot: annually

Cleaning Tips: gently shower

Origins: rainforests, tropical and subtropical regions

Notes: A good substitute for Boston fern if space is a concern.

Brazilian Tree Fern
Blechnum brasilience

This upright fern develops a distinct trunk with age. New fronds are pinkish-red changing to dark green. Height: 1–1.5m; Spread: 1–1.5m. Bright indirect light.

Ease of Care: moderate

Water: moist (keep soil consistently moist but not soggy)

Fertilizer: heavy (10-6-16 once every 2 weeks, February to October)

Propagation: spores

Common Plant Problems: mealy bugs, scale insects

Growth Rate: medium

Repot: annually

Cleaning Tips: gently shower

Origins: South America

Notes: Upright ferns can be displayed directly on the floor or on a stand. Sought after by collectors.

Button Fern
Pellaea rotundifolia

This compact fern with an arching habit prefers moist but well-drained soil. Foliage is leathery and dark green, and its shape is round when new, changing to narrowly oblong with scalloped margins. Height: 30cm; Spread: 40cm. Bright indirect light.

Ease of Care: moderate

Water: moist (keep soil consistently moist but not soggy)

Fertilizer: heavy (10-6-16 once every 2 weeks, February to October)

Propagation: spores, division

Common Plant Problems: mealy bugs, fungal spots, root rot

Growth Rate: medium

Repot: annually

Cleaning Tips: gently shower

Origins: Australia, New Zealand

Notes: An unusual looking fern with a creeping rootstock. Sought after by collectors.

Crocodile Fern
Microsorium musifolium crocodyllus

An upright fern with lance-shaped, puckered, pale-green foliage displaying prominent dark veins. Height: 25–50cm; Spread: 20cm. Bright indirect light.

Button Fern

Crocodile Fern

Ease of Care: easy

Water: moist (keep soil consistently moist but not soggy)

Fertilizer: heavy (10-6-16 once every 2 weeks, February to October)

Propagation: division

Common Plant Problems: mealy bugs, scale insects

Growth Rate: medium

Repot: annually

Cleaning Tips: gently shower

Origins: Malaysia, Philippines, Indonesia, New Guinea

Notes: Mist regularly. Sought after by collectors.

Foxtail Fern
Plume Asparagus
Asparagus densiflorus 'Myersii'

Dense, arching foliage resembles a fox's tail. Height: 30–40cm; Spread: 60cm. Bright indirect light.

Ease of Care: moderate

Water: medium (allow 1cm of the soil to dry out)

Fertilizer: heavy (10-6-16 once every 2 weeks, February to October)

Propagation: seed, division

Common Plant Problems: mealy bugs, spider mites

Growth Rate: medium

Repot: annually

Cleaning Tips: gently shower

Origins: Europe, Asia, Africa

Notes: Adds texture and form to mixed houseplant arrangements.

Giant Sword Fern 'Macho'
Broad Sword Fern
Nephrolepis biserrata

This trailing fern displays long, dark-green, arching fronds. Height: 45cm–1m; Spread: 90cm. Bright indirect light.

Ease of Care: moderate

Water: moist (keep soil consistently moist but not soggy)

Fertilizer: heavy (10-6-16 once every 2 weeks, February to October)

Propagation: division, offsets

Common Plant Problems: infrequent

Growth Rate: medium

Repot: annually

Cleaning Tips: gently shower

Origins: Sri Lanka, the Maldives, south-east Asia

Notes: Display on a stand that allows fronds to arch freely. Sought after by collectors.

Kimberly Queen Sword Fern
Australian Sword Fern
Nephrolepis obliterata 'Kimberly Queen'

A large fern with an upright and arch-ing habit. Foliage is dark green. Excel-lent floor plant; looks good in group-ings. Height: 1m; Spread: 1m. Bright indirect light.

Ease of Care: moderate

Water: moist (keep soil consistently moist but not soggy)

Fertilizer: heavy (10-6-16 once every 2 weeks, February to October)

Propagation: division

Common Plant Problems: infrequent

Growth Rate: fast

Repot: annually

Cleaning Tips: gently shower

Origins: Australia

Notes: More tolerant of dry air and sun than many other ferns.

Maidenhair Fern
Delta Maidenhair Fern
Adiantum raddianum

Wiry black stalks that darken with age support pale-green fronds of lacy foliage. Height: 60cm; Spread: 81cm. Bright indirect light.

Ease of Care: moderate

Water: moist (keep soil consistently moist but not soggy)

Maidenhair Fern

Fertilizer: heavy (10-6-16 once every 2 weeks, February to October)

Propagation: spores, divide rhizomes

Growth Rate: medium

Repot: annually

Cleaning Tips: gently shower

Origins: tropical north and South Africa

Notes: Good companion plant to orchids. Requires high humidity. Sought after by collectors.

Kimberly Queen Sword Fern

Rabbit's Foot Fern

Rabbit's Foot Fern
Hare's Foot
Davallia fejeensis

The furry rhizomes of this fern push out of the soil and spill over the edge of the pot. Produces dark-green, feathery fronds. Height: 20–50cm; Spread: 30–100cm. Bright indirect light.

Ease of Care: easy

Water: moist (keep soil consistently moist but not soggy)

Fertilizer: heavy (10-6-16 once every 2 weeks, February to October)

Propagation: division, spores

Common Plant Problems: scale insects, grey mould

Growth Rate: medium

Repot: annually

Cleaning Tips: gently shower

Origins: south-west Europe, North America

Notes: Often sold in hanging baskets so that the rhizomes can hang freely.

Staghorn Fern

Staghorn Fern

Antelope Ears, Elk's Horn Fern
Platycerium bifuricatum

A really interesting fern displaying large, greyish–green fronds shaped like staghorns and covered with soft felt–like growth. Height: 1m; Spread: 60cm. Bright indirect light.

Ease of Care: moderate

Water: medium (allow 1cm of the soil to dry out)

Fertilizer: heavy (10-6-16 once every 2 weeks, February to October)

Propagation: spores

Common Plant Problems: scale insects

Growth Rate: medium

Repot: annually

Cleaning Tips: gently shower

Origins: tropical rain forests in Africa, Asia and Australia

Notes: These plants are epiphytes and are best grown on bark or in wooden hanging baskets. Do not wipe the fronds as the attractive, felt-like scurf will be removed. Sought after by collectors.

Table Fern
Pteris cretica

An upright fern with a variety of foliage colours. Fronds may be dark green or variegated and toothed. Height: 48–60cm; Spread: 30–40cm. Bright indirect light.

Ease of Care: moderate

Water: moist (keep soil consistently moist but not soggy)

Fertilizer: heavy (10-6-16 once every 2 weeks, February to October)

Propagation: spores, division

Common Plant Problems: mealy bugs, scale

Growth Rate: medium

Repot: annually

Cleaning Tips: gently shower

Origins: tropical and subtropical forests worldwide

Notes: Great for container gardens.

Walking Fern
Asplenium rhizophyllum

A spreading fern with mid-green, pointed and oblong foliage. Height: 15cm; Spread: 15–30.5cm. Bright indirect light.

Ease of Care: moderate

Water: moist (keep soil consistently moist but not soggy)

Fertilizer: light (10-6-16 at half-strength once per month, February to October)

Propagation: spores

Growth Rate: medium

Repot: annually

Cleaning Tips: gently shower

Origins: North America

Notes: When tips of fronds touch moist ground, they root and a new fern can be grown. Sought after by collectors.

Table Fern

Ornamental Fig Group

This group consists of 2 types: low plants that can either be grown as climbers or creepers and tall upright trees; some of the tallest and most successfully grown indoor trees. All prefer consistent moisture and bright indirect light. Height: 1–5+m; Spread: 30cm–3+m.

Creeping Fig
Climbing Fig
Ficus pumila

Displays a spreading habit with small, green or variegated foliage. Height: 1m; Spread: 30cm. Bright indirect light.

Ease of Care: easy

Water: moist (keep soil consistently moist but not soggy)

Fertilizer: heavy (10-6-16 once every 2 weeks, February to October)

Propagation: cutting

Common Plant Problems: spider mites

Growth Rate: medium

Repot: annually

Cleaning Tips: gently shower

Origins: China, Vietnam, Japan

Notes: Do not allow to dry out. Good plant for terrariums. Provide support if grown as a climber.

Fiddleleaf Fig
Banjo Fig
Ficus lyrata

An upright fig with broad, fiddle-shaped, leathery foliage that is glossy and dark-green. Height: 3+m; Spread: 1+m. Bright indirect light.

Ease of Care: easy

Water: medium (allow 1cm of the soil to dry out)

Fertilizer: heavy (10-6-16 once every 2 weeks, February to October)

Propagation: cutting

Common Plant Problems: mealy bugs, scale insects, spider mites

Growth Rate: fast

Repot: annually

Cleaning Tips: wipe leaves with a soft cloth or gently shower

Origins: West and Central Africa

Notes: A very large indoor plant.

Fig 'Amstel King'
Ficus binnendijkii

A large upright tree form, with long, oval leaves that are reddish-brown when new, changing to green with age. Height: 3m+; Spread: 2m. Bright indirect light.

Ease of Care: easy

Water: moist (keep soil consistently moist but not soggy)

Fiddleleaf Fig

Fertilizer: heavy (10-6-16 once every 2 weeks, February to October)

Propagation: cutting

Common Plant Problems: scale insects

Growth Rate: medium

Repot: annually

Cleaning Tips: wipe leaves with a soft cloth or gently shower

Origins: hybrid

Notes: Rotate plant for even, fuller growth.

Rubber Tree
India Rubber Fig, India Rubber Tree
Ficus elastica

A number of varieties of this popular plant are available. Fleshy foliage varies from deep-green or black-green to variegated and tri-colour. Height: 2–3m; Spread: 1+m. Bright indirect light.

Ease of Care: easy

Water: medium (allow 1cm of the soil to dry out)

Fertilizer: heavy (10-6-16 once every 2 weeks, February to October)

Propagation: cutting

Common Plant Problems: mealy bugs, scale insects, spider mites

Fig 'Amstel King'

Rubber Tree

Growth Rate: medium

Repot: annually

Cleaning Tips: wipe leaves with a soft cloth or gently shower

Origins: India

Notes: Varieties with green leaves are less fussy than variegated or tricolour selections.

Saber Fig
Narrow Leaf Fig, Long Leaf Fig
Ficus alii

An upright tree with narrow, pointed, lance-shaped foliage. Height: 3+m; Spread: 2m. Bright indirect light.

Ease of Care: easy

Water: moist (keep soil consistently moist but not soggy)

Fertilizer: heavy (10-6-16 once every 2 weeks, February to October)

Propagation: cutting

Common Plant Problems: scale insects

Growth Rate: medium

Repot: annually

Cleaning Tips: gently shower

Origins: hybrid

Notes: Rotate plant for even, full growth.

Weeping Fig
Ficus benjamina

Enormously popular in homes, malls and offices, this upright fig is long-lived and tolerant of slightly rootbound conditions. Produces small, ovate, glossy, mid-green leaves. Height: 2–3+m; Spread: 1m. Bright indirect light.

Ease of Care: moderate

Water: medium (allow 1cm of the soil to dry out)

Fertilizer: heavy (10-6-16 once every 2 weeks, February to October)

Propagation: cutting

Common Plant Problems: mealy bugs, scale insects, leaf drop (caused by stress, change of light conditions), galls (caused by pruning with infected tools)

Growth Rate: medium

Repot: biennially

Cleaning Tips: wipe leaves with a soft cloth or gently shower

Origins: tropical Asia, North Australia, south-west Pacific

Notes: Do not overpot—when maximum pot size has been reached, top dress annually. Turn for even, full growth.

Weeping Fig

Flamingo Flower

Flamingo Flower
Anthurium

An upright plant with tall stems bearing ovate, reflexed, glossy, dark-green foliage. Continually produces waxy, colourful, spathe-type blooms in pink, white, red or orange with prominent straight or curly tails. Height: 50–60cm; Spread: 30cm. Bright indirect light.

Ease of Care: easy

Water: moist (keep soil consistently moist but not soggy)

Fertilizer: heavy (10-6-16 once every 2 weeks, February to October)

Propagation: seed, divisions, cuttings, offsets

Common Plant Problems: mealy bugs, scale insects, fungal leaf spots, bacterial soft rot

Growth Rate: medium

Repot: annually

Cleaning Tips: wipe leaves with a soft cloth or gently shower

Origins: tropical and subtropical North and South America

Notes: Interesting cutflower. Water sparingly in winter. Contact with sap may irritate skin. Sought after by collectors.

Flowering Maple
Abutilon pictum 'Thompsonii'

A short-lived, large plant with a weeping habit. Five to nine-lobed leaves are dark-green and richly mottled with yellow. Produces single, orange, flushed with salmon-pink, blooms in summer. Height: 3+m; Spread: 2–5m. Direct light.

Ease of Care: easy

Water: medium (allow 1cm of the soil to dry out)

Fertilizer: heavy (15-30-15 once every 2 weeks, February to October)

Propagation: cutting

Common Plant Problems: mealy bugs, scale insects, spider mites, whiteflies, rust, abutilon mosaic virus, leaf spots

Repot: annually

Cleaning Tips: gently shower, remove dead foliage and spent flowers

Origins: tropical and subtropical regions of Africa, Asia, Australia, North and South America

Notes: Cut back to half its size in spring to ensure a bushy plant next year.

Trailing Flowering Maple
Trailing Abutilon
Abutilon megapotamicum

A short-lived, large plant with a weeping habit. Three to five-lobed leaves are medium to dark green (*A. megapotamicum 'Variegata'* foliage is splashed with yellow). Produces single, pendant, yellow flowers with bright-red calyx in summer. Height: 2m; Spread: 2m. Direct light.

Ease of Care: easy

Water: medium (allow 1cm of the soil to dry out)

Fertilizer: heavy (15-30-15 once every 2 weeks, February to October)

Propagation: seed, cutting

Common Plant Problems: mealy bugs, scale insects, spider mites, whiteflies, rust, abutilon mosaic virus, leaf spots

Repot: annually

Cleaning Tips: gently shower, remove dead foliage and spent flowers

Freesia

Origins: tropical and subtropical regions of Africa, Asia, Australia, North and South America

Notes: Cut back to half its size in spring to ensure a bushy plant next year. Often grown in hanging baskets or tied to supports.

Freesia

Freesia

An upright plant grown from a bulb. Narrow, sword- to lance-shaped foliage is mid green. Funnel-shaped, single blooms, which appear in summer, are available in many colours, and some hybrids are fragrant. Height: 40cm; Spread: 15cm. Direct light.

Ease of Care: easy

Water: moist (keep soil consistently moist but not soggy)

Fertilizer: moderate (15-30-15 once every 2 weeks, February to October)

Propagation: seed, offsets

Common Plant Problems: aphids, spider mites

Growth Rate: medium

Repot: annually

Cleaning Tips: wipe leaves with a soft cloth or gently shower

Origins: South Africa

Notes: Flower spikes may need staking. Let foliage die down, then cut off and store bulb in a cool dry place. Repot in spring.

Gardenia

Gardenia jasminoides

This flowering plant has an upright habit. Dark-green foliage is shiny and leathery. Produces fragrant, semi-double to double, waxy-petalled, white blooms in summer. Fussy about temperature and water when budding. Height: 45cm; Spread: 25–30cm. Direct light (but shade from hot summer sun).

Ease of Care: difficult

Water: moist (keep soil consistently moist but not soggy, see Notes)

Fertilizer: heavy (30-10-10 once every 2 weeks, February to October)

Propagation: seed, cutting

Common Plant Problems: aphids, spider mites

Growth Rate: medium

Repot: annually

Cleaning Tips: wipe with a soft cloth or gently shower

Origins: tropical regions of Asia and Africa

Notes: Flowers best when rootbound. Use tepid, lime-free water for this plant. Reduce water in winter, allowing 1cm of the soil to dry out. Sought after by collectors.

Gardenia

Gerbera Daisy
Barberton Daisy
Gerbera jamesonii

Compact in habit, gerberas display toothed, lance-shaped foliage. Produces big daisy-like, double, yellow, orange, red, pink or white blooms in summer with prominent centres. Height: 25–60cm; Spread: 25cm. Direct light (but shade from hot summer sun).

Ease of Care: easy

Water: moist (keep soil consistently moist but not soggy)

Fertilizer: heavy (15-30-15 once every 2 weeks, February to October)

Propagation: seed

Common Plant Problems: aphids, thrips, powdery mildew

Growth Rate: medium

Repot: annually

Cleaning Tips: remove spent blooms

Origins: South Africa, Madagascar, Asia, Indonesia

Notes: Requires lots of direct light to flower.

Gloriosa Lily
Climbing Lily, Glory Lily
Gloriosa superba

This plant's vining habit requires support. Lance-shaped, mid-green foliage bears tendrils at the tips. Produces lily-like, single, red blooms with yellow centres in summer. Height: 2m; Spread: 30cm. Bright indirect light.

Ease of Care: moderate

Water: moist during growing season (keep soil consistently moist but not soggy)

Fertilizer: heavy (10-6-16 once every 2 weeks, February to October)

Propagation: seed, separate tubers

Common Plant Problems: aphids, viral diseases

Growth Rate: medium

Repot: annually

Origins: Africa, India

Gerbera Daisy

Notes: Highly toxic if ingested, and handling tubers may irritate skin. Store tubers dry in their pot in a cool, dry place in winter. Sought after by collectors.

Glory Bower
Bleeding Heart Vine
Clerodendrum thomsoniae

A climbing plant with ovate, rich-green foliage. Produces single, bell-shaped calyx with crimson, star-shaped blooms in summer. Height: up to 4m. Bright indirect light.

Ease of Care: moderate

Water: moist (keep soil consistently moist but not soggy)

Fertilizer: heavy (15-30-15 once every 2 weeks, February to October)

Propagation: seed, cutting

Common Plant Problems: aphids, mealy bugs, whiteflies

Growth Rate: fast

Repot: annually

Origins: tropical and subtropical areas in Africa and Asia

Notes: Needs extra humidity during active growth period to promote flowering. Flowers best if potbound. At beginning of growing season, cut back at least $1/2$ of previous year's growth. Sought after by collectors.

Gloxinia

Gloxinia
Sinningia speciosa

A compact flowering plant. Foliage is large, velvety, ovate, scalloped and dark green. Produces single or double, red, violet-blue or white blooms in summer. Height: 20–30cm; Spread: 30–45cm. Bright indirect light.

Water: moist (keep soil consistently moist but not soggy)

Fertilizer: heavy (15-30-15 once every 2 weeks, February to October)

Propagation: seed, leaf cuttings

Common Plant Problems: large leaves are easily damaged

Growth Rate: medium

Repot: annually; see Notes

Cleaning Tips: remove spent blooms

Origins: Central and South America

Notes: Water from the bottom. After flowering, stop feeding and reduce water. Allow to dry out when leaves turn yellow. Store in a cool, dry location. Repot in spring, keeping warm and dry until leaves appear, then provide light and moisture.

Golden Trumpet
Allamanda cathartica

An upright plant that requires support. Foliage is glossy, dark green and point-ed. Single, yellow blooms appear in summer. Height: 2–3m; Spread: 2–3m. Direct light.

Ease of Care: moderate

Water: medium (allow 1cm of the soil to dry out)

Fertilizer: heavy (15-30-15 once every 2 weeks, February to October)

Propagation: seed, greenwood cuttings in late spring or early summer

Common Plant Problems: spider mites, whiteflies

Growth Rate: medium

Repot: annually

Cleaning Tips: remove spent blooms

Origins: North, Central and South America

Notes: Prefers warmth and high humidity. Sap may irritate skin. Water sparingly in winter. Sought after by collectors.

Goldfish Plant
Columnea banksii

Best in a hanging basket or in a pot where it can trail freely. Displays smooth or hairy, mid-green to dark-green foliage. Produces tubular, yellow-orange or red blooms in summer. Height: 15cm; Trails: 1.5m. Bright indirect light.

Ease of Care: moderate

Water: medium in growing season (allow 1cm of the soil to dry out), sparingly in winter

Fertilizer: heavy (15-30-15 once every 2 weeks, February to October)

Propagation: cutting

Common Plant Problems: aphids, mealy bugs, spider mites, botrytis

Repot: annually

Cleaning Tips: wipe with a soft cloth or gently shower

Origins: West Indies, Mexico, Central America, tropical South America

Notes: Can be fussy about flowering—frequently mist to promote blooming. Trim stems back after flowering.

Curled Parsley

Herbs

Growing herbs indoors allows you to enjoy the flavours and scents they impart all year. There are many available; be adventurous. All will require direct light as close to a window as possible. Place containers outdoors in summer and scrupulously check for bugs before bringing back indoors.

Curled Parsley
Petroselinum crispum crispum

This lovely herb has bright-green, curled foliage. Snip some to add flavour to all kinds of dishes. Height: 30–45cm; Spread: 15–30cm. Direct light.

Ease of Care: easy

Water: medium (allow 1cm of the soil to dry out)

Fertilizer: no

Propagation: seed

Common Plant Problems: aphids

Growth Rate: medium

Repot: no

Cleaning Tips: gently shower

Notes: Parsley can be used fresh, frozen or dried. Parsley may irritate sensitive skin on some individuals.

Lemon Balm
Melissa officinalis

A loosely branched, upright plant. Foliage has a bright, fresh lemon taste. Height: 20–80cm; Spread: 60cm. Direct light.

Ease of Care: easy

Water: medium (allow 1cm of the soil to dry out)

Fertilizer: no

Propagation: seed

Common Plant Problems: rare

Growth Rate: medium

Repot: no

Cleaning Tips: gently shower

Notes: Pinch plants regularly to promote bushiness. Harvest only young leaves for the best flavour.

Lemon Geranium
Pelargonium crispum

An upright plant with rough, crinkled, serrated, rounded or lobed leaves about 1cm in length. The leaves may be used for teas, sauces, sorbets and vinegars. Height: 30–100cm; Spread: 30–45cm. Direct light.

Ease of Care: easy

Water: medium (allow 1cm of the soil to dry out)

Mint

Fertilizer: no
Propagation: cutting
Common Plant Problems: over-watering
Growth Rate: medium
Repot: no
Cleaning Tips: gently shower
Origins: South Africa
Notes: Pretty flowers are edible but not as tasty as the leaves.

Lemon Verbena
Aloysia triphylla
An upright plant with stiff, apple-green, willowy leaves and small, pale-lilac flowers in pyramid-shaped clusters. Leaves have a strong lemon fragrance and flavour. Height: 1–2m; Spread: 45cm–1m. Direct light.

Lemon Verbena

Ease of Care: easy
Water: medium (allow 1cm of the soil to dry out)
Fertilizer: no
Propagation: seed, cutting
Common Plant Problems: dislikes being wet
Growth Rate: medium
Repot: no
Cleaning Tips: gently shower
Notes: Harvest leaves and flowers from mature plants and discard stalks. This plant loves light and heat.

Mint
Mentha
Mint comes in a huge variety of enticing scents and flavours. Harvest the leaves and use fresh for teas, jelly and other culinary delights. Height: 15–60cm; Spread: indefinite. Direct light.

Ease of Care: easy
Water: medium (allow 1cm of the soil to dry out)
Fertilizer: no
Propagation: cuttings, division
Common Plant Problems: rust
Growth Rate: fast
Repot: no
Cleaning Tips: gently shower
Notes: Harvest the leaves and use fresh for teas and jelly

Rosemary
Rosmarinus officinalis
Upright in habit, this plant has hundreds of straight, needle-shaped, succulent, green leaves. Foliage can be harvested for cooking, potpourris and sachets. Height: 30–100cm; Spread: 30–60cm. Direct light.

Ease of Care: easy
Water: medium (allow 1cm of the soil to dry out)
Fertilizer: no
Propagation: seed
Common Plant Problems: spider mites
Growth Rate: slow
Repot: annually

Sage

Cleaning Tips: gently shower
Origins: Mediterranean
Notes: Young plants require more water than older, established ones. Harvest leaves sparingly in winter because plants get less light and produce fewer leaves.

Sage
Salvia officinalis

Sage is a valuable culinary herb said to aid in digesting fatty foods. Foliage is ovate and can be mid green to purplish green. Height: 45–60cm; Spread: 1m. Direct light.

Ease of Care: easy
Water: medium (allow 1cm of the soil to dry out)
Fertilizer: no
Propagation: cutting, division
Common Plant Problems: powdery mildew
Growth Rate: medium

Repot: no
Cleaning Tips: gently shower
Origins: Mediterranean
Notes: Never over-water. Plants get woody with age and should be replaced.

Sweet Basil
Ocimum basilicum

An upright herb useful in cooking. There are many varieties with different coloured leaves and slightly different flavours. Height: 30–60cm; Spread: 30–45cm. Direct light.

Ease of Care: easy
Water: medium (allow 1cm of the soil to dry out)
Fertilizer: no
Propagation: seed, cutting
Common Plant Problems: root rot (caused by over-watering)
Growth Rate: fast
Repot: annually
Cleaning Tips: gently shower
Origins: Mediterranean
Notes: Older plants become woody; replace with new plants. Pinch to promote new growth.

Sweet Basil

Hibiscus

Hibiscus rosa-sinensis

An upright plant often available in a lollipop-like tree or standard form. Glossy, dark-green foliage highlights the single, semi-double or double, white, yellow, orange, pink or red flowers that bloom continually. Height: 1.5m; Spread: 1m. Direct light.

Ease of Care: moderate

Water: moist (keep soil consistently moist but not soggy)

Fertilizer: heavy (15-30-15 once every 2 weeks, February to October)

Propagation: cutting

Common Plant Problems: aphids, spider mites, yellow leaves (caused by underwatering)

Growth Rate: fast

Repot: annually

Cleaning Tips: wipe with a soft cloth or gently shower

Origins: tropical and subtropical regions

Notes: Often grown outdoors in summer—be vigilant about checking for bugs before returning to indoors. Can live 20 years or more. Flowers last 1 to 2 days but are quickly replaced by more blooms.

Hindu Rope Hoya

Hoya

Wax Flower

Hoya carnosa

A vining plant with rigid, fleshy, mid-green foliage. Produces single, fragrant white blooms with red coronas in summer. Trails: 2+m; Spread: indefinite. Direct light.

Ease of Care: easy

Water: medium (allow 1cm of the soil to dry out)

Fertilizer: heavy (tomato fertilizer once every 2 weeks, February to October)

Propagation: seed, cutting

Common Plant Problems: mealy bugs, scale insects

Growth Rate: medium

Repot: only if potbound

Cleaning Tips: wipe with a soft cloth or gently shower

Origins: India, South China, Burma

Notes: Do not remove old flower stems because new inflorescences develop on them.

Hibiscus

Hindu Rope Hoya
Krinkle Kurl
Hoya carnosa compacta

An interesting trailing plant with contorted, crowded, fleshy leaves folded along their lengths. Produces fragrant, single, pink, white or red blooms with a darker corona in summer. Height: 30cm; Trails: up to 2+m. Direct light.

Ease of Care: easy

Water: medium (allow 1cm of the soil to dry out)

Fertilizer: heavy (tomato fertilizer once every 2 weeks, February to October)

Propagation: seed

Common Plant Problems: mealy bugs, scale insects

Growth Rate: medium

Repot: only if potbound

Cleaning Tips: wipe with a soft cloth or gently shower

Notes: Do not remove old flower stems because new inflorescences develop on them. Sought after by collectors.

Hyacinth
Hyacinthus

One of the most commonly forced bulbs. Bulbs must be pre-chilled. Foliage is long and lance shaped. Produces a single stem of very fragrant, single white, pink or blue blooms about 2 weeks after forcing. Height: 30cm. Direct light.

Ease of Care: easy

Water: medium (allow 1cm of the soil to dry out)

Fertilizer: no

Propagation: offsets

Growth Rate: fast

Origins: western Europe, North Africa

Notes: Plant in garden when blooming is finished. Can be grown in soil or water.

Hydrangea

Hydrangea
Hydrangea macrophylla

An upright, flowering plant with broad, oval, coarsely toothed foliage. Produces showy, mop-like heads of white, pink or blue blooms in spring. Height: 60cm; Spread: 45cm. Bright indirect light.

Ease of Care: moderate

Water: moist (keep soil consistently moist but not soggy)

Fertilizer: heavy (30-10-10 once every 2 weeks, February to October)

Propagation: cutting

Common Plant Problems: yellow leaves (caused by underwatering)

Growth Rate: medium

Repot: no

Cleaning Tips: remove spent blooms

Origins: East Asia, North and South America

Notes: Prefers cool locations. Difficult to over-winter indoors—usually discarded once finished blooming.

Hyacinth

Ivy Group

A number of trailing and vining plants are grouped together by garden centres as 'Ivy' although many of these are not the English ivy that generally comes to mind.

Marengo Ivy
Hedera algeriensis
'Gloire de Marengo'

A vining plant with large, lobe-shaped, light-green and white foliage. Trails: 1.5–2m; Spread: 1m. Bright indirect light.

Ease of Care: easy

Water: medium (allow 1cm of the soil to dry out)

Fertilizer: heavy (10-6-16 once every 2 weeks, February to October)

Propagation: cutting

Common Plant Problems: mealy bugs, spider mites

Growth Rate: medium

Repot: biennially

Cleaning Tips: gently shower, remove dead foliage

Origins: North Africa, Canary Islands, Azores, Madeira, western Europe, China, Korea, Japan

Notes: The largest-leaved ivy. Can be trained along a wall, on a form or grafted as topiary.

Grape Ivy

English Ivy

English Ivy
Hedera helix

A popular vine displaying flat, 3 to 5-lobed leaves that are green or variegated white or yellow. Trails: 2m; Spread: 1m. Bright indirect light.

Ease of Care: easy

Water: medium (allow 1cm of the soil to dry out)

Fertilizer: heavy (10-6-16 once every 2 weeks, February to October)

Propagation: cutting

Common Plant Problems: aphids, scale insects, spider mites

Growth Rate: medium

Repot: annually

Cleaning Tips: gently shower, remove dead foliage

Origins: North Africa, Canary Islands, Azores, Madeira, western Europe, Himalayas, China, Korea, Japan

Notes: Can be trained along a wall, on a form or grafted as topiary.

Grape Ivy
Cissus rhombifolia

An easy and lovely versatile plant with a climbing habit and tendrils that cling to supports. Foliage is palmate and dark green. Trails: 4m; Spread: 1m. Bright indirect light.

Ease of Care: easy

Water: medium (allow 1cm of the soil to dry out)

Fertilizer: heavy (10-6-16 once every 2 weeks, February to October)

Propagation: cutting

Common Plant Problems: mealy bugs, powdery mildew

Growth Rate: fast

Repot: annually

Cleaning Tips: gently shower

Origins: tropical America

Notes: Although it prefers bright indirect light, this vine is surprisingly tolerant of lower light levels.

Grape Ivy 'Ellen Danica'
Cissus rhombifolia

A small variety of grape ivy, this lovely, versatile plant displays a climbing habit and tendrils that cling to supports. Foliage is deeply lobed and dark green. Trails: 1m; Spread: 1m. Bright indirect light.

Ease of Care: easy

Water: medium (allow 1cm of the soil to dry out)

Fertilizer: heavy (10-6-16 once every 2 weeks, February to October)

Propagation: cutting

Grape Ivy 'Ellen Danica'

Swedish Ivy

Common Plant Problems: mealy bugs, powdery mildew

Growth Rate: medium

Repot: annually

Cleaning Tips: gently shower

Origins: tropical America

Notes: Bushier and slower growing than grape ivy.

Swedish Ivy
Candle Plant
Plectranthus

Typically grown in a hanging basket where the attractive foliage spills over the sides freely. Foliage is heart shaped to ovate with scalloped edges and may be green with white veins, green with white edges or just solid green. Trails: 25cm; Spread: 1m. Bright indirect light.

Ease of Care: easy

Water: moist (keep soil consistently moist but not soggy)

Fertilizer: heavy (10-6-16 once every 2 weeks, February to October)

Propagation: cutting

Common Plant Problems: mealy bugs, spider mites, leaf spot, root rot

Growth Rate: medium

Repot: annually

Cleaning Tips: gently shower

Origins: Africa, Madagascar, Asia, Australia, Pacific islands

Notes: Remove growing tips to encourage branching and bushy growth. More tolerant of dry air than English ivy is.

Jacaranda
Jacaranda mimosifolia

A beautiful, upright plant. Ferny foliage is mid green and arches away from the central stem. Height: 1–2m; Spread: 30cm. Direct light.

Ease of Care: moderate

Water: medium (allow 1cm of the soil to dry out)

Fertilizer: heavy (10-6-16 once every 2 weeks, February to October)

Propagation: seed, cuttings

Common Plant Problems: spider mites

Growth Rate: medium

Repot: annually

Cleaning Tips: gently shower

Origins: tropical America

Notes: Plants lose their lower leaves with age. Use tepid water. Water sparingly in winter. Unlikely to produce its purple-blue flowers indoors. Sought after by collectors.

Japanese Aralia
Japanese Fatsia
Fatsia japonica

An excellent upright, feature plant with large, leathery, 7 to 11-lobed leaves. Height: 1.5m; Spread: 1m. Bright indirect light.

Ease of Care: moderate

Water: moist (keep soil consistently moist but not soggy)

Fertilizer: heavy (10-6-16 once every 2 weeks, February to October)

Jacaranda

Jasmine

Propagation: cutting, seed, air layering

Common Plant Problems: mealy bugs, scale insects, spider mites, fungal and bacterial leaf spots

Growth Rate: medium

Repot: annually

Cleaning Tips: wipe with a soft cloth or gently shower

Origins: east Asia

Notes: Turn to promote even, full growth. Sought after by collectors.

Jasmine
Jasminum polyanthum

A climbing and vining plant prized for its lovely, fragrant flowers. Dark-green foliage is oval to lance shaped. Produces pink buds that open to very fragrant, single, white blooms in summer. Height: 3m. Direct light.

Ease of Care: moderate

Water: moist (keep soil consistently moist but not soggy)

Fertilizer: heavy (15-30-15 once every 2 weeks, February to October)

Propagation: seed, cutting

Common Plant Problems: aphids, mealy bugs, spider mites

Repot: annually

Cleaning Tips: gently shower

Origins: China

Notes: Keep plants cool in winter. Provide support and do not allow to dry out. Sought after by collectors.

Jerusalem Cherry

Jerusalem Cherry
Christmas Cherry, Winter Cherry
Solanum pseudocapsicum

A stocky, upright plant usually sold laden with berries. Wavy-margined foliage is elliptical and dark green. Produces single, white blooms in summer, followed by green (ripening to red), round to oval berries. Height: 30–45cm; Spread: 30–45cm. Direct light.

Ease of Care: moderate

Water: moist (keep soil consistently moist but not soggy)

Fertilizer: heavy (10-6-16 once every 2 weeks, February to October)

Propagation: seed, cutting

Common Plant Problems: aphids, spider mites

Growth Rate: medium

Repot: annually

Origins: eastern South America

Notes: All parts of plant can cause skin irritation and sickness if ingested. Prolong the time the berries stay on by growing it on a sunny windowsill.

Kafir Lily
Clivia miniata

An upright plant with strap-shaped, dark-green foliage. Produces tubular, orange-yellow blooms in clusters in early spring. Height: 45cm; Spread: 30cm. Bright indirect light.

Ease of Care: easy

Water: medium (allow 1cm of the soil to dry out)

Fertilizer: heavy (15-30-15 once every 2 weeks, February to October)

Propagation: seed, division

Common Plant Problems: mealy bugs, spider mites, bacterial and fungal spots, viral diseases

Growth Rate: medium

Repot: biennially

Cleaning Tips: wipe with a soft cloth or gently shower

Origins: South Africa

Notes: Sap may irritate skin. Needs cool nights in fall and winter to promote flowering. Flowers best if rootbound. Sought after by collectors.

Kafir Lily

Kalanchoe
Kalanchoe blossfeldiana

A compact, upright flowering plant with fleshy, glossy, dark-green foliage. Produces clusters of single, tubular-shaped, white, yellow, pink or red blooms primarily in summer (although growers induce blooming throughout the year). Height: 25cm; Spread: 15cm. Direct light.

Ease of Care: easy

Water: medium (allow 1cm of the soil to dry out)

Fertilizer: moderate (15–30–15 once every 2 weeks, February to October)

Propagation: seed, cutting

Kalanchoe

Common Plant Problems: aphids, mealy bugs

Growth Rate: medium

Repot: annually

Cleaning Tips: wipe with a soft cloth or gently shower, remove spent blooms

Origins: Madagascar

Notes: To promote reblooming, trim off spent blooms and move pot into bright indirect light, reducing water for about a month. Move back into direct light and increase water.

Kangaroo Paw
Anigozanthos flavidus

A compact plant with spiky, grey-green foliage. Continually produces clusters of unusual, two-lipped, tubular blooms thought to resemble a kangaroo's paw. Height: 30cm; Spread: 30cm. Direct light (but avoid hot summer sun).

Ease of Care: moderate

Water: moist (keep soil consistently moist but not soggy)

Fertilizer: heavy (15-30-15 once every 2 weeks, February to October)

Propagation: seed, division

Growth Rate: medium

Repot: annually

Cleaning Tips: gently shower, remove spent blooms

Origins: south-west Australia

Notes: Water freely spring and summer but keep almost dry in winter. Sought after by collectors.

Kangaroo Vine
Cissus antarctica

A vigorous vining plant with glossy, ovate, rich-green foliage. Height: 2–3m; Spread: 60cm. Bright indirect light.

Ease of Care: easy

Water: medium (allow 1cm of the soil to dry out)

Fertilizer: heavy (10-6-16 once every 2 weeks, February to October)

Propagation: seed

Common Plant Problems: infrequent

Growth Rate: fast

Repot: annually

Cleaning Tips: gently shower

Origins: tropical and subtropical areas of North Australia

Notes: Curly tendrils attach to supports. Pinch out growing tips to control height and spread. Sought after by collectors.

Lipstick Vine
Basket Plant
Aeschynanthus lobbianus

A trailing plant with fleshy, mid-green to dark-green, ovate to lance-shaped foliage. Produces clusters of tubular, orange, red and dark-red blooms from summer to winter. Trails: 20–30cm; Spread: 40–60cm. Bright indirect light.

Ease of Care: easy

Water: medium (allow 1cm of the soil to dry out)

Lipstick Vine

Fertilizer: heavy (15-30-15 once every 2 weeks, February to October)

Propagation: seed, cutting

Common Plant Problems: aphids, mealy bugs, thrips

Growth Rate: medium

Repot: annually

Cleaning Tips: gently shower, remove spent blooms

Origins: Himalayas, south China, Malaysia, Indonesia, New Guinea

Notes: Water freely in growing season, sparingly in winter.

Mexican Hat Plant

Lisianthus
Prairie Gentian
Eustoma grandiflorum (syn. *Lisianthus russelianus*)

This compact, upright plant has mid-green, oval foliage. Produces single or double, blue, purple, mauve or white blooms in summer. Height: 30–45cm; Spread: 20cm. Bright indirect light.

Ease of Care: difficult

Water: medium (allow 1cm of the soil to dry out)

Fertilizer: heavy (15-30-15 once every 2 weeks, February to October)

Propagation: seed, division

Common Plant Problems: gray mould, stem cankers, fusarium wilt, viral diseases

Growth Rate: medium

Lisianthus

Repot: no

Cleaning Tips: remove spent blooms

Origins: central and southern United States to northern South America

Notes: Mist leaves frequently to prolong blooming. Usually discarded after blooming. Sought after by collectors.

Mexican Hat Plant
Devil's Backbone, Mexican Hat Plant
Kalanchoe daigremontiana

An upright plant often grouped with succulents at garden centres. Fleshy, lance-shaped foliage produces plantlets on toothed margins. Height: 1m; Spread: 30cm. Direct light.

Ease of Care: easy

Water: dry (allow 3cm of soil to dry out thoroughly before watering)

Fertilizer: heavy (cactus fertilizer once every 2 weeks, February to October)

Propagation: plantlets

Common Plant Problems: mealy bugs

Growth Rate: slow

Repot: biennially

Cleaning Tips: wipe with a soft paintbrush

Origins: south-west Madagascar

Notes: Plantlets will drop from mother plant and root at the plant's base.

Money Tree
Good Luck Plant
Pachira

An upright plant with large, round-shaped leaves divided into fingers. Often sold with a braided trunk. Height: 2m; Spread: 1m. Direct light.

Ease of Care: easy

Water: moist (keep soil consistently moist but not soggy)

Fertilizer: heavy (10-6-16 once every 2 weeks, February to October)

Propagation: cutting, side shoots

Common Plant Problems: spider mites

Growth Rate: medium

Repot: annually

Cleaning Tips: wipe leaves with a soft cloth or gently shower

Origins: tropical America

Notes: A plant used in *feng shui* to bring good luck and money into the home. Sought after by collectors.

Money Plant

Monkey Plant
Ruellia makoyana

An attractive, upright plant that may require staking if stems become floppy. Displays velvety, ovate, silver-veined, green foliage with purple undersides. Produces single, carmine-pink blooms in summer. Height: 30–60cm; Spread: 30–45cm. Bright indirect light.

Ease of Care: easy

Water: moist (keep soil consistently moist but not soggy)

Fertilizer: heavy (10-6-16 once every 2 weeks, February to October)

Propagation: cutting

Common Plant Problems: aphids, bacterial and fungal leaf spots, rust, root rot

Growth Rate: medium

Repot: annually

Cleaning Tips: wipe with a soft paintbrush

Origins: Brazil

Notes: Pinch growing tips to promote bushiness. Reduce water after flowering.

Mother of Thousands
Strawberry Begonia
Saxifraga stolonifera

A lovely plant that produces plantlets on long, thread-like stolons. Foliage is hairy, deep olive-green with reddish-purple undersides. Produces single, white with yellow centred blooms in summer. Height: 20cm; Spread: 20cm. Bright indirect light.

Ease of Care: easy

Water: medium (allow 1cm of the soil to dry out)

Fertilizer: heavy (10-6-16 once every 2 weeks, February to October)

Propagation: plantlets

Common Plant Problems: aphids, spider mites

Growth Rate: medium

Repot: annually if necessary

Cleaning Tips: remove dead foliage

Origins: mountains in northern hemisphere

Notes: Prefers fairly cool conditions 10–16°C. Mist regularly in higher temperatures. A short-lived plant (2–3 years) that is easily propagated by plantlets.

Myrtle
Myrtus communis

A compact, upright habit makes myrtle an excellent plant for topiary shapes.

Norfolk Island Pine

Displays small, dark–green, oval foliage. Produces double, white blooms in summer. Height: as trained; Spread: as trained. Direct light.

Ease of Care: moderate

Water: moist (keep soil consistently moist but not soggy)

Fertilizer: heavy (10-6-16 once every 2 weeks, February to October)

Propagation: seed, cutting

Common Plant Problems: scale insects

Growth Rate: medium

Repot: annually

Cleaning Tips: gently shower

Origins: Mediterranean, North Africa, South America, Falkland Islands

Notes: Leaves are aromatic when crushed. Sought after by collectors.

Nerve Plant
Painted Net Leaf
Fittonia albivenis

A creeping plant with oval foliage covered with a fine network of pink or white veins. Height: 15cm; Spread: indefinite. Indirect light.

Ease of Care: moderate

Water: moist (keep soil consistently moist but not soggy)

Fertilizer: heavy (10-6-16 once every 2 weeks, February to October)

Propagation: cutting

Common Plant Problems: bacterial and fungal leaf spots

Growth Rate: medium

Repot: annually

Cleaning Tips: gently shower

Origins: Peru

Notes: Prefers high humidity— good plant for terrariums.

Norfolk Island Pine
Araucaria heterophylla

A beautiful upright plant that is not a pine as its common name suggests (it is a conifer). Soft needles of foliage are displayed on long, outward spreading branches. Height: 2–3+m; Spread: 1–2m. Bright indirect light.

Ease of Care: moderate

Water: medium (allow 1cm of the soil to dry out)

Fertilizer: heavy (10-6-16 once every 2 weeks, February to October)

Propagation: cutting

Common Plant Problems: mealy bugs, spider mites, needle drop and loss of lower branches (caused by dry air and dry soil)

Growth Rate: slow

Repot: biennially

Cleaning Tips: shower gently, remove dead needles and branches

Origins: New Guinea, Australia, New Hebrides, New Caledonia, Norfolk Island, Brazil

Notes: Keep potbound to restrict growth. Prefers cool light conditions.

Nerve Plant

Oleander

Oleander
Nerium oleander

A large, upright plant with lance-shaped, leathery foliage. Produces single, white, pink or red blooms in summer. Height: 2–6m; Spread: 1–3m. Direct light.

Ease of Care: moderate to difficult

Water: moist (keep soil consistently moist but not soggy)

Fertilizer: heavy (15-30-15 once every 2 weeks, February to October)

Propagation: seed, cutting, air layer

Common Plant Problems: aphids, mealy bugs, scale insects, spider mites

Growth Rate: medium

Repot: annually

Cleaning Tips: wipe leaves with a soft cloth or gently shower

Origins: Mediterranean to China

Notes: Wood and sap are poisonous, and contact with foliage may irritate skin. Water sparingly in winter. Sought after by collectors.

Olive Tree
Olea europaea

An upright plant with grey-green, leathery, elliptical to lance-shaped foliage. Produces panicles of creamy-white, fragrant blooms in spring. Height: 3m; Spread: 3m. Direct light.

Ease of Care: moderate

Water: medium (allow 1cm of the soil to dry out)

Fertilizer: heavy (10-6-16 once every 2 weeks, February to October)

Propagation: cutting, seeds

Common Plant Problems: scale insects, olive knot, verticillium wilt, mushroom root rot, lesion nematode, southern blight

Growth Rate: slow

Repot: biennially

Cleaning Tips: wipe leaves with a soft cloth or gently shower

Origins: Mediterranean

Notes: Keep small by pruning in spring. Sought after by collectors.

Orchid Group

Orchids are often thought of as fussy plants, but quite a few can be easily grown indoors provided they have the right growing conditions. Start with the easiest types (*Phalaenopsis* and *Paphiopedilum* are two). Orchids are expensive because they take a number of years to reach saleable size and, in some cases, are rare. Height: 15–120cm; Spread: 15–120cm. Bright indirect light.

Brassia Orchid
Spider Orchid
Brassia

A compact plant with an arching habit. Displays large, spherical pseudobulbs, each with long, green, strap-shaped leaves. Produces spider-like, fragrant, yellow-green blooms on 1–1.5m long spikes in May, lasting 4–8 weeks. Height: 45cm; Spread: 45cm. Bright indirect light.

Ease of Care: easy

Water: medium (allow 1cm of the orchid mix to dry out February to October; see Notes)

Fertilizer: heavy (orchid food once every 2 weeks, February to October)

Propagation: divide when plant fills the pot

Common Plant Problems: aphids, mealy bugs, scale insects, spider mites, fungal leaf and viral diseases

Growth Rate: medium

Repot: every 3 years in orchid mix

Cleaning Tips: wipe leaves with a soft cloth or gently shower, remove spent blooms

Origins: North, Central and South America

Notes: A cool-growing orchid that dislikes having its roots disturbed. Water freely in summer. Keep almost dry and lightly shaded in winter. Sought after by collectors.

Brassia Orchid

Cattleya Orchid

Cattleya Orchid
Corsage orchid
Cattleya

An upright plant with semi-rigid, leathery, oblong to ovate, medium-green foliage. Produces large, showy, waxy, single, white, yellow, green or pink blooms between spring and fall. Some varieties are fragrant. Height: 30cm–1.5m; Spread: 30–60cm. Direct light (but protect from hot sun).

Ease of Care: moderate
Water: medium (allow 1cm of the orchid mix to dry out)
Fertilizer: heavy (orchid food once every 2 weeks, February to October; see Notes)
Propagation: division
Common Plant Problems: aphids, mealy bugs, scale insects, spider mites, whiteflies, fungal and bacterial pseudobulb, leaf rot, viral diseases
Growth Rate: medium
Repot: biennially in orchid mix

Cleaning Tips: wipe leaves with a soft cloth or gently shower, remove spent blooms
Origins: Central and South America
Notes: Flowers last up to 2 weeks. Requires a 6-week rest period after flowering—water sparingly. Best time to repot is after flowering and rest period. Sought after by collectors.

Cymbidium Orchid
Cymbidium

An upright plant with mid-green, strap-shaped foliage and single, white, yellow, pink or red blooms in late winter or spring. Height: 30–90cm; Spread: 30–90cm. Bright indirect light.

Ease of Care: medium
Water: medium (allow 1cm of the orchid mix to dry out)
Fertilizer: heavy (orchid food once every 2 weeks, February to October)
Propagation: division
Common Plant Problems: mealy bugs, scale insects, spider mites
Growth Rate: medium
Repot: annually in orchid mix

Cymbidium Orchid

Moth Orchid

Cleaning Tips: wipe leaves with a soft cloth or gently shower, remove spent flower spikes

Origins: India, China, Japan, south-east Asia, Australia

Notes: Prefers cool temperatures (especially cool nights in fall to promote flowering). Sought after by collectors.

Dendrobium Orchid
Dendrobium

An upright plant with mid-green, strap-shaped foliage and single, white, yellow, pink or purple blooms appearing sporadically. Height: 30–120cm; Spread: 15–120cm. Bright indirect light.

Ease of Care: moderate

Water: medium (allow 1cm of the orchid mix to dry out)

Fertilizer: heavy (orchid food once every 2 weeks, February to October)

Propagation: division, stem cuttings, keikis (plantlets)

Common Plant Problems: aphids, mealy bugs, mites, whiteflies, leaf spots, viral diseases

Growth Rate: medium

Repot: biennially in orchid mix

Cleaning Tips: wipe leaves with a soft cloth or gently shower, remove spent blooms

Origins: India, south-east Asia, New Guinea, Australia, Pacific Islands

Notes: Flowers best in small containers. Sought after by collectors.

Moth Orchid
Phalaenopsis

A compact plant with oval, fleshy, medium-green foliage and flat-faced, single, white, yellow, pink, purple or red blooms that may appear continually. Height: 20–60cm; Spread: 20–30cm. Bright indirect light.

Ease of Care: easy

Water: medium (allow 1cm of the orchid mix to dry out)

Fertilizer: heavy (orchid food once every 2 weeks, February to October)

Propagation: keikis (plantlets)

Common Plant Problems: aphids, petal blight, bacterial soft rot, pseudobulb rots, cymbidium mosaic viral diseases, edema, iron deficiency

Growth Rate: medium

Repot: annually in orchid mix

Cleaning Tips: wipe leaves with a soft cloth or gently shower, remove spent flower spikes; see Notes

Origins: Himalayas, south-east Asia, North Australia

Notes: Flowers can last 1–6 months. When all flowers have finished blooming, cut back to the last node, before the scar left by the first flower that bloomed, and usually a new spike will develop. When repotting, make sure to soak orchid medium well. Do not force aerial roots down into potting mix. Sought after by collectors.

Odontoglossum Orchid
Tiger Orchid
Odontoglossum

An upright plant with green, strap-shaped foliage and single, white, yellow, olive-green, mauve or brown blooms in spring or summer. Height: 30–60cm; Spread: 30cm. Bright indirect light.

Ease of Care: moderate

Water: medium (allow 1cm of the orchid mix to dry out)

Fertilizer: heavy (orchid food once every 2 weeks, February to October)

Propagation: division

Common Plant Problems: aphids, mealy bugs, spider mites

Growth Rate: medium

Repot: biennially in orchid mix

Cleaning Tips: wipe leaves with a soft cloth or gently shower, remove spent flower spikes

Origins: Central and South America

Notes: Some varieties are fragrant. High humidity and a rest period promote reblooming. Sought after by collectors.

Oncidioda Orchid
Oncidioda sphacetante

An upright plant with mid-green, strap-shaped foliage and orange-red, dark-pink blooms in late summer. Height: 60cm; Spread: 20cm. Bright indirect light.

Ease of Care: moderate

Water: medium (allow 1cm of the orchid mix to dry out)

Fertilizer: heavy (orchid food once every 2 weeks, February to October)

Common Plant Problems: aphids, mealy bugs, spider mites

Growth Rate: medium

Repot: annually in orchid mix

Cleaning Tips: wipe leaves with a soft cloth or gently shower, remove spent flower spikes

Origins: man-made

Notes: Sought after by collectors.

Oncidium Orchid

Oncidium Orchid
Golden Shower Orchid, Dancing Ladies Orchid
Oncidium

A compact, upright plant with lance-shaped foliage. Produces single yellow, pink, maroon, yellow and brown blooms in summer. Some may bloom year-round. Height: 15–60cm; Spread: 30cm. Bright indirect light.

Ease of Care: easy

Water: medium (allow 1cm of the orchid mix to dry out)

Fertilizer: heavy (orchid food once every 2 weeks, February to October)

Propagation: division

Common Plant Problems: aphids, mealy bugs, scale insects, spider mites, leaf and bulb rots, grey mould, viral diseases

Growth Rate: medium

Repot: biennially in orchid mix

Cleaning Tips: wipe leaves with a soft cloth or gently shower, remove spent flower spikes

Origins: Mexico, Central and South America, West Indies

Notes: Some flowers last 1–2 months. Miniature Oncidium bears many spikes and blooms. Some varieties are fragrant. Sought after by collectors.

Slipper Orchid
Paphiopedilum

A compact, upright plant with green or mottled, ovate to lance-shaped foliage and single, yellow, rose, green, white, mahogany blooms between spring and fall. Height: 30cm; Spread: 15cm. Bright indirect light.

Ease of Care: easy

Water: medium (allow 1cm of the orchid mix to dry out)

Fertilizer: heavy (orchid food once every 2 weeks, February to October)

Propagation: division

Common Plant Problems: aphids, mealy bugs, spider mites, whiteflies, anthracnose, grey mould, bacterial rot, root rot, iron deficiency, cymbidium mosiac viral diseases

Growth Rate: slow

Repot: biennially in orchid mix

Cleaning Tips: wipe leaves with a soft cloth or gently shower, remove spent flower spikes

Origins: India, China, south-east Asia, Papua New Guinea

Notes: Good orchid for beginners. Do not over-water. Blooms can last 2–3 months. Sought after by collectors.

Slipper Orchid

Ornamental Pepper
Chili pepper
Capsicum anuum

This upright plant displays lance-shaped, slightly hairy, dark-green foliage. Produces single, white, insignificant blooms followed by small, brightly coloured fruit. Height: up to 45cm; Spread: up to 45cm. Direct light.

Ease of Care: easy

Water: moist (keep soil consistently moist but not soggy)

Fertilizer: heavy (10-6-16 once every 2 weeks, February to October)

Propagation: seed

Common Plant Problems: aphids, mites

Growth Rate: medium

Repot: no

Cleaning Tips: gently shower

Origins: tropical North and South America

Notes: Mist flowers daily to encourage fruiting. Pinch out growing tips to promote branching. Plant is usually discarded after fruit are finished.

Areca Palm

Palm Group

Many palms make wonderful house-plants, adding a tropical feel to our rooms and vertical interest. Leaf forms vary, as do heights, so you are sure to find a size to fit your needs. Height: 1–5+m; Spread: 1+m. Bright indirect light.

Areca Palm
Butterfly Plant, Golden Feather Palm
Chrysalidocarpus lutescens
An upright plant with narrow, mid-green foliage on tall, reed-like, arching stems. Height: 2m; Spread: 1m. Bright indirect light.

Ease of Care: easy
Water: moist (keep soil consistently moist but not soggy)
Fertilizer: heavy (10-6-16 once every 2 weeks, February to October)
Propagation: seed, rooted suckers
Common Plant Problems: mealy bugs, scale insects, spider mites
Growth Rate: slow
Repot: annually
Cleaning Tips: gently shower
Origins: Madagascar
Notes: Great feature plants, nicely fitting in bright corners. Display small specimens on stands if height is required.

Bamboo Palm
Chamaedorea erumpens
An upright plant with broad, ovate, dark-green foliage on arching stems. Height: 3+m; Spread: 1m. Bright indirect light.

Ease of Care: easy
Water: moist (keep soil consistently moist but not soggy)
Fertilizer: heavy (10-6-16 once every 2 weeks, February to October)
Propagation: seed
Common Plant Problems: mealy bugs, scale insects, spider mites
Growth Rate: medium
Repot: annually
Cleaning Tips: gently shower
Origins: Mexico, Central and South America
Notes: Stems are sectional and knotted like bamboo. Sought after by collectors.

Chinese Fan Palm
Livistona chinensis

This large upright plant displays its long foliage in a fan shape on toothed stalks. Height: 2m; Spread: 1m. Bright indirect light.

Ease of Care: moderate

Water: moist (keep soil consistently moist but not soggy)

Fertilizer: heavy (10-6-16 once every 2 weeks, February to October)

Propagation: seed

Common Plant Problems: scale insects, spider mites

Growth Rate: medium

Repot: biennially

Cleaning Tips: gently shower

Origins: Asia, Australia

Notes: Foliage tips droop—interesting looking. Sought after by collectors.

Fishtail Palm
Caryota mitis

This big palm has long, arching stems covered in mid-green, fishtail-shaped foliage, divided herring bone fashion, with tattered edges. Height: 3m; Spread: 2m. Bright indirect light.

Ease of Care: moderate

Water: moist (keep soil consistently moist but not soggy)

Fertilizer: heavy (10-6-16 once every 2 weeks, February to October)

Propagation: seed, offsets

Common Plant Problems: scale insects, spider mites, fungal leaf spots

Growth Rate: slow

Repot: biennially

Cleaning Tips: gently shower

Origins: India and Sri Lanka to southeast Asia, North Australia and the Solomon Islands

Notes: Fishtail palms like to have their roots restricted—repot only as needed. Sought after by collectors.

Fishtail Palm

Kentia Palm
Sentry Palm, Thatch Leaf Palm
Howea forsteriana

A wide-spreading palm with foliage displayed on large fronds up to 3m long. Height: 3m; Spread: 3m. Bright indirect light.

Ease of Care: moderate

Water: medium (allow 1cm of the soil to dry out)

Fertilizer: heavy (10-6-16 once every 2 weeks, February to October)

Propagation: seed

Common Plant Problems: scale insects, spider mites

Growth Rate: medium

Repot: annually

Cleaning Tips: gently shower

Origins: Australia

Notes: This slow-growing palm is only grown from seed and may take up to 6 years to reach a saleable-size, resulting in an expensive plant. Sought after by collectors.

Lady Palm
Miniature Fan Palm
Rhapis excelsa

Attractive, upright fan palm with dark-green foliage arranged in whorls on top of stems. Height: 1.5–5m; Spread: 1.5–5m. Bright indirect light.

Kentia Palm

Ease of Care: moderate

Water: medium (allow 1cm of the soil to dry out)

Fertilizer: heavy (10-6-16 once every 2 weeks, February to October)

Propagation: seed, suckers

Common Plant Problems: scale insects, spider mites, leaf spots

Growth Rate: medium

Repot: biennially

Cleaning Tips: gently shower

Origins: south China to south-east Asia

Notes: Excellent indoor palm—tolerant of indoor conditions. Sought after by collectors.

Majesty Palm
Ravenea rivularis

An upright plant with elegant, feather-like foliage. Height: 2–3m; Spread: 1.5m. Bright indirect light.

Ease of Care: moderate

Water: moist (keep soil consistently moist but not soggy)

Fertilizer: heavy (10-6-16 once every 2 weeks, February to October)

Common Plant Problems: spider mites

Growth Rate: medium

Repot: biennially

Cleaning Tips: gently shower

Origins: Madagascar

Notes: Tolerates low light and cool conditions.

Parlor Palm
Neanthe Bella Palm,
Good Luck Palm
Chamaedorea elegans

A very popular, compact, upright and small palm with medium-green foliage on arching stems. Height: 1m; Spread: 1m. Bright indirect light.

Ease of Care: easy

Water: moist (keep soil consistently moist but not soggy)

Fertilizer: heavy (10-6-16 once every 2 weeks, February to October)

Propagation: seed, not practical in the home

Common Plant Problems: mealy bugs, scale insects, spider mites

Growth Rate: slow

Repot: annually

Cleaning Tips: gently shower

Origins: Mexico, Central and South America

Notes: Excellent palm for lower light areas. Grows very slowly and may take several years to reach 1m. Sought after by collectors.

Majesty Palm

Ponytail Palm
Beaucarnea recurvata

Interesting long, strap-like, dark-green foliage arches up and out of a large, swollen, bulb-like base. Height: 2m; Spread: 1m. Direct light.

Ease of Care: easy

Water: medium (allow 1cm of the soil to dry out)

Fertilizer: heavy (10-6-16 once every 2 weeks, February to October)

Propagation: seed, offsets

Common Plant Problems: mealy bugs, scale insects, spider mites

Growth Rate: slow

Repot: annually

Cleaning Tips: gently shower

Origins: semi-desert and scrub from the southern United States to Guatemala

Notes: Do not over-water. Sought after by collectors.

Pygmy Date Palm
Miniature Date Palm
Phoenix roebelenii

This upright plant displays very narrow, arching, mid-green foliage on long stems. Height: 1m; Spread: 1.5m. Bright indirect light.

Ease of Care: easy

Water: medium (allow 1cm of the soil to dry out)

Fertilizer: heavy (10-6-16 once every 2 weeks, February to October)

Propagation: seed

Common Plant Problems: mealy bugs, scale insects, spider mites

Growth Rate: slow

Repot: biennially

Cleaning Tips: gently shower

Origins: Laos, south-east Asia

Notes: A very slow-growing palm. Mist regularly. Sought after by collectors.

Reed Palm
Chamaedorea siefrizii

A small, clump-forming, upright palm with lacy, delicate-looking, deep bluish-green leaves on slender reed-like stems. Height: 1.5m; Spread: 1m. Bright indirect light.

Ease of Care: easy

Water: medium (allow 1cm of the soil to dry out)

Fertilizer: heavy (10-6-16 once every 2 weeks, February to October)

Propagation: seed

Common Plant Problems: mealy bugs, scale insects, spider mites

Growth Rate: medium

Repot: annually

Cleaning Tips: gently shower

Origins: Mexico, Central and South America

Notes: A good choice for rooms where a larger palm would not fit. Sought after by collectors.

Ponytail Palm

Sago Palm
Fern Palm
Cycas revoluta

An extremely slow-growing cycad with dark-green, fan-shaped foliage on arching stems. Height: 60cm; Spread: 60cm. Bright indirect light.

Ease of Care: moderate

Water: medium (allow 1cm of the soil to dry out)

Fertilizer: heavy (10-6-16 once every 2 weeks, February to October)

Propagation: seed

Common Plant Problems: mealy bugs, scale insects, spider mites

Growth Rate: slow

Repot: biennially

Cleaning Tips: gently shower

Origins: Madagascar, south and southeast Asia, Australia, Pacific islands

Notes: A good palm to purchase in the size that closely meets your needs, as it is very slow growing, producing only one leaf a year. Sought after by collectors.

Windmill Palm
Trachycarpus fortunei

A large, upright plant with long foliage displayed in a fan shape on finely toothed stalks. Height: 2–3+m; Spread: 1+m. Bright indirect light.

Ease of Care: moderate

Water: moist (keep soil consistently moist but not soggy)

Fertilizer: heavy (10-6-16 once every 2 weeks, February to October)

Propagation: seed

Common Plant Problems: scale insects, spider mites

Growth Rate: medium

Repot: annually

Cleaning Tips: gently shower

Origins: Asia

Notes: Young leaves are pleated and covered with fine grey hair. As the leaf ages, the hair disappears and the pleats divide into segments.

Zamia Palm

Zamia Palm
Cardboard Palm
Zamia

A small cycad with dark-green, oblong to ovate leaflets on swollen stems. Height: 1.5m; Spread: 1m. Bright indirect light.

Ease of Care: moderate

Water: medium (allow 1cm of the soil to dry out)

Fertilizer: moderate (10-6-16 full strength once per month, February to October)

Propagation: seed

Common Plant Problems: mealy bugs, scale insects, leaf spots

Growth Rate: slow

Repot: annually

Cleaning Tips: gently shower

Origins: North to South America

Notes: Leaves grow in whorls that are pale-green as they open, aging to olive-green with a rusty coating. Sought after by collectors.

Paperwhite
Narcissus

A popular bulb to force for indoor floral displays. Foliage is lance-shaped and the single, white blooms held atop stems are very fragrant. Each bulb may produce as many as 3 or 4 bloom stalks per bulb. A good bulb for forcing in water. Height: 35cm. Direct light.

Ease of Care: easy

Water: medium (allow 1cm of the soil to dry out)

Fertilizer: no

Propagation: separate bulbs

Common Plant Problems: bulb fly, bulb scale mite

Growth Rate: medium

Repot: no

Origins: south France, south Spain, North Africa

Notes: Plant outdoors in spring.

Parrot Plant
Congo Cockatoo
Impatiens niamniamensis

An upright plant with dark-green, oval leaves. Produces hooded, single, bright-red and yellow blooms in summer, each with a distinctive spur. Height: 60cm; Spread: 30cm. Bright indirect light.

Ease of Care: moderate

Water: moist (keep soil consistently moist but not soggy)

Fertilizer: Moderate (15-30-15 once every 2 weeks, February to October)

Propagation: seed, cutting

Common Plant Problems: aphids

Growth Rate: medium

Repot: annually

Cleaning Tips: remove spent blooms

Origins: tropical and warm temperate regions

Notes: A short-lived novelty plant. Sought after by collectors.

Passion Flower
Passiflora caerulea

This vining plant is usually grown outdoors, but it can be grown inside over winter (normally will not flower indoors). Produces roundly ovate, 3 to 5-lobed leaves. White blooms are unusual with reflexed petals fully showing the flowers' blue corollas in summer. Height: 3+m; Spread: 3+m. Direct light.

Ease of Care: moderate

Water: moist (keep soil consistently moist but not soggy)

Fertilizer: heavy (15-30-15 once every 2 weeks, February to October)

Propagation: seed, cutting, air layer

Common Plant Problems: scale insects, spider mites, whiteflies, leaf spots, viral diseases, iron deficiency

Growth Rate: fast

Repot: annually

Cleaning Tips: shower gently

Origins: tropical North, Central and South America, tropical Asia, Australia, New Zealand, Pacific islands

Paperwhite

Passion Flower

Ease of Care: easy

Water: medium (allow 1cm of the soil to dry out)

Fertilizer: heavy (10-6-16 once every 2 weeks, February to October)

Propagation: division

Common Plant Problems: leaf spot, root rot, bacterial soft rot

Growth Rate: medium

Repot: annually

Cleaning Tips: wipe with a soft cloth or gently shower, remove spent blooms

Origins: Indonesia, Philippines, tropical North, Central and South America

Notes: Because it is easily divided, this plant is an economical choice. Blooms drop pollen.

Peace Lily 'Domino'
Spathiphyllum

A very useful, bushy plant for lower light areas, this upright plant displays glossy, lance-shaped, mottled green and white foliage. Produces single, white to cream blooms heavily in spring and sporadically throughout year. Height: 60cm; Spread: 45cm. Bright indirect light.

Peace Lily

Notes: Can be trained around hoops or be supported by a trellis. Cut down to 15cm in early spring. Repot annually, but use a pot no bigger than 20cm as overpotting will produce lots of leaves and no flowers. Sought after by collectors.

Peace Lily
Spathiphyllum

A very useful, bushy plant for lower light areas, this upright plant displays glossy, lance-shaped, dark-green foliage. Produces single, white to cream blooms heavily in spring and sporadically throughout the year. Height: 60–90cm; Spread: 60cm. Bright indirect light.

Peperomia

Growth Rate: medium

Repot: annually

Cleaning Tips: wipe fleshy smooth types with a soft cloth or gently shower, gently shower textured types, remove spent blooms

Origins: tropical and subtropical regions worldwide

Notes: Bushy types are useful plants for container gardens. Trailing types are best grown in hanging baskets or on a stand where stems can hang freely.

Persian Buttercup
Ranunculus asiaticus

An upright, spring flowering plant with dark-green, shiny foliage. Produces buttercup-shaped, white, yellow, orange or red blooms in spring. Height: 20–30cm; Spread: 15cm. Bright indirect light.

Ease of Care: moderate

Water: moist (keep soil consistently moist but not soggy)

Fertilizer: no

Propagation: seed

Growth Rate: medium

Repot: no

Cleaning Tips: remove spent blooms

Origins: worldwide

Notes: Prefers a cool location. Usually discarded after blooming.

Peperomia Group
Peperomia

An attractive group of plants comprising bushy, trailing and upright types. Foliage varies from textured with prominent veins to thick, fleshy leaves, and includes many shapes and colours. Some produce white spikes of blooms in summer. Height: 20–30cm; Spread: 20–30cm; Trails: 30cm. Bright indirect light.

Ease of Care: easy

Water: medium (allow 1cm of the soil to dry out)

Fertilizer: heavy (10-6-16 once every 2 weeks, February to October)

Propagation: cutting

Common Plant Problems: leaf drop, leaf rot (caused by over-watering), leaf browning (caused by allowing plant to wilt before watering)

Persian Buttercup

Persian Shield
Strobilanthes dyerianus

This upright plant has become quite popular as an outdoor annual foliage plant. Foliage is long, pointed and dark green with a silvery-purple sheen. Height: 1–2m; Spread: 1m. Bright indirect light.

Ease of Care: difficult

Water: medium (allow 1cm of the soil to dry out)

Fertilizer: heavy (10-6-16 once every 2 weeks, February to October)

Propagation: cutting

Common Plant Problems: spider mites

Growth Rate: medium

Repot: annually

Cleaning Tips: gently shower

Origins: Burma

Notes: Prefers high humidity—mist often. Old plants get straggly—start new plants with cuttings. Sought after by collectors.

Persian Violet
Exacum affine

A small, compact and tidy plant, often given as a gift. Displays small, oval, medium-green foliage and produces fragrant, single, violet to blue, pink or white blooms in summer. Height: 25–30cm; Spread: 25–30cm. Bright indirect light.

Ease of Care: easy

Water: moist (keep soil consistently moist but not soggy)

Fertilizer: no

Propagation: seed

Common Plant Problems: aphids

Growth Rate: slow

Repot: no

Cleaning Tips: remove spent blooms

Origins: Yemen, India

Notes: Usually discarded once flowering has finished. Purchase plants that include some unopened buds to help prolong flowering period.

Persian Violet

Peruvian Lily
Peruvian Lily
Alstroemeria

Sold as a flowering plant, Peruvian lily is upright in habit with lance-shaped, mid-green foliage. Produces single, white, pink or yellow blooms in summer. Height: 45cm; Spread: 30–60cm. Direct light.

Ease of Care: easy

Water: moist (keep soil consistently moist but not soggy)

Fertilizer: heavy (15-30-15 once every 2 weeks, February to October)

Propagation: seed, divide tubers in spring

Common Plant Problems: aphids, mites

Growth Rate: medium

Repot: annually

Cleaning Tips: remove spent blooms

Origins: South America

Notes: Rhizomes can be stored over winter in a cool dry location. Sought after by collectors.

Heart Leaf Philodendron

Philodendron Group

A very popular group of plants that include climbing and non-climbing types. Climbing types require support and may produce aerial roots on their stems (grow them on a moss stick and push the aerial roots into the moss). Non-climbing types can become very large plants. Height: 1–3.5+m; Spread: 30cm–2+m. Bright indirect light (give variegated types more light).

Ease of Care: easy

Water: medium (allow 1cm of the soil to dry out)

Fertilizer: heavy (10-6-16 once every 2 weeks, February to October)

Propagation: cutting, air layering

Common Plant Problems: mealy bugs, scale insects, spider mites, fungal and bacterial leaf spots, root rot (caused by over-watering in winter)

Growth Rate: fast

Repot: annually

Cleaning Tips: wipe leaves with a soft cloth or gently shower

Origins: Florida, Mexico, West Indies, Central and tropical South America

Notes: All philodendrons prefer fairly high humidity.

Heart Leaf Philodendron
Sweetheart Plant
Philodendron scandens

A climbing type with a vining habit. Displays heart-shaped, glossy, dark-green foliage. An excellent plant for low-light areas. Can be grown in a hanging basket or on a moss pole or frame. Trails: 3m; Spread: 3m. Bright indirect light.

Philodendron 'Autumn'
Philodendron x 'Autumn'

This non-climbing, new hybrid variety has foliage that emerges copper-bronze and ages to glossy, dark olive. Height: 60cm; Spread: 60cm. Bright indirect light.

Philodendron 'Brazil'
Philodendron

A climbing hybrid variety that grows best on a moss pole or in a hanging basket. Foliage is rounded and splashed with creams and greens. Trails: 3–3.5m; Spread: 1m. Bright indirect light.

Origins: rainforest in Florida, Mexico, West Indies, Central and tropical South America

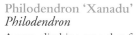

Philodendron 'Brazil'

Philodendron 'Prince Albert'
Philodendron

An upright, bushy plant with large, burgundy-coloured leaves. Makes an excellent contrast plant in groupings. Height: 60cm; Spread: 1m. Bright indirect light.

Notes: Sought after by collectors.

Philodendron 'Xanadu'
Philodendron

A non-climbing type that forms a large neat clump in the pot. Foliage is oval, pointed and dark green. Height: 90cm; Spread: 90cm. Bright indirect light.

Origins: Australia

Philodendron 'Xanadu'

Philodendron Monstera
Monstera, Splitleaf Philodendron,
Swiss Cheese Plant
Monstera deliciosa

A large, fast-growing, upright plant
with gigantic, dark-green leaves that
are perforated and deeply cut. Requires
sturdy support (grow on a moss stick
and push aerial roots into the moss
or tuck into soil). Height: 3m. Bright
indirect light.

Origins: Mexico to Panama

Philodendron Selloum
Lacy Tree Philodendron
Philodendron selloum

A non-climbing, tree type plant with
glossy, green, large, deeply cut, ovate
foliage with ruffled edges. A good
specimen plant for a large area. Height:
2+m; Spread: 2m. Bright indirect light.

Origins: south-east Brazil

Notes: Sought after by collectors.

Philodendron Selloum

Piggyback Plant
Thousand Mothers, Youth-on-Age
Tolmiea menziesii

A lovely, spreading plant that performs
well in a cool, shady environment.
Downy, bright-green, mature foliage
support tiny plantlets in piggyback-
fashion. Height: 30cm; Spread: 30cm.
Bright indirect light.

Ease of Care: easy

Water: moist (keep soil consistently
moist but not soggy)

Fertilizer: heavy (10-6-16 once every
2 weeks, February to October)

Propagation: plantlets

Common Plant Problems: mealy bugs,
rust

Growth Rate: medium

Repot: annually

Cleaning Tips: gently shower

Origins: western North America

Notes: Dislikes hot, dry air—keep away
from heat vents. Can be grown in a
hanging basket.

Pilea Group
Friendship Plant
Pilea

This group of plants has an upright and spreading to trailing habit. Produces textured oval foliage that is attractively marked. Height: 3–30cm; Spread: 15–30cm. Bright indirect light.

Aluminum Plant
Friendship Plant
Pilea cadierei

Upright in habit, this tough plant's textured oval foliage is green and at-tractively marked with silver patches. Height: 30cm; Spread: 15–20cm. Bright indirect light.

Ease of Care: easy

Water: medium (allow 1cm of the soil to dry out)

Fertilizer: heavy (10-6-16 once every 2 weeks, February to October)

Propagation: cutting

Common Plant Problems: mealy bugs, spider mites

Growth Rate: slow

Repot: biennially

Cleaning Tips: gently shower

Origins: rainforests in tropical regions

Notes: A useful plant for container gardens. Because these plants deteriorate with age, it is best to start fresh with cuttings.

Friendship Plant
Pilea involvcrata

An upright plant that produces quilted, oval foliage with dark, visible veins and clustered white blooms. Height: 30cm; Spread: 15–30cm. Bright indirect light.

Ease of Care: easy

Water: medium (allow 1cm of the soil to dry out)

Fertilizer: heavy (10-6-16 once every 2 weeks, February to October)

Propagation: cutting

Common Plant Problems: mealy bugs, spider mites

Growth Rate: medium

Repot: annually

Cleaning Tips: gently shower

Origins: rainforests in tropical regions

Notes: Because these plants deteriorate with age, it is best to start fresh with cuttings.

Pilea involucrata

Pineapple Plant

Pineapple Lily
Eucomis

Grown from a true bulb, this unusual plant has an upright habit with lance-shaped, light-green foliage. Produces masses of tiny, star-like, green, white or pink blooms in summer borne on a thick stalk tipped with a rosette of small, green leaves. Height: 30–60cm. Direct light.

Ease of Care: easy

Water: medium (allow 1cm of the soil to dry out)

Fertilizer: heavy (10-6-16 once every 2 weeks, February to October)

Propagation: offsets

Common Plant Problems: infrequent

Growth Rate: medium

Repot: annually

Cleaning Tips: wipe with a soft cloth

Origins: South Africa

Notes: As plants go dormant, over-winter them in a cool, frost-free place. Sought after by collectors.

Pineapple Plant
Ananas comosus variegatus

An upright plant with spiny, lance shaped foliage that is dark green or dark green with yellow stripes. Mature plants produce reddish-yellow bracts on long stalks with violet blooms in summer, followed by bright-red, inedible fruit. Garden centres often group this plant with bromeliads. Height: 1m; Spread: 50cm. Direct light.

Ease of Care: moderate

Water: dry (allow 3cm of soil to dry out thoroughly before watering)

Fertilizer: moderate (10-6-16 full strength once per month, February to October)

Propagation: basal offsets, cuttings

Common Plant Problems: mealy bugs, scale insects, fruit rot

Growth Rate: medium

Repot: annually

Cleaning Tips: wipe leaves with a soft cloth or gently shower

Origins: Brazil

Notes: Water freely during growing season, but keep barely moist for the rest of the year. Root basal offsets in early summer, or sever leafy rosette at top of fruit and allow to callus before rooting in a mix of peat and sand. Sought after by collectors.

Pineapple Lily

Plumbago

Cape Leadwort

Plumbago auriculata

A vigorous climber with bright matte-green, oblong to spoon-shaped leaves and single, sky-blue or white blooms in summer. Height: 3m; Spread: 1m. Direct light.

Ease of Care: moderate

Water: moist (keep soil consistently moist but not soggy)

Fertilizer: heavy (15-30-15 once every 2 weeks, February to October)

Propagation: cutting

Common Plant Problems: mealy bugs, spider mites

Growth Rate: fast

Repot: annually

Cleaning Tips: wipe leaves with a soft cloth or gently shower

Origins: South Africa

Notes: Flowers are produced on current year's growth. Cut back by 2/3rds in spring. This plant's weak stems can reach 1.5m and need support. Sought after by collectors.

Plush Vine

Mikania dentata (syn. M. ternata)

A very pretty trailing plant with hairy, greenish-purple, palmate foliage with purple veins and purple undersides. Height: 20–25cm; Trails: 30+cm. Bright indirect light.

Ease of Care: moderate

Water: moist (keep soil consistently moist but not soggy)

Fertilizer: heavy (10-6-16 once every 2 weeks, February to October)

Propagation: cutting

Common Plant Problems: spider mites

Growth Rate: fast

Repot: annually

Cleaning Tips: blow on gently or brush carefully with a soft paintbrush

Origins: central and south Brazil

Notes: Although this plant prefers high humidity it doesn't like to be misted— try growing in a humid room.

Poinsettia

Euphorbia pulcherrima

An upright plant, traditionally grown for the Christmas season. Foliage is a deep green with colourful bracts available in shades of white, pink, red, burgundy and other variations. Height: 60cm; Spread: 60cm. Direct light.

Ease of Care: easy

Water: medium (allow 1cm of the soil to dry out)

Fertilizer: no

Propagation: cutting

Common Plant Problems: spider mites, whiteflies

Growth Rate: medium

Repot: no

Cleaning Tips: remove dead foliage

Origins: Mexico

Notes: Very susceptible to cold— keep away from cold drafts. Usually discarded at the end of season.

Plumbago

Polka Dot Plant
Freckle Face
Hypoestes phyllostachya
A pretty little plant with oval, green foliage spotted with pink, white or red. Height: 30cm; Spread: 25cm. Bright indirect light.

Ease of Care: easy

Water: moist (keep soil consistently moist but not soggy)

Fertilizer: heavy (10-6-16 once every 2 weeks, February to October)

Propagation: seed, cutting

Common Plant Problems: infrequent

Growth Rate: medium

Repot: annually

Cleaning Tips: gently shower

Origins: Madagascar

Notes: A useful plant for providing contrast in houseplant arrangements. Pinch growing tips to promote bushiness. Older plants may get straggly—take cuttings to start new ones.

Pot Mum
Chrysanthemum morifolium
A compact, upright, flowering plant. Foliage is mid-green to dark-green and deeply lobed. Produces single or double, white, pink, purple or yellow blooms usually only once indoors. Height: 30–45cm; Spread: 30cm. Bright indirect light.

Ease of Care: easy

Water: moist (keep soil consistently moist but not soggy)

Fertilizer: no

Growth Rate: medium

Repot: no

Cleaning Tips: remove spent blooms

Origins: Mediterranean

Notes: Usually discarded once finished blooming.

Polka Dot Plant

Polyantha Primrose

Primula Group
Primrose
Primula

A very popular group of spring-flowering plants prized for their pretty blooms that are, more often than not, quite fragrant. Usually these plants are treated the same as long-lasting flower arrangements and discarded once blooming has finished. Bright, cool rooms will help prolong blooming. Keep them tidy by pinching off spent blooms and foliage. Height: 15–45cm; Spread: 15–30cm. Bright indirect light.

Ease of Care: easy

Water: moist (keep soil consistently moist but not soggy)

Fertilizer: no

Propagation: seed

Common Plant Problems: aphids, spider mites

Growth Rate: medium

Repot: no

Cleaning Tips: remove spent blooms

Origins: China

Notes: A cool location will help prolong blooming. Most can be replanted outdoors in a shady, moist area.

Fairy Primrose
Primrose
Primula malacoides

A tall primrose with flowers borne above the foliage on long stalks. Foliage is hairy and pale green with a scalloped edge. Produces small, fragrant, single, white, pink, mauve, purple, yellow or red blooms in spring. Height: 30–45cm; Spread: 20cm. Bright indirect light.

German Primrose
Poison Primrose
Primula obconica

A compact, upright primrose with flowers borne above the foliage on long stalks. Mid-green foliage is coarse and oval to heart shaped and on contact can cause a skin rash. Produces large, fragrant, single, pink, lilac-blue, red or white blooms in spring. Height: 25–40cm; Spread: 25cm. Bright indirect light.

Polyantha Primrose
Primrose
Primula x *polyantha*

A lovely small, flowering plant with oval, heavily veined, dark-green foliage. Produces single, white, yellow, orange, red or purple blooms in spring. Yellow blooms are fragrant. Height: 15–20cm; Spread: 15cm. Bright indirect light.

Fairy Primrose

Pothos

Pothos Group

Epipremnum sp. *(syn. Scindapsus* sp.)

This group of climbing plants is best grown on a moss stick for support or in a hanging basket. Glossy foliage varies from green with yellow markings to green with creamy-white markings. Trails: 2+m. Bright indirect light.

Ease of Care: moderate

Water: medium (allow 1cm of the soil to dry out)

Fertilizer: heavy (10-6-16 once every 2 weeks, February to October)

Propagation: cutting

Common Plant Problems: mealy bugs, scale insects, spider mites, leaf spot

Growth Rate: medium

Repot: annually

Cleaning Tips: wipe with a soft cloth or gently shower

Origins: south-east Asia to west Pacific

Notes: Take care not to over-water in winter.

Golden Pothos
Devil's Ivy
Epipremnum aureus
(syn. Scindapsus aureus)

A popular climbing plant with heart-shaped green foliage marked with yellow. Trails: 2+m. Bright indirect light.

Pothos 'Lemon Lime'
Epipremnum aureum
(syn. Scindapsus aureus)

A great plant for adding contrast to a grouping. Produces heart-shaped, lime-coloured foliage with lemon markings. Trails: 2+m. Bright indirect light.

Pothos 'Marble Queen'
Epipremnum aureum pinnatum
(syn. Scindapsus aureus)

A pothos with heart-shaped foliage that is more white than green, giving the appearance the leaves have been splashed. Trails: 2m. Bright indirect light.

Satin Pothos
Satin Pothos 'Argyraeus'
Scindapsus pictus

Bearing smaller leaves than other pothos, this plant is also slower growing and only requires repotting biennially. Produces olive-green, satin-textured foliage marked with silver. Trails: 45–90cm. Bright indirect light.

Golden Pothos

Prayer Plant

Prayer Plant
Maranta leuconeura

Commonly named prayer plant because the foliage has a habit of folding upwards at night. Produces elliptic to ovate, dark-green foliage with striking bright-red mid ribs and veins. Height: 20cm; Spread: 20cm. Bright indirect light.

Ease of Care: easy

Water: moist (keep soil consistently moist but not soggy)

Fertilizer: heavy (10-6-16 once every 2 weeks, February to October)

Propagation: cutting, division

Common Plant Problems: mealy bugs, spider mites

Growth Rate: medium

Repot: biennially

Cleaning Tips: wipe with a soft cloth or gently shower

Origins: Brazil

Notes: Reduce watering in winter and keep out of cold drafts. Prefers high humidity.

Purple Passion Vine
Purple Velvet Plant
Gynura aurantiaca
(syn. *G. sarmentosa*)

A very pretty trailing plant with hairy, velvety, purple foliage. It produces smelly, single, yellow blooms in summer that are usually pinched off. Height: 1–3m; Trails: 1m. Direct light.

Ease of Care: moderate

Water: medium (allow 1cm of the soil to dry out)

Fertilizer: heavy (10-6-16 once every 2 weeks, February to October)

Propagation: cutting

Common Plant Problems: aphids, spider mites

Growth Rate: medium

Repot: annually

Cleaning Tips: wipe with a soft paintbrush

Origins: Java, Africa, Asia

Notes: If not grown in bright light, the leaves will revert to dark green. Pinch back growing tips to encourage a compact, full plant.

Pussy Ears
Teddy Bear Vine
Cyanotis somaliensis

A pretty trailing plant with deep olive-green, hairy foliage flushed with purple. Produces single, mauve-blue blooms in summer. Height: 15cm; Spread: 40cm. Bright indirect light.

Ease of Care: moderate

Water: medium (allow 1cm of the soil to dry out)

Fertilizer: heavy (10-6-16 once every 2 weeks, February to October)

Propagation: cutting

Common Plant Problems: infrequent

Growth Rate: medium

Repot: annually

Cleaning Tips: remove spent blooms and dead foliage

Origins: Africa, Asia

Notes: Grow in a hanging basket or on a stand that allows the plants to trail freely.

Pussy Ears

Sensitive Plant

Sensitive Plant
Humble Plant, Touch Me Not
Mimosa pudica

This upright plant gets its common names because it reacts to touch by folding up its leaves. Long, thin, bright-green to greyish-green foliage is divided into sections. Produces fluffy, pompon, mauve-pink blooms in summer. Height: 50cm; Spread: 25–40cm. Direct light.

Ease of Care: moderate

Water: moist (keep soil consistently moist but not soggy)

Fertilizer: heavy (10-6-16 once every 2 weeks, February to October)

Propagation: seed, cutting

Common Plant Problems: rust, spider mites

Growth Rate: slow

Repot: biennially as required

Cleaning Tips: no

Origins: forest to dry savanna in tropical regions

Notes: Leaves can take up to one hour to recover from being touched. Sought after by collectors.

Shamrock
Good Luck Plant
Oxalis regnelli

This little, upright plant produces clover-like foliage on top of slender stalks. Single, white or pink blooms appear in spring and summer and sporadically throughout the year. Height: 25cm; Spread: 15cm. Bright indirect light.

Ease of Care: easy

Water: moist (keep soil consistently moist but not soggy)

Fertilizer: heavy (15-30-15 once every 2 weeks, February to October)

Propagation: seed, division

Common Plant Problems: spider mites, powdery mildew, fungal leaf spots

Growth Rate: medium

Repot: annually

Cleaning Tips: gently shower

Origins: Africa, South America

Notes: Leaves close up at night or if touched. If leaves start to die back, the plant is entering dormancy. Stop watering and store in a cool dark place for 1 to 3 months. When new leaves emerge, put in sun and start watering again.

Shamrock

Silk Oak Tree
Grevillea robusta

An upright plant with pretty fern-like foliage that is dark green above with pale undersides. Height: 1.5–2+m; Spread: 60cm. Direct light.

Ease of Care: easy

Water: moist (keep soil consistently moist but not soggy)

Fertilizer: heavy (10-6-16 once every 2 weeks, February to October)

Propagation: seed

Common Plant Problems: mealy bugs, scale insects

Growth Rate: fast

Repot: annually

Cleaning Tips: gently shower

Origins: Queensland, New South Wales

Notes: Smaller sizes of this plant are useful in houseplant arrangements. Enjoys a cool, bright spot. This fast-growing plant can reach 2m in 2 or 3 years. Sought after by collectors.

Silver Shield
King of Hearts
Homalomena wallisii

Displaying a compact, upright habit this plant has dark-green, heart-shaped leaves on long stalks. Height: 65cm; Spread: 45cm. Bright indirect light.

Ease of Care: moderate

Water: moist (keep soil consistently moist but not soggy)

Fertilizer: heavy (10-6-16 once every 2 weeks, February to October)

Propagation: division

Common Plant Problems: spider mites

Growth Rate: slow

Repot: biennially

Cleaning Tips: wipe leaves with a soft cloth or gently shower

Origins: tropical regions of Asia and the Americas

Notes: Sought after by collectors.

Slipper Flower
Pouch Flower, Slipperwort
Calceolaria Herbeohybrida Group

Sold in garden centres as a spring-flowering plant prized for its unusual pouch-shaped blooms. Produces soft, hairy, mid-green foliage and yellow, orange or red blooms with spots in spring. Flowers annually. Height: 20–45cm; Spread: 15–30cm. Bright indirect light.

Ease of Care: moderate

Water: moist (keep soil consistently moist but not soggy)

Fertilizer: no

Propagation: seed

Common Plant Problems: spider mites

Growth Rate: slow

Repot: no

Cleaning Tips: remove spent blooms

Origins: Mexico, Central and South America

Notes: Usually discarded when plant is finished blooming.

Silver Shield

Snake Plant

Snake Plant
Mother-in-Law's Tongue
Sansevieria trifasciata

An excellent plant that can withstand neglect—perfect for beginners. Fleshy, rigid foliage is upright, dark green and attractively mottled and striped. The tip of each leaf is slightly barbed, hence the nasty common name mother-in-law's tongue. Height: 1.5m; Spread: 50cm. Bright indirect light.

Ease of Care: easy

Water: medium (allow 1cm of the soil to dry out)

Fertilizer: heavy (10-6-16 once every 2 weeks, February to October)

Propagation: division, leaf cuttings

Common Plant Problems: mealy bugs, spider mites

Growth Rate: slow

Repot: biennially

Cleaning Tips: wipe leaves with a soft cloth or gently shower

Origins: Africa, Madagascar, India, Indonesia

Notes: Do not repot until the plant completely fills the pot.

Spider Plant
Chlorophytum comosum

An extremely popular plant with lance- or strap-shaped, arching foliage that can be striped with white or cream. Produces single, white, insignificant blooms on long, arching stems throughout the year that develop into plantlets. Height: 15–20cm; Spread: 15–30cm. Bright indirect light.

Ease of Care: easy

Water: moist (keep soil consistently moist but not soggy)

Fertilizer: heavy (10-6-16 once every 2 weeks, February to October)

Propagation: seed, root plantlets

Common Plant Problems: tip burn (caused by excess salts, fluoride or dry soil)

Growth Rate: medium

Repot: annually

Cleaning Tips: gently shower, remove dead foliage

Origins: South and West Africa

Notes: Best in a hanging basket or on a stand where the foliage and stems can hang freely. Do not hang over heat registers.

Spider Plant Chlorophytum comosum

Spider Plant

Chlorophytum orchidastrum

An upright plant displaying broad, lance-shaped, dark-green foliage with a prominent orange centre stripe and stem. Height: 35cm; Spread: 35cm. Bright indirect light.

Ease of Care: easy

Water: moist (keep soil consistently moist but not soggy)

Fertilizer: heavy (10-6-16 once every 2 weeks, February to October)

Propagation: seed, cutting

Common Plant Problems: black leaf tips (caused by drying out between watering)

Growth Rate: medium

Repot: annually

Cleaning Tips: wipe with a soft cloth or gently shower

Origins: South and West Africa

Notes: Dislikes cold drafts. Sought after by collectors.

Stephanotis

Floradora, Madagascar Jasmine
Stephanotis floribunda

A large, flowering vine with oval, thick, glossy, mid-green to dark-green foliage. Produces fragrant, single, white blooms in summer. Height: 3–6m; Spread: indefinite. Direct light.

Ease of Care: moderate

Water: moist (keep soil consistently moist but not soggy)

Fertilizer: heavy (15-30-15 once every 2 weeks, February to October)

Propagation: cutting, seed

Common Plant Problems: mealy bugs, scale insects, viral diseases

Growth Rate: medium

Repot: annually

Cleaning Tips: gently shower

Origins: Madagascar

Notes: Support climbing stems with a trellis. Often used in corsages and boutonnières. Sought after by collectors.

Stephanotis

Succulents

Succulent is a catchall term for a very large group of plants that share the ability to store water in their leaves and stems. This single characteristic allows the inclusion of plants with vastly different shapes, forms and sizes. This is a very easy group of plants to grow and they are seriously collected around the globe. They all require well-drained soil and more water in active growth periods and less in resting periods. Height: 3cm–2+m; Spread: 5cm–1m. Direct light.

Aloe
Medicine Plant
Aloe vera

Best known for the use of the gel within its fleshy leaves, there are many types of aloe. All have upright, lance-shaped, semi-rigid foliage. Some have thorns. Some produce small, yellow blooms in summer. Height: 10–60cm; Spread: indefinite. Direct light.

Ease of Care: easy

Water: medium (allow 1cm of the soil to dry out)

Fertilizer: heavy (cactus fertilizer once every 2 weeks, February to October)

Propagation: seed, offsets in spring, early summer

Common Plant Problems: aphids, mealy bugs, scale insects

Growth Rate: medium

Repot: biennially

Cleaning Tips: wipe with a soft paintbrush

Origins: unknown but widespread in tropical and subtropical regions

Notes: Large types can get top heavy and will naturally grow over the side of pots. All prefer clay pots.

Echeveria
Echeveria

Echeverias are pretty plants with fleshy leaves arranged in a rosette pattern. Their succulent foliage can be greenish-blue, red, purple or burgundy pink. Single blooms that appear in summer range from yellow to red. Height: 5–30cm; Spread: 10–50cm. Direct light.

Aloe

Ease of Care: easy
Water: medium (allow 1cm of the soil to dry out)
Fertilizer: heavy (cactus fertilizer once every 2 weeks, February to October)
Propagation: seed, cutting, offsets
Common Plant Problems: mealy bugs, soft rot
Growth Rate: medium
Repot: annually
Cleaning Tips: wipe with a soft paintbrush, remove dead foliage from base of stem
Origins: Mexico to Central America to the Andes
Notes: Do not water into the 'rosettes' as the plant may rot. Keep cool and drier in winter. Sought after by collectors.

Jade Plant
Crassula ovata

Just one of many *Crassula*, jade plants are popular, long-lived plants with fleshy, mid-green foliage distributed along upright, fleshy stems. When grown indoors they rarely produce single, white to pale-pink blooms in summer. Height: 80+cm; Spread: 80+cm. Direct light.

Ease of Care: easy
Water: medium (allow 1cm of the soil to dry out)
Fertilizer: heavy (cactus fertilizer once every 2 weeks, February to October)
Propagation: seed, cutting
Common Plant Problems: aphids, mealy bugs, fungal leaf spots, root rot, leaf drop (caused by over-watering and low light)
Growth Rate: slow
Repot: biennially
Cleaning Tips: gently shower
Origins: South Africa
Notes: Leaves that break off and land in soil will readily root to form new plants.

Jade Plant

Living Stones
Lithops

Fascinating succulent plants that resemble stones. Foliage consists of a pair of very thick, fleshy leaves fused together. Produces daisy-like, single, pink, white or yellow blooms in fall. Height: 3–4cm; Spread: 8–15cm. Direct light.

Ease of Care: easy
Water: dry (allow 3cm of soil to dry out thoroughly before watering; see Notes)
Fertilizer: no
Propagation: seed, offsets
Common Plant Problems: soft rot
Growth Rate: slow
Repot: biennially as needed
Cleaning Tips: wipe with a soft paintbrush or swab
Origins: Namibia, South Africa
Notes: These interesting plants require a rest period from fall to spring—give no water at this time. Divide in early spring. Sought after by collectors.

Rosary Vine

Madagascar Palm
Pachypodium lamerei

An upright plant with dark-green, lance-shaped foliage held atop a spiny columnar stem. Grown indoors, this plant rarely produces single, creamy-white blooms in summer. Height: 2m; Spread: 1.5m. Direct light.

Ease of Care: easy

Water: medium (allow 1cm of the soil to dry out)

Fertilizer: heavy (cactus fertilizer once every 2 weeks, February to October)

Common Plant Problems: various leaf spots

Growth Rate: medium

Repot: biennially

Cleaning Tips: wipe with a soft paintbrush or swab

Origins: south and south-west Madagascar

Notes: Lower leaves gradually die leaving a tree-like shape. Sought after by collectors.

Rosary Vine
Hearts on a String, Sweetheart Vine
Ceropegia linearis ssp. *woodii*

A pretty trailing plant with sparsely spaced, heart-shaped, fleshy, green foliage with purple markings and purple undersides on wiry stems. Produces insignificant, tubular, lantern-like, purplish-brown blooms in summer. Trails: indefinitely. Direct light.

Ease of Care: easy

Water: medium (allow 1cm of the soil to dry out)

Fertilizer: heavy (cactus fertilizer once every 2 weeks, February to October)

Propagation: seed, cutting

Common Plant Problems: aphids, mealy bugs, scale insects

Growth Rate: medium

Repot: biennially

Cleaning Tips: gently shower

Origins: subtropical areas of Canary Islands, Africa, Madagascar, Asia, Australia

Notes: Don't expect a full, lush plant no matter how happy this plant is—it will always appear sparsely leafed. Sought after by collectors.

Living Stones

String of Pearls
String of Beads
Senecio rowleyanus
A trailing plant with spherical, mid-green foliage on pendant thread-like stems. Produces single, white blooms in summer. Height: 8cm. Direct light.

Ease of Care: easy
Water: medium (allow 1cm of the soil to dry out)
Fertilizer: heavy (cactus fertilizer once every 2 weeks, February to October)
Propagation: seed, cutting
Common Plant Problems: mealy bugs
Growth Rate: medium
Repot: biennially
Cleaning Tips: gently shower
Origins: south-west Africa
Notes: Best grown in a hanging basket. Sought after by collectors.

Euphorbia
Many shapes and forms of *Euphorbia* are available in garden centres today. They are most often grouped for sale with succulents. All require direct light.

African Milk Tree
Euphorbia trigona
An upright plant with 3-sided stems, lined with small green leaves. Height: 1.5m; Spread: 1m. Direct light.

Ease of Care: easy
Water: medium (allow 1cm of the soil to dry out)
Fertilizer: heavy (cactus fertilizer once every 2 weeks, February to October)
Propagation: cutting
Growth Rate: medium
Repot: annually
Cleaning Tips: wipe with a soft paintbrush
Origins: Namibia
Notes: Leaves will fall at the end of summer and grow back at the end of the resting period. Sought after by collectors.

Candelabra Plant
Elkhorn
Euphorbia lactea 'Cristata'
This upright, very odd-looking plant is sometimes referred to as a false cactus. Produces fan-shaped, crested foliage on branches. Height: 60cm; Spread: 40cm. Direct light.

Ease of Care: easy
Water: dry (allow 3cm of soil to dry out thoroughly between watering)
Fertilizer: heavy (cactus fertilizer once every 2 weeks, February to October)
Common Plant Problems: mealy bugs
Growth Rate: slow
Repot: every 2–3 years
Cleaning Tips: wipe with a soft cloth or paintbrush
Notes: A novelty plant—the fan-shaped *cristata* is grafted onto a piece of *Euphorbia*. Water only once in the winter months (over-watering at this time will cause certain death). Sought after by collectors.

Madagascar Palm

Pencil Tree
Milkbush, Fingertree, Rubber Euphorbia
Euphorbia tirucallii

An interesting upright euphorbia that produces pencil-thick, fleshy, green foliage that branches, looking much like a tree with no leaves. Height: 60cm; Spread: 1m. Direct light.

Ease of Care: easy

Water: dry (allow 3cm of soil to dry out thoroughly before watering)

Fertilizer: heavy (cactus fertilizer once every 2 weeks, February to October)

Propagation: cutting

Common Plant Problems: mealy bugs

Growth Rate: medium

Repot: biennially

Cleaning Tips: wipe with a soft paintbrush

Origins: tropical east and South Africa

Notes: This plant produces a lot of milky sap when cut—allow cut ends to dry completely for a couple of days before planting to propagate. Water only enough to stop drying out completely in winter. Sought after by collectors.

Sedum

The sedums or stonecrops are considered succulents and are fleshy-leaved plants that are prized by novices and collectors alike. There are upright and trailing types and their leaf form varies from flat, paddle-shaped to round and pea-like. All prefer direct light indoors.

Burro's Tail
Donkey's, Horse's or Lamb's Tail
Sedum morganianum

A trailing sedum with stems that are covered in small, overlapping, cylindrical, fleshy leaves. These stems hang over the edges of pots, looking like tails or ropes. Produces single, pink blooms in early spring. Height: 30cm; Spread: 30cm. Direct light.

Ease of Care: easy

Water: medium (allow 1cm of the soil to dry out)

Fertilizer: heavy (cactus fertilizer once every 2 weeks, February to October)

Propagation: cutting

Common Plant Problems: mealy bugs

Growth Rate: medium

Repot: annually

Cleaning Tips: gently shower

Origins: Mexico

Notes: Take care handling as stems break easily. Discard old plants (juvenile forms look better) and start again with cuttings. Best grown in a hanging basket.

Burro's Tail

Tahitian Bridal Veil

Tahitian Bridal Veil
Gibasis geniculata
A very popular trailing plant with tiny, dark-green leaves with purple undersides. Produces single, tiny, white blooms in summer and throughout the year. Height: 45–60cm; Spread: 60–90cm. Direct light.

Ease of Care: moderate
Water: medium (allow 1cm of the soil to dry out)
Fertilizer: heavy (15-30-15 once every 2 weeks, February to October)
Propagation: seed, cutting
Common Plant Problems: aphids, spider mites
Growth Rate: medium
Repot: annually
Cleaning Tips: gently shower
Notes: Best in a hanging basket or on a plant stand that allows stems to trail freely.

Tapestry Vine
Cissus discolor
A vining plant with pointed, heart-shaped, velvety-green foliage with silver and pale-purple markings and maroon undersides. Height: up to 2m. Bright indirect light.

Ease of Care: difficult

Water: medium (allow 1cm of the soil to dry out)
Fertilizer: heavy (10-6-16 once every 2 weeks, February to October)
Propagation: cutting
Common Plant Problems: spider mites, powdery mildew
Repot: annually
Cleaning Tips: gently shower, remove dead foliage
Origins: south-east Asia
Notes: Difficult plant to grow as it needs a large window with warmth, high humidity, freedom from drafts, direct sunlight and a precise watering program. Sought after by collectors.

Ti-Plant
Cabbage Tree, Palm Lily, Good Luck Plant
Cordyline fruitcosa
An attractive, upright plant that displays lance-shaped, purple foliage or green foliage striped with purple. Height: 1–2.5m; Spread: 2m. Bright indirect light.

Ease of Care: moderate
Water: medium (allow 1cm of the soil to dry out)
Fertilizer: heavy (10-6-16 once every 2 weeks, February to October)
Propagation: seed, suckers
Common Plant Problems: mealy bugs, scale insects, spider mites, bacterial and fungal spots
Growth Rate: medium
Repot: annually
Cleaning Tips: wipe with a soft cloth or gently shower
Origins: south-east Asia, the Pacific
Notes: Provides nice colour contrast in an arrangement of houseplants. Sensitive to excessive fluoride.

Tapestry Vine

Tradescantia Group

Tradescantia encompasses a number of trailing plants primarily grown in hanging baskets so that their stems hang freely. Foliage colour and markings differ, but they commonly share a lance-shaped leaf. Bright direct light.

Moses in a Cradle

Moses in a Cradle
Boat Lily, Three Men in a Boat
Tradescantia spathacea (syn. Rhoeo)
A compact plant with long, lance-shaped, dark-green foliage with purple undersides. Single, white blooms appear sporadically. Height: 20–30cm; Spread: 20–30cm. Bright indirect light.

Ease of Care: moderate
Water: medium (allow 1cm of the soil to dry out)
Fertilizer: heavy (10-6-16 once every 2 weeks, February to October)
Propagation: side shoots
Growth Rate: medium
Repot: annually
Cleaning Tips: wipe with a soft cloth or gently shower
Origins: Central America
Notes: Has small white flowers in purple 'boats' at base of lower leaves.

Purple Heart
Purple Queen
Tradescantia pallida 'purpurea'
A trailing plant with dark–purple, pointed and oblong leaves. Produces single pink blooms in summer. Height: 60cm; Spread: 40cm. Bright indirect light.

Ease of Care: easy
Water: medium (allow 1cm of the soil to dry out)
Fertilizer: heavy (10-6-16 once every 2 weeks, February to October)
Propagation: cutting, division
Common Plant Problems: aphids, spider mites, viral diseases
Growth Rate: fast
Repot: annually
Cleaning Tips: shower gently
Origins: eastern Mexico
Notes: Pinch growing tips to encourage bushiness. Leaves develop best colour in bright light.

Wandering Jew
Inch Plant, Luck Plant
Tradescantia zebrina
A trailing plant with fleshy, oval leaves available in many forms of variegation. Produces single, purple blooms in spring and summer. Height: 15cm; Spread: 25cm. Bright indirect light with some direct light.

Ease of Care: easy
Water: medium (allow 1cm of the soil to dry out)
Fertilizer: heavy (10-6-16 once every 2 weeks, February to October)
Propagation: cutting
Growth Rate: medium
Repot: annually
Cleaning Tips: shower gently
Origins: North, Central and South America
Notes: Older plants lose their lower leaves—start new plants yearly. Good plant for children to propagate as it roots very easily.

Wandering Jew

Umbrella Plant 'Gracilis'
Cyperus involucratus

An upright plant with interesting grassy foliage radiating like umbrella spokes from the top of tall stems. Height: 30cm; Spread: 25cm. Bright indirect light.

Ease of Care: easy

Water: moist (keep soil consistently moist)

Fertilizer: moderate (10-6-16 full strength once per month, February to October)

Propagation: division

Growth Rate: medium

Repot: annually

Cleaning Tips: gently shower

Origins: Africa

Notes: Keep plant sitting in saucer of water or in a water bowl. A good plant for a beginner as it cannot be over-watered.

Umbrella Tree
Queensland Umbrella Tree, Octopus Tree
Schefflera actinophylla

An upright plant that is often sold as a bushy plant or trained as a single-stem specimen. Glossy, green foliage is divided to form an umbrella-like appearance. Height: 3m; Spread: 1.5m. Bright indirect light.

Ease of Care: easy

Water: medium (allow 1cm of the soil to dry out)

Fertilizer: heavy (10-6-16 once every 2 weeks, February to October)

Propagation: cutting, air layering

Common Plant Problems: mealy bugs, scale insects, thrips

Growth Rate: medium

Repot: annually

Cleaning Tips: wipe leaves with a sponge or soft cloth or gently shower

Origins: North and north-east Australia, south and south-east New Guinea

Notes: Rarely blooms indoors.

Umbrella Tree Schefflera arboricola

Umbrella Tree
Schefflera arboricola

Smaller than *S. actinophylla*, this plant displays the same glossy, green foliage divided to form an umbrella-like appearance. Height: 2m; Spread: 1m. Bright indirect light.

Ease of Care: easy

Water: medium (allow 1cm of the soil to dry out)

Fertilizer: heavy (10-6-16 once every 2 weeks, February to October)

Propagation: cutting, air layering

Common Plant Problems: mealy bugs, scale insects, thrips

Growth Rate: medium

Repot: annually

Cleaning Tips: wipe leaves with a sponge or soft cloth or gently shower

Origins: south-east Asia to Pacific islands, Taiwan

Notes: Rarely blooms indoors.

Venus Fly Trap
Dionaea muscipula

A fascinating insectivore with a compact habit of growth. Two-lobed foliage is hinged and has spines along the outer edge, giving the appearance of

Venus Fly Trap

Ease of Care: easy
Water: moist (keep soil consistently moist but not soggy)
Fertilizer: heavy (10-6-16 once every 2 weeks, February to October)
Propagation: cutting
Common Plant Problems: infrequent
Growth Rate: medium
Repot: annually
Cleaning Tips: gently shower
Origins: tropical Asia
Notes: Pinch back growing tips to encourage bushier growth. Useful for adding texture and colour to plant arrangements.

teeth (called traps). Insects are trapped and ingested between the hinged leaves. Produces single, white blooms in summer. Height: 15cm; Spread: 15cm. Bright indirect light.

Ease of Care: moderate
Water: moist (keep soil consistently moist but not soggy)
Fertilizer: no
Propagation: seed, leaf cuttings
Common Plant Problems: leaf spot, crown rot
Growth Rate: slow
Repot: biennially
Origins: coastal areas of North and South Carolina
Notes: To encourage the development of more traps, pinch out emerging flowers and remove dead traps. Requires high humidity. Sought after by collectors.

Waffle Plant 'Red Ivy'
Purple Waffle Plant
Hemigraphis 'Exotica'
This plant displays ovate, purplish-green foliage with puckering between the veins. Produces single, white blooms in spring to summer. Height: 25cm; Spread: 50cm. Bright indirect light.

West Indian Holly 'Burgundy'
Leea guineensis
An upright plant with pointed, bronze-coloured, young foliage that ages to purplish-green. Height: 1.5m; Spread: 1m. Bright indirect light.

Ease of Care: moderate
Water: medium (allow 1cm of the soil to dry out)
Fertilizer: heavy (10-6-16 once every 2 weeks, February to October)
Propagation: cutting, air layering
Common Plant Problems: mealy bugs, spider mites, bacterial leaf spot
Repot: annually
Cleaning Tips: gently shower
Origins: Burma
Notes: This attractive plant maintains its best foliage colour when grown in good light. Sought after by collectors.

Yucca

Yucca
Spineless Yucca
Yucca elephantipes

An easy, large plant to grow indoors. Light-green to mid-green foliage is narrow and lance-shaped, sometimes growing as long as 90cm. Grown indoors it rarely produces single, white to cream blooms in summer and only when the plant reaches maturity. Height: 3+m; Spread: 1.5m. Direct light.

Ease of Care: easy

Water: medium (allow 1cm of the soil to dry out)

Fertilizer: heavy (10-6-16 once every 2 weeks, February to October)

Propagation: cutting

Common Plant Problems: scale insects, fungal leaf spots

Growth Rate: medium

Repot: annually

Cleaning Tips: wipe with a soft cloth, gently shower

Origins: North and Central America, West Indies

Notes: Can become very large over time and may drop lower foliage.

Zebra Plant

Zebra Plant
Saffron Spike
Aphelandra squarrosa

An attractive, upright plant with ovate to elliptical, dark-green foliage with prominent white veins and mid ribs. Produces waxy, yellow blooms on terminal spikes in summer. Height: 45cm; Spread: 30cm. Bright indirect light.

Ease of Care: easy

Water: moist (keep soil consistently moist but not soggy)

Fertilizer: heavy (10-6-16 once every 2 weeks, February to October)

Propagation: cutting

Common Plant Problems: aphids, mealy bugs, mites, scale insects, fungal diseases

Growth Rate: medium

Repot: annually

Cleaning Tips: wipe with a soft cloth or gently shower, remove spent blooms

Origins: tropical North, Central and South America

Notes: Adds contrast to houseplant arrangements.

ZZ Plant
Aroid Palm, Fat Boy, Eternity Plant
Zamioculcas zamiifolia

An upright plant with glossy, dark-green foliage displayed on fleshy stems in a prominent pattern. Height: 45–80cm; Spread: 50–95cm. Bright indirect light.

Ease of Care: easy

Water: medium (allow 1cm of the soil to dry out)

Fertilizer: moderate (10-6-16 full strength once per month, February to October)

Propagation: leaf cutting, division

Common Plant Problems: infrequent

Growth Rate: slow

Repot: annually

Cleaning Tips: gently shower

Origins: East Africa, Zanzibar

Notes: All parts of plant are poisonous if ingested. Can survive without being watered for 3–4 months. Sought after by collectors.

ZZ Plant

Glossary of Terms

Anther: The pollen-bearing portion of the stamen. It's also the portion of the stamen that will leave a yellow stain on your nose if you lean in too close to smell an Easter lily.

Bract: A modified leaf structure associated with a flower. It's sometimes thought of incorrectly as a petal, as in the case of poinsettias.

Calyx: Refers collectively to the green, leaf-like parts (sepals) that protect the flowerbud; typically found beneath the open flower.

Chloroplasts: The structures that contain chlorophyll and give plants their green colour. The primary duty of chlorophyll is to take electromagnetic energy (sunlight) and change it into chemical energy (photosynthesis).

Corona: An interior flower structure, found between the corolla and the stamens, that resembles a crown.

Deadheading: Removing spent blooms from a plant.

Diapause: A state of rest that insects and insect-like creatures go into when their living environments are poor.

Direct sunlight: Plants that are in unobstructed sunlight (the light rays that pass through the glass and strike leaves directly) for at least three hours a day are said to be in direct sunlight.

Duration (of light): The amount of time plants are exposed to light in a 24-hour period.

Epiphytes: A plant that grows on another plant but does not derive its nourishment from it, such as many ferns, orchids and bromeliads.

Fecundity: The capacity for producing young (fruitfulness or fertility).

Foot-candle: This is the illuminance provided by one candle at a distance of one foot.

Honeydew: A clear, sticky secretion that some insect pests (like aphids and scale) leave behind on leaves.

Hydroponics: Growing plants exclusively in a water solution that contains nutrients.

Indirect sunlight: Plants that are in a bright sunlit room but not near a window receive what is referred to as indirect sunlight.

(Bright) indirect sunlight: Plants that are very close to a sunny window but that aren't in direct sunlight receive what is referred to as bright indirect light.

Inflorescence: The flowering structure; an arrangement of flowers on the plant.

Keiki: A plantlet that forms on the flower of an orchid.

Leachate: The water and excess fertilizer that flows out through the holes at the bottom of a plant pot.

Light meter: An instrument used for measuring light.

Micronutrients: Essential plant nutrients required in very small quantities.

Palmate: Having three or more lobes, leaflets or nerves radiating from a common point.

Panicles: A loosely branched, pyramidal flower cluster.

Parthenogenetic: A form of reproduction in which an unfertilized egg develops into a new individual.

Photosynthesis: The conversion of light energy into chemical energy.

Photosynthetic photon flux: The total useable light energy for plants.

Polyphagous: Feeding on many types of foods.

Pythium: A root destroying fungi that loves to invade plant roots that have been growing in cool, wet soil.

Quality (of light): The wavelength or colour of light.

Quantity (of light): The total amount of light available for a plant.

Relative humidity: A measure of the amount of water the air will hold at a certain temperature. A preferred relative humidity for a plant is about 60%, but a much more realistic percentage to aim for indoors is 25%.

Rhizome: A thick, horizontal, elongated underground stem that produces upright shoots.

Scurf: A bran-like scale or powder covering a plant.

Spathe: A showy, modified leaf that encloses a flower cluster.

Stolons: A horizontally growing stem that produces adventitious roots.

Stomata: Pores found, primarily, on the underside of a leaf's surface.

Thigmotactic: Pests that love living in tight spaces—literally being hugged by plant tissue—are referred to as thigmotactic.

Transpiration: The loss of water from plants, primarily, through the pores (stomata) on the surface of leaves.

Wavelengths (of visible light): The distance between one peak or crest of a wave of light.

Whorl: A circular collection of three or more leaves, branches or flower stalks arising from the same point.

Index

ABOUT THE AUTHOR

If you want to see Jim Hole practise patience, just explain something to him by saying, "That's just the way it is." After he stops grimacing, you'll quickly understand how heartfelt his love for learning and teaching is.

Jim inherited a love of plants and knowledge from his mother, Lois Hole. After spending his formative years in St. Albert, Alberta, Jim attended the U of A and earned a Bachelor of Science in Agriculture with a major in plant science.

Today, Jim writes a weekly gardening column for both the *Edmonton Journal* and *The Star Phoenix* and is the author of three bestselling *What Grows Here?* books: *Locations, Problems* and *Solutions*. He is also the co-author, with his mother, of six *Question & Answer* books. His latest book, *Hole's Dictionary of Hardy Perennials*, is a project that brings together Hole's decades of experience in growing and selling perennials.

Jim also appears regularly on CBC radio and television call-in shows. His specialty is talking about the science of nature. He knows what makes a garden tick and can distill complicated information into engaging conversations—all without losing sight of the joy of gardening.

For more from Jim Hole, including his speaking schedule, columns and weekly newsletter, visit www.enjoygardening.com

ABOUT THE PHOTOGRAPHER

Akemi Matsubuchi was born in Montreal, Quebec, and lived on several continents before settling in St. Albert, Alberta. She attended Ryerson University where she received a Bachelor of Applied Arts in Still Photography. She has worked as a commercial and portrait photographer and photographed *Edmonton, Secrets of the City*. Akemi has been the primary photographer for 21 Hole's books, including the best-selling *Favorite* series and *Herbs and Edible Flowers*, which won an Alberta Book Illustration Award. Her work is regularly featured in the annual *Spring Gardening* magazine.

Akemi loves to travel and record the images that inspire her. She has taken up the challenge of teaching photography and says that if she can do one thing, she'd like to encourage everyone to pick up a camera and record their view of the world.

The success of this book is due entirely
to the hard work of the staff of Hole's Greenhouses and Gardens
over the years, including, but not limited to...

Christina McDonald
EDITOR

Gregory Brown
DESIGN

Akemi Matsubuchi
PRINCIPAL PHOTOGRAPHY

Carmen D. Hrynchuk
PRINCIPAL WRITER

Christina McDonald
CONTRIBUTING WRITER

Leslie Vermeer, Bruce Timothy Keith
CONTRIBUTING EDITORS

Judith Fraser, Arlene Hancock, Sandra Klien, Suzanne Letawsky,
Sharon McDonald, Stephen Raven, Marcie Wheele
HORTICULTURAL RESEARCH & CONSULTATION